MW01134842

"I learned a lot from this wonderful book. Some delightful things about elephant-whispering and turning up the treble. But also some profound things that I have been thinking and writing about for decades. Scott Burson showed me in these pages that I still have much to learn about cultivating Christian civility."

—**Richard Mouw**, President Emeritus, Fuller Theological Seminary

"*All about the Bass* is like a course on listening: it will enlighten, challenge, inspire, and—most important—equip you to understand more people better. And I can't think of anything the world needs more right now than this effort, these skills, and this vision."

—**Karen Swallow Prior**, author of *On Reading Well: Finding the Good Life through Great Books*

"I wish I could take Scott Burson's book back in time and give it to myself when I was a young Christian. It would have saved me from so many communication mistakes. It would have helped me be a better family member, friend, citizen, and pastor. It would have helped me be less of a 'noisy gong and clanging symbol,' and more of a person whose communication conveys the sweet music of love. It's never too late to learn the valuable lessons offered in this practical, readable, intelligent book."

—**Brian D. McLaren**, author of *Faith After Doubt*

"This is a remarkable and insightful book that invites readers to live their convictions courageously, with humility and civility. Burson applies Moral Foundations Theory, bass and treble, to help us understand the intuitions and stories behind the music of today's culture wars. This book should be essential reading for anyone seeking to expand the circle and love their enemies."

—**Doug Daugherty**, Dean of Rosemead School of Psychology, Biola University

"In our increasingly tribalized culture, Scott Burson's *All about the Bass* offers a compelling way forward. This is a marvelously clear Christian adaptation of Moral Foundations Theory (MFT), which is a valuable gift in itself, but Burson does more. Guided by the gospel, Burson leans on the insights of MFT to cast a winsome vision for remaining faithful to our convictions while compassionately sowing peace, empathetically building bridges, and courageously seeking reconciliation. This is essential reading!"

—**Kent Eilers**, Professor of Theology, Huntington University

"Here is a wonderful book that can help heal the fractious dialogue in our churches and society. It clearly presents the keys for how to accomplish this and the inspiring stories provide hope for success."

—**John Sanders**, Professor of Religious Studies, Hendrix College

"In a culture defined by greater anger, louder voices, and stronger indignation, Scott Burson offers a different way for Christians to engage the world around them. He counters the fallacies of our time with a call for humility, empathy, and relational generosity—in other words, with the way of Jesus. Our interactions, both in person and online, will benefit greatly if we heed his words."

—**Rod Reed**, Chancellor, Indiana Wesleyan University

"In a noisy culture longing for radical hospitality and extra measures of kindness, Scott Burson offers a quiet voice with practical wisdom and personal messages that keep the reader turning the pages. Read, reflect, and apply, then repeat the cycle to discover new rhythms of grace and bridge the generational and relational divides. I highly recommend!"

—**Keith Newman**, President, Southern Nazarene University

"In *All about the Bass*, Scott Burson persuasively argues for a higher calling of conviction and compassion, beginning with the search to find common ground and culminating with loving your enemies."

—**Arthur C. Brooks**, Professor, Harvard Kennedy School and Harvard Business School

"In a time when the messengers have often upstaged the message, and conflated being right with leading others to the light, what a timely call for Christ-followers to imitate the gospel of reconciliation. Peppered with powerful stories, weighty points of theology, practical application, and whimsical pop cultural awareness, Scott's thoughts could not have come sooner, nor cut me more deeply."

—**Steve Wood**, Associate Professor of Theatre, Indiana Wesleyan University

All about the Bass

All about the Bass

Searching for Treble in the Midst of a Pounding Culture War

Scott R. Burson

FOREWORD BY
Russ Gunsalus

CASCADE *Books* • Eugene, Oregon

ALL ABOUT THE BASS
Searching for Treble in the Midst of a Pounding Culture War

Cascade Books
An Imprint of Wipf and Stock Publishers
199 W. 8th Ave., Suite 3
Eugene, OR 97401

www.wipfandstock.com

PAPERBACK ISBN: 978-1-7252-5511-1
HARDCOVER ISBN: 978-1-7252-5512-8
EBOOK ISBN: 978-1-7252-5513-5

Cataloguing-in-Publication data:

Names: Burson, Scott R., author. | Gunsalus, Russ, foreword.

Title: All about the bass : searching for treble in the midst of a pounding culture war / by Scott R. Burson ; foreword by Russ Gunsalus.

Description: Eugene, OR: Cascade Books, 2021 | Includes bibliographical references and index.

Identifiers: ISBN 978-1-7252-5511-1 (paperback) | ISBN 978-1-7252-5512-8 (hardcover) | ISBN 978-1-7252-5513-5 (ebook)

Subjects: LCSH: Social psychology. | Psychology, Religious. | Interpersonal relations. | Christianity and culture.

Classification: BJ45 .B80 2021 (print) | BJ45 (ebook)

06/09/21

To my parents, who spent a lifetime of faithful service as music and physical education instructors. Together they introduced me to the beauty and drama of song and sport—both of which take center stage in the following pages.

Contents

Foreword

In every age and every culture there exist divisive issues and rancorous rhetoric. And in every age and every culture there is a tendency to think these dynamics are worse than they have ever been. It is no different for us today. We too experience these universal and timeless dynamics of vitriol, divisive dissent, and contentious conversations that prevent productive dialogue around a myriad of topics and issues. However, today there truly seems to be significant differences from the past.

For the first time in history almost anyone can communicate with everyone and everyone can communicate back. In addition to the world shrinking via globalization and the Internet, there has been an explosive growth of communication networks, social media platforms, and the personal devices to use them. The only limitations seem to be language and bandwidth—both of which technological progress is quickly diminishing.

These globalized communication realities exacerbate our differences and divisions. They amplify and even incentivize a particular type of public vitriol and social conflict. This destructive mode of communication has spread to almost every issue and disseminated its destructive seeds in every corner of our culture and around the globe.

For millennia, the village idiot, town crier, and local genius were all basically confined to a limited geographical area. Their voices rarely reached beyond one valley, forest, or mountain. Now, for good and ill every one of those folks can communicate together and be their own town crier with a cheap phone and spotty Wi-Fi. On one hand this has given rise to global scientific collaborations to solve world problems, access to every library around the globe, and instantly being able to see and relate to people from other cultures and countries. On the other hand, it has enabled global terrorist networks, ubiquitous disinformation campaigns, and cynical cyber trolls.

While we may all celebrate the positive effects of this phenomenon, the negative elements have been weaponized and metastasized across and into all realms of society—from politics, corporations, sports, media, and the academy to communities, churches, families, and even personal relationships. Broadly speaking, we seemingly are unable to find common ground outside of our tribal bubbles. We struggle to engage in respectful dialogue that genuinely listens to the views and perspectives of the other, while still faithfully communicating our own convictions and beliefs.

We have come to a point where there is a critical need for parties on all sides on all kinds of issues to achieve some kind of rapprochement across these cultural, political, and social divides. We need genuine and productive conversations to move us forward toward livable, manageable, and constructive solutions.

It is into this moment that Scott Burson has delivered *All about the Bass: Searching for Treble in the Midst of a Pounding Culture War*. With prescient and practical insights, Burson offers an immensely helpful remedy to our contentious public square and lays out a clear path toward restoring civil and constructive discourse. Engaging Jonathan Haidt's moral psychology from a Christian perspective, Burson delivers substantive guidance grounded in academic research, insightful analysis, and shared human experience.

When I first encountered Haidt's work in *The Righteous Mind: Why Good People Are Divided by Politics and Religion* in 2012 I believed it would be an important book for anyone interested in restoring civil discourse to the public square. This would be especially true for Christians who found themselves in the middle of the cacophony of culture wars, religious disputes, and political polarization, yet still wished to live by the proverb "a gentle word turns away wrath." I had no idea how much greater the need for this kind of Christlike discourse would become in the ensuing years.

The implications of Haidt's work for Christian thought, evangelism, apologetics, and communication seemed significant and hopeful. But to explore the intersections of Haidt's social and moral psychology with Christian theology and practices would take some work. So, I turned to my friend and colleague Scott Burson to discuss Haidt's research as well as the possibilities it had for Christians and the church's engagement with the world. Fortunately for me then and all of us now, he had already begun that work. Scott's insights and engagement with these ideas continued to germinate until the seeds of his thought were planted in a presentation at Indiana Wesleyan University's inaugural Day of Courageous Conversations on Valentine's Day 2017. Those initial seeds have now grown and delivered the fruit of his labor in *All about the Bass*.

I knew Scott to be a quality philosopher and theologian. His bachelor's degree in Communication as well as an MA in Theology and Philosophy of Religion from Asbury Seminary and PhD in Philosophical Theology from Brunel University in London, coupled with his work in marketing, writing, and teaching, gave him a multi-dimensional perspective that he has demonstrated in his Christian apologetics work. As an apologist, Scott had already made the turn from the usual syllogisms and argumentation in defense of Christianity to the persuasive power of relational dialogue and conversational exploration of theology and faith to advance the Christian message. This is a turn that invites persons into a relationship with Christ and his church.

This winsome approach exudes through his thinking and writing in this book. I also witnessed it in his teaching of undergraduate students. Scott has always been able to blend philosophy, theology, psychology, communication, sports, and popular culture to communicate sound academic work and its practical implications for students, pastors, and people in the pew. In *All about the Bass* he continues that practice and delivers profound, yet accessible analysis with down-to-earth strategies for reaching across any divide with charity without compromise.

Furthermore, Burson has provided the first sustained Christian engagement with Haidt's three principles of moral psychology. In addition to a straightforward and insightful analysis of Haidt's work he has also delivered clear and practical guidance for how it can be used from a Christian perspective to winsomely engage all voices and views around us. *All about the Bass* provides a pathway to understand the perspectives and convictions of others while maintaining our own in a way that reflects Christlike listening and love.

While this book is written for a broader Christian audience its Wesleyan theological and ethical roots are unmistakable. These roots are seen in Burson's emphasis on divine goodness and God's heart for all people, our ability to cooperate with God's grace in the transformational process of sanctification, an optimistic theology of hope, and the recognition of the *imago dei* and prevenient grace imprinted by God at the core of every person.

These strong theological underpinnings are expressed throughout the book in beautiful illuminating stories from Scott's personal life, experiences in the classroom, popular culture, and the Bible. The stories are as timeless as the Exodus narrative and as timely as the Samaritan's Purse COVID care field hospital in New York City and the controversy surrounding quarterback Drew Brees's comments about the Black Lives Matter NFL protests. In each illustration, Burson delivers deeper insight into how these stories reflect the challenges we all face in difficult conversations and strategies for faithful peacemaking and bridge-building.

All about the Bass is practical, accessible, and eminently useful for anyone who wishes to productively engage others in sincere and respectful dialogue. Whether you tend to dial up the treble or double down on the bass, Burson's advice will help us balance out the music of our conversations so we can listen and engage in empathetic and constructive dialogue.

Then we may even be able to hear and share our aspirations and discover that though we have diverse ideas about how to achieve them we may share more common hopes and dreams than we ever imagined. Dreams that foster genuine relationships that draw both parties toward the greater good, deeper into the gospel of Christ, and closer to realizing God's vision of achieving "on earth as it is in heaven."

Rev. Russ Gunsalus

Executive Director of Education and Clergy Development
The Wesleyan Church

Acknowledgments

I want to thank Jonathan Haidt for his gracious interaction through the years. His bold yet nuanced work as a researcher, writer, educator, and public intellectual is shining a bright light during a dark time in our country. The seeds for this book were sown on Valentine's Day 2017 when I gave a talk at the inaugural Indiana Wesleyan University Day of Courageous Conversations. Much thanks to Steve Wood for envisioning and organizing this important mind- and heart-stretching event, which is now an annual fixture on the IWU campus. Thanks also to several colleagues—Ken Schenck, Russ Gunsalus, David Vardaman, Steve Horst, Doug Daugherty, Brian Fry, Rod Reed, Phoenix Park-Kim, Ashley DeMichael, and Kent Eilers. Each of you helped make this project a reality through illuminating conversations, helpful feedback, and words of encouragement. I am indebted to my students, who have helped sharpen my thinking through their inspiring engagement with this material. Special thanks to the team at Cascade Books. It was an honor to work again with Rodney Clapp, one of the most adroit editors in the Christian publishing world. I also want to thank my children: Ashley, Lindsey, and Ryan, who each in their own way have inspired and challenged me to turn up the treble in my own life. Finally, much of this book was written during the coronavirus pandemic, so I am deeply indebted to my *quaranteam*: the love of my life and wife, Deb, whose constant support and encouragement made this book possible, and our three very spoiled canines: Burley, Pokey, and Bean. As Richard Rohr once wrote, "The only people who can say dogs do not have souls are those who do not know what a soul is or who have never been loved by a dog!"[1]

1. Rohr, *Eager to Love*, vii.

Introduction

All about the Bass

Searching for Treble in the Midst of a Pounding Culture War

"Because you know I'm all about that bass. 'Bout that bass, no treble."[1]

—MEGHAN TRAINOR

Teaching philosophy to college students can be challenging. Especially at night. This was never more apparent than on the evening of February 26, 2015, when a picture of a dress took Twitter by storm and redirected the attention of all sixty students away from my lecture on David Hume.

While I teach in Indiana, this story begins in Hume's homeland of Scotland. There the mother of a bride-to-be went shopping for a dress to wear to her daughter's wedding and sent a picture to the happy couple for feedback. The bride and bridegroom, however, disagreed on the color. Was the dress white and gold or blue and black? Soon others in the wedding party, including members of the wedding band, were embroiled in a vigorous debate. One band member asked fans on social media to settle the dispute. Within a few hours the image of the dress soared to the number one trending topic on Twitter, garnering tens of millions of views.

Like Cinderella arriving at the ball, the dress made its grand entrance into my classroom at 7 PM—about the time that several pop culture icons were chiming in on the controversy. In an homage to the *Seinfeld* Soup

1. Trainor, "All About That Bass."

Nazi, Julia Louis-Dreyfus tweeted, "It's blue and brown. Period. Next?" The Los Angeles Dodgers simply asserted, "It's blue." Anna Kendrick and Rob Lowe supported the white and gold team, while Ellen DeGeneres offered the following prediction: "From this day on, the world will be divided into two people. Blue & black, or white & gold." One spiritually-minded average Joe wondered if the dispute held eternal significance: "Is this how we find out who goes to heaven and who goes to hell? #TheDress."[2] I don't know if the mother of the bride wore the controversial dress to her daughter's wedding, but for one night it got more attention than a Luis Vuitton red carpet gown.

This American Strife

Just a few weeks before, a different optical illusion raised a ruckus on the Internet. In an episode entitled "If You Don't Have Anything Nice to Say, SAY IT IN ALL CAPS," *This American Life* host Ira Glass described an MIT-created graphic featuring two small side-by-side gray boxes. One was surrounded by a lighter shade, making the left gray box appear darker. The other was surrounded by a darker shade, making the right gray box appear lighter. But contrary to appearances, both gray boxes are identical. This is easily confirmed by checking the RGB values in Microsoft Paint.

But if you think this settled the matter, think again. This is the Internet after all. Despite the straightforward evidence, one discussion board was laced with petulant posts like: "Not the same ****ing shade" and "Not convinced!" Midway through the thread another person naively observed, "The second square looks brighter to me," which prompted: "It's definitely brighter *than* you!" This exchange quickly devolved into all manner of incivility, punctuated by the following grandiose pronouncement: "If after reading this thread, you refuse to actually test it and choose to stick with your dogmatic belief, then you are everything that is wrong with America!"[3]

While humorous, these vignettes illustrate how little it takes to stir the pot these days. We are a quarrelsome and divided country. I mean, if the shade of a square or color of a dress can leave us black and blue, what hope do we have for adjudicating divisive issues like race relations, immigration, abortion, marriage equality, and interreligious dialogue?

2. McCoy, "Inside story."
3. Glass, "SAY IT IN ALL CAPS."

How an "Apostate" and an Atheist Helped Me See the Light

In our highly contentious world, there are two typical ways of explaining those who disagree with us: they are either ignorant or evil. If ignorant, they need education. If evil, vilification. And, of course, we are the enlightened ones who must function as both teacher and judge. This simplistic outlook casts the world into black and white, hard and fast, "us" versus "them" teams. Whether it is community spirit, athletics, religion, or politics, we naturally gravitate toward those on *our* team and view *others* with suspicion or even contempt.

While the psychology of teams produces powerful and pleasurable bonding with fellow teammates, it also creates an obvious problem for Christ-followers who are commanded to love not only family and friends, but folks on other teams, as well. Given our tribal nature, how are we to faithfully respond to the most difficult moral command ever uttered—the command to love our enemies? And how do we do this without compromising our most cherished and deeply held beliefs? In short, how are we to live our lives with compassionate conviction? These are the questions this book seeks to answer.

In the following pages, we will interact with several guides. If you identify as an evangelical Christian, like me, you would likely welcome without hesitation the advice of teammates like Lee Strobel, Richard Mouw, C. S. Lewis, and Francis Schaeffer.[4] In fact, these men are more than teammates, they are evangelical all-stars, even hall-of-famers. Many would view them as some of the best the Christian movement has to offer, so why wouldn't we heed their sagacious guidance?

That said, you might not feel as much initial warmth toward some of the other guides that will appear in this book. Guides like Brian McLaren, whom some evangelicals view as an apostate, and Jonathan Haidt, a New York University (NYU) social psychologist and atheist. Now, you might wonder why an evangelical author/professor would choose to favorably cite a so-called apostate and self-proclaimed atheist. Why not play it safe and rely solely on fellow evangelical team members? After all, if human beings (and Christians are no exception) are naturally tribal, isn't

4. For more on these two defenders of Christian truth, see my co-authored *Lewis and Schaeffer*.

honoring fellow tribe members the tried and true road to generous royalties and glowing reviews?

Well, yes, I suppose that's true if generous royalties and glowing reviews were my primary motivations (not that there is anything wrong with cold cash and positive ink; I will gladly accept both!). But the aim of this book is higher, namely, to help Christ-followers move beyond binary us-versus-them thinking and toward a more holistically biblical mind-set. What better way to do this than by honoring truth, goodness, and beauty wherever it is found, even if it means looking beyond the boundaries of the evangelical fold? After all, every expression of truth, goodness, and beauty can be traced back to one source, namely, Jesus Christ. The doctrine of common grace tells us that all people are made in God's image and consequently capable of positively impacting our shared life together through words of wisdom, acts of virtue, and expressions of creativity. So, despite points of theological and philosophical disagreement, McLaren and Haidt have helped me see the light on some important issues. I believe they can do the same for you.

Haidt's thinking will be central in the following pages. I read his first book, *The Happiness Hypothesis*, while researching and writing my PhD thesis on the theology and apologetics of McLaren, who was once an influential leader in a controversial movement called the Emerging Church.[5] Upon exploring the work of these two men, I located a key intersection point—the role of intuition in human thought and behavior. I realized that McLaren wasn't questioning all of the doctrinal tenets of Christianity, but rather the morally counterintuitive way in which the Christian story is often told. At the same time, Haidt's work was helping me see that most humans live their day-to-day lives at the intuitive level. So if we are interested in persuading people, we need to connect with their intuitions. As someone who has studied and written about evangelism and apologetics for many years, this insight got me thinking deeply about the relationship between logic, argumentation, and moral intuition.

In 2012, Haidt developed his work on intuition further in *The New York Times* best-selling book *The Righteous Mind: Why Good People Are Divided by Politics and Religion*. This book is structured around three main principles of moral psychology: intuitions come first, strategic reasoning second; morality binds and blinds; and morality is more than

5. A version of my PhD thesis was published as *Brian McLaren in Focus*.

harm and fairness.[6] Grasping these three principles, as well as a few associated metaphors, will position us to understand why we are so divided and what can be done about it.

Principle One: Intuitions Come First, Strategic Reasoning Second

Key Metaphor: The mind is divided, like a rider on an elephant, and the rider's job is to serve the elephant.[7]

One of Haidt's main areas of expertise is identifying the relationship between intuition and reason in moral decision-making.[8] He is especially interested in issues related to purity and disgust. For one particular study, he concocted several shocking vignettes designed to trigger strong revulsion. In each story, the fictitious characters make disgusting or disrespectful choices in private.[9] These stories range from eating human cadaver flesh to using scraps of the American flag to clean the bathroom. But perhaps the most unsettling fictitious tale involves a brother and sister on a summer European holiday:

> Julie and Mark, who are sister and brother, are traveling together in France. They are both on summer vacation from college. One night they are staying alone in a cabin near the beach. They decide that it would be interesting and fun if they tried making love. At the very least it would be a new experience for each of them. Julie is already taking birth control pills, but Mark uses a condom too, just to be safe. They both enjoy it, but they decide not to do it again. They keep that night as a special secret between them, which makes them feel even closer to each other.[10]

6. In *Righteous Mind*, Haidt lists "morality is more than harm and fairness" as the second principle and "morality binds and blinds" as the third principle of moral psychology. I've flipped the order of these two for literary reasons. This liberty on my part does not alter the content of either principle.

7. Haidt, *Righteous Mind*, xiv.

8. Haidt, *Righteous Mind*, 40.

9. Haidt explains the significance of isolation in the disgust vignettes as follows, "If you want to give people a quick flash of revulsion but deprive them of any victim they can use to justify moral condemnation, ask them about people who do disgusting or disrespectful things, but make sure the actions are done in private so that nobody else is offended." Haidt, *Righteous Mind*, 19.

10. Haidt, *Righteous Mind*, 19.

After reading the above, participants in the study were then asked some questions. Here is an excerpt from a typical follow-up interview:

EXPERIMENTER: So what do you think about this, was it wrong for Julie and Mark to have sex?

SUBJECT: Yeah, I think it's totally wrong to have sex. You know, because I'm pretty religious and I just think incest is wrong anyway. But, I don't know.

EXPERIMENTER: What's wrong with incest, would you say?

SUBJECT: Um, the whole idea of, well, I've heard—I don't even know if this is true, but in the case, if she did get pregnant, the kids become deformed, most of the time, in cases like that.

EXPERIMENTER: But they used a condom and birth control pills—

SUBJECT: Oh, OK. Yeah, you did say that.

EXPERIMENTER: —so there's no way they're going to have a kid.

SUBJECT: Well, I guess the safest sex is abstinence, but, um, uh . . . um, I don't know, I just think that's wrong. I don't know, what did you ask me?

EXPERIMENTER: Was it wrong for them to have sex?

SUBJECT: Yeah, I think it's wrong.

EXPERIMENTER: And I'm trying to find out why, what you think is wrong with it.

SUBJECT: OK, um . . . well . . . let's see, let me think about this. Um—how old were they?

EXPERIMENTER: They were college age, around 20 or so.

SUBJECT: Oh, oh [looks disappointed]. I don't know, I just . . . it's just not something you're brought up to do. It's just not—well, I mean I wasn't. I assume most people aren't [laughs]. I just think that you shouldn't—I don't—I guess my reason is, um . . . just that, um . . . you're not brought up to it. You don't see it. It's not, um—I don't think it's accepted. That's pretty much it.

EXPERIMENTER: You wouldn't say anything you're not brought up to see is wrong, would you? For example, if you're not brought

> up to see women working outside the home, would you say that makes it wrong for women to work?
>
> **SUBJECT:** Um . . . well . . . oh, gosh. This is hard. I really—um, I mean, there's just no way I could change my mind but I just don't know how to—how to show what I'm feeling, what I feel about it. It's crazy![11]

Not surprisingly, the incest vignette registers an initial flash of moral revulsion for the subject (as it almost certainly did for you, too!). When asked by the experimenter to explain why the behavior is wrong, however, the subject flounders and casts about for readily available arguments. After the experimenter pokes holes in each post-hoc rationalization, however, the dumbfounded subject remains fully committed to the initial gut-level flash of moral revulsion. In short, the study participant instantaneously *knows* incestuous behavior is wrong even while struggling to articulate a rational argument for this unshakable conviction.

Haidt's research confirmed what is now widely accepted in psychology and neuroscience, namely, that the brain is comprised of distinct, but related dual circuitry that Princeton psychologist Daniel Kahneman calls "System 1" and "System 2."[12] NYU Neuroscientist Joseph LeDoux somewhat more colorfully labels these systems the "low road" and "high road."[13] Daniel Goleman offers a vivid clarification of these systems:

> The low road can be seen as "wet," dripping with emotion, and the high road as relatively "dry," coolly rational. The low road traffics in raw feelings, the high in a considered understanding of what's going on. The low road lets us immediately feel with someone else; the high road can think about what we feel. Ordinarily they mesh seamlessly. Our social lives are governed by the interplay of these two modes.[14]

Consider the final comment in the above interview transcript, in which the subject declared, "*There's just no way I could change my mind* but I just don't know how to—how to show what I'm *feeling*, what I feel about it. It's crazy!"[15] Dual systems are operating in the brain—the automatic, intuitive

11. Haidt, *Righteous Mind*, 39–40.
12. Kahneman, *Thinking, Fast and Slow*, 21–24.
13. LeDoux, *Emotional Brain*, 161–65.
14. Goleman, *Social Intelligence*, 16–17.
15. Haidt, *Righteous Mind*, 40. Emphasis mine.

low road and the reflective, strategic high road, but when push comes to shove, jettisoning our commitment to the low road is simply not an option. So not only do we find two cognitive systems in the brain, but the intuitive low road is, as Haidt puts it, "where most of the action is."[16]

While Plato famously envisioned the relationship between reason and emotions as a charioteer (reason) steering two winged horses (representing our noble and base passions), Haidt likens our strategic reasoning to a rider sitting atop an enormous emotional and intuitive elephant.[17] Haidt rejects the Platonic notion that reason holds the reins. Instead, he argues that intuition sets the agenda. While the elephant is occasionally open to taking advice from the rider, most of the time our pachyderm has a mind of its own and is on a mission well before the rider engages. Instead of telling the elephant where to go, Haidt believes "the rider is an attentive servant, always trying to anticipate the elephant's next move. If the elephant leans even slightly to the left, as though preparing to take a step, the rider looks to the left and starts preparing to assist the elephant on its imminent leftward journey. The rider loses interest in everything to the right."[18] In short, human beings are wired to feel and intuit before they think. This is the first principle of moral psychology.

Principle Two: Morality Binds and Blinds

Key Metaphor: Human beings are 90 percent chimp and 10 percent bee.

My father was a basketball coach, so as a kid I accompanied him to practice every day. As I grew older, you could find me on the indoor hardwood or outdoor asphalt from dawn to dusk. This investment of time and energy eventually led to a basketball scholarship at a university in southern Ohio. As a basketball player, I learned very early about the paradox of team sports—the tension between individual and collective competition. During practice, athletes compete with fellow teammates for playing time. When game day rolls around, however, teammates are required to put all of the intra-squad competition aside and come together as a cohesive unit for the higher purpose of defeating the opposing foe. While this is difficult to

16. Haidt, *Righteous Mind*, 71.

17. Haidt, *Righteous Mind*, 44–49.

18. Haidt, *Righteous Mind*, 56.

accomplish, humans possess the equipment to pull this off under the right conditions. We can do this because we are by nature *homo duplex*. That is to say, we possess a dual nature: while primarily selfish, we are also capable of transcending our own interests for the sake of the team. As Haidt puts it, we are 90 percent chimp (primarily selfish) and 10 percent bee (capable of personal sacrifice for the sake of the hive).[19]

Participating in a hive or on a team can be highly pleasurable and can lead to great accomplishments. Think about all that a hive of bees can accomplish by working cohesively and sacrificially together. Likewise, a cohesive basketball team with less individual talent can often defeat a group of very athletic players who fail to perform as a unit. There is no shortage of elevating stories to illustrate this point. Living in Indiana, the first that comes to mind is the movie *Hoosiers*!

Good things happen when we transcend our individual interests and rally around our team's higher sacred purpose; but in the moral domain, there can be an underbelly, as well. Shared values and causes *bind* us into cohesive moral tribes, while simultaneously *blinding* us to the genuine insights of competing tribes. Once we join a tribe and accept the group's collective mind-set, Haidt believes we are constitutionally incapable of seeing other perspectives. We become convinced that our tribe sees the world with perfect clarity, while the other side is completely obtuse. This is the second principle of moral psychology: morality binds and blinds.

Principle Three: Morality Is More than Harm and Fairness

Key Metaphor: The righteous mind is like a tongue with six taste receptors.[20]

A few years ago, Haidt stumbled upon a new restaurant called The True Taste. He was immediately struck by the stark white décor and the arrangement of five small spoons at each table setting. If the lack of serrated cutlery was not enough, the menu quickly confirmed that chewing would be an unlikely part of his impending dining experience. Instead, Haidt would be sampling sweeteners from around the world.

19. Haidt, *Righteous Mind*, 225.

20. Haidt, *Righteous Mind*, xiv–xv.

The waiter, who doubled as the owner and tripled as the only employee, explained the restaurant's novel concept. Instead of a seasoned restaurateur, the waiter/owner/sole employee was actually a skilled biologist with an expertise in the sense of taste. He explained to Haidt the glories of the tongue; specifically, how each bud could discern five tastes (sweet, sour, salty, bitter, and savory). His research revealed that humans are hardwired to pursue sweetness above all else because sugary tastes trigger the most dopamine in the pleasure centers of the brain. Then one day it hit him. Why not open an eatery that caters entirely to the sugary hedonists of the world? At least they will be happy while dining; the sugar crash won't come until after they've paid the bill! Haidt looked around the empty room and asked him how his business was doing. The biologist/waiter/owner/sole employee responded, "Terrible . . . but at least I'm doing better than the chemist down the street who opened a salt-tasting bar."[21]

Now, don't go looking for The True Taste restaurant, because you won't find it. As you might have guessed, this story is a metaphor that Haidt devised to illustrate the reductionist tendencies so prevalent in moral psychology and philosophy. Haidt observes:

> Many authors reduce morality to a single principle, usually some variant of welfare maximization (basically help people, don't hurt them). Or sometimes it's justice or related notions of fairness, rights, or respect for individuals and their autonomy. There's The Utilitarian Grill, serving only sweeteners (welfare), and The Deontological Diner, serving only salts (rights). Those are your options.[22]

Years of research, however, have convinced Haidt that morality is actually quite broad and cannot be narrowed to one or two principles. While Haidt used to condemn any ideas coming from the right end of the political or ideological spectrum, he now believes conservatives hold a more accurate view of human nature and often see things in the moral domain that liberals cannot.[23] This is because conservatives possess a broad-based morality, while liberals tend to narrow morality to issues of harm,

21. Haidt, *Righteous Mind*, 112–13.

22. Haidt, *Righteous Mind*, 113.

23. Haidt acknowledges that liberals also can see things that conservatives cannot. Since both have blind spots, a yin-yang relationship is the best way forward. This is why Haidt and some of his colleagues have started Heterodox Academy, which was launched to promote viewpoint diversity in higher education. For more, see http://heterodoxacademy.org/.

autonomy, and fairness.[24] This restriction can block liberals from seeing the full scope of the moral terrain.

Haidt, who identifies as a centrist, calls this truncated liberal approach to morality WEIRD (Western, Educated, Industrialized, Rich, and Democratic), in part because it is a catchy acronym, but also because it is "unusual" or "odd" when compared to the moral values of most of the world.[25] This claim is supported by extensive cross-cultural research, which reveals that morality in most cultures extends well beyond individual harm, autonomy, and fairness to include a broader range of communal concerns. Haidt found that WEIRD and non-WEIRD moral visions tend to correspond to individualistic and collectivistic cultures, respectively. As he puts it, "The WEIRDer you are, the more you see a world full of separate objects, rather than relationships."[26]

As Haidt and colleague Craig Joseph began comparing the moral sensibilities of various cultures, a common set of universal moral intuitions began to emerge. This research culminated in the development of Moral Foundations Theory, which claims that properly functioning human beings come into the world with a range of diverse moral intuitions already in place—what Haidt calls the "first draft of the moral mind."[27] Specifically, Haidt and Joseph have identified six distinct foundational moral intuition pairings. According to their theory, humans are naturally wired to resonate with expressions of the first concept in each pairing and to recoil from instantiations of the second.[28] Here are the six pairings:

1. The *Care/Harm* foundation equips humans to protect and nurture the vulnerable members of society and to fight against cruelty and abuse.
2. The *Liberty/Oppression* foundation equips humans to recognize the inherent value of freedom and to fight against the suppression of individual and collective rights.

24. This approach to morality can be summed up with the following phrase, "As long as I am not hurting anyone else, then I should be free to do as I please."

25. Haidt, *Righteous Mind*, 96. Haidt did not coin this acronym. He credits the following journal article: Henrich, et al., "Weirdest people."

26. Haidt, *Righteous Mind*, 96.

27. Haidt, *Righteous Mind*, 131.

28. For the sake of brevity, I will generally use the first term in each pairing for the remainder of this book.

3. The *Fairness/Cheating* foundation equips humans with a concern to see rewards and punishments justly administered.[29]
4. The *Loyalty/Betrayal* foundation equips humans to trust and honor those who are faithful to our in-group, while ostracizing and punishing the treacherous.
5. The *Authority/Subversion* foundation equips humans to honor appropriate hierarchy and to oppose disrespectful attitudes and behavior.
6. The *Sanctity/Degradation* foundation equips humans to respond to the challenge of living in a world that is clean and unclean both literally and figuratively.[30]

With these six foundational moral intuition pairings in mind, the differences between the conservative and liberal paradigms can be seen. According to Haidt, the conservative narrative is thick and tends to activate all six moral intuitions with an emphasis on the last three (in-group loyalty, authority, and sanctity). Liberals, on the other hand, typically honor the first three intuitions listed above (care, liberty, and fairness), while undervaluing or altogether ignoring the last three (in-group loyalty, authority, and sanctity). In fact, when Haidt first began writing and speaking about Moral Foundations Theory, many liberals rejected the claim that in-group loyalty, authority, and sanctity even belong on the positive side of the moral ledger. Instead, they argue that these are vices rather than virtues, oppressive concepts that contribute to many personal and systemic evils. However, cross-cultural research, including a three-month immersion experience in India, convinced Haidt that WEIRD morality ignores important aspects of the moral landscape. He has since spent a good deal of energy trying to persuade liberals to expand their palate when it comes to moral and political issues. This has begun to happen, specifically with the sanctity intuition. While conservatives have traditionally championed sanctity-of-life issues (e.g., abortion and euthanasia), many liberals have started to activate this built-in yet previously dormant intuition by discussing food in sacred terms. This leads to a crucial point. While Moral Foundations Theory identifies the basic intuitive building blocks of the moral mind, Haidt is quick to explain that these modules can be activated in a variety of ways. While the first draft of the moral mind is essentially the same for all people, the interaction

29. Haidt believes conservatives understand this intuition in terms of proportionality, while liberals tend to think of it as inclusion. See Haidt, *Righteous Mind*, 176–81.

30. Haidt, *Righteous Mind*, 153–54, 185.

between these universal intuitions and subsequent life experiences (which includes socialization and cultural norms) will ultimately determine the final shape of each person's moral matrix.

All about the Bass

In 2014, singer-songwriter Meghan Trainor released a song entitled "All About That Bass," which spent eight weeks as the number-one song on the US Billboard Hot 100. By several measures, the song was a massive hit. Less obvious is whether the lyrics achieved its social goal of communicating a positive body image message to young women who do not possess a Barbie-doll physique. Nevertheless, the title of the song is also useful in describing our current culture war moment. While we've likened Moral Foundations Theory to human taste buds, we can also use a musical metaphor. Imagine a six-channel audio equalizer, with the first three channels managing the treble and the last three channels modulating the bass.[31] In this metaphor, the treble channels represent the compassion intuitions of care, liberty, and fairness, while the bass channels represent the conviction intuitions of in-group loyalty, authority, and sanctity. When placing this image within a Christian framework, the compassion and conviction intuitions work together as a holistic expression of holy triune love. Consequently, if each of these moral intuitions plays a necessary role in God's intricate moral design and collectively reflect the depth, richness, and fullness of God's character, then the song we are singing to the world should include a proper balance of treble and bass. In short, as faithful Christ-followers, we should aspire to a symphonic, six-channel, holistic form of Christianity (see below).

31. A version of the audio equalizer metaphor can be found in Haidt, "Moral roots."

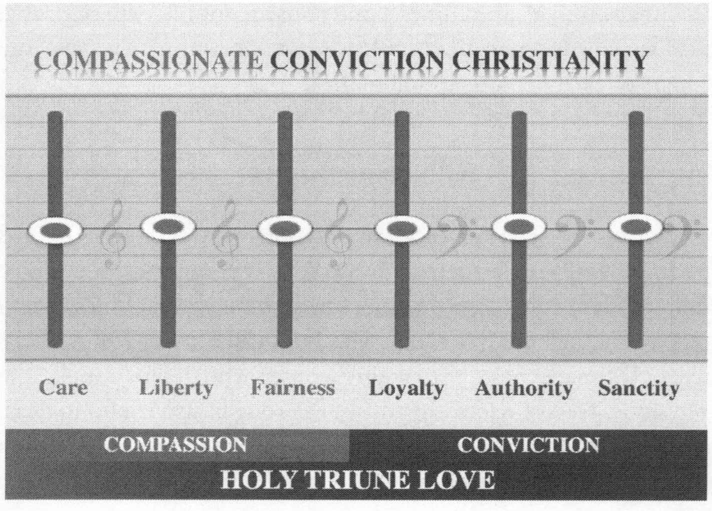

But Christians have often struggled to achieve this harmonious balance of compassionate treble and righteous conviction bass. Some progressive Christian streams increase the treble as an expression of tolerance, acceptance, and good will toward those outside the Christian fold. In so doing, however, this approach can diminish the bass of orthodox Christian teaching. This results in a truncated three-channel compassionate Christianity that is thin and tinny, lacking in substance and faithful conviction (see below).

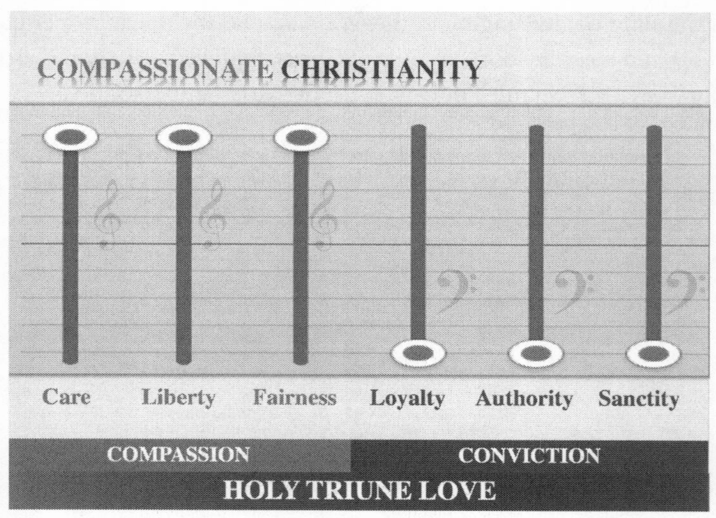

In the midst of the current culture war, however, many evangelicals have struggled with a different imbalance. Instead of overemphasizing compassion, many have elevated the bass to deafening decibel levels. In so doing, the treble of care, liberty, and fairness is overwhelmed by pounding culture-war rhetoric that triggers the intuitions of in-group loyalty, authority, and sanctity. While often motivated by good intentions, this approach, nevertheless, leads to a cacophonic, three-channel righteous conviction form of Christianity that can come across as pharisaical self-righteousness (see below). It is like that annoying tricked-out car that you can hear and feel coming toward you from a mile away. All bass, no treble.

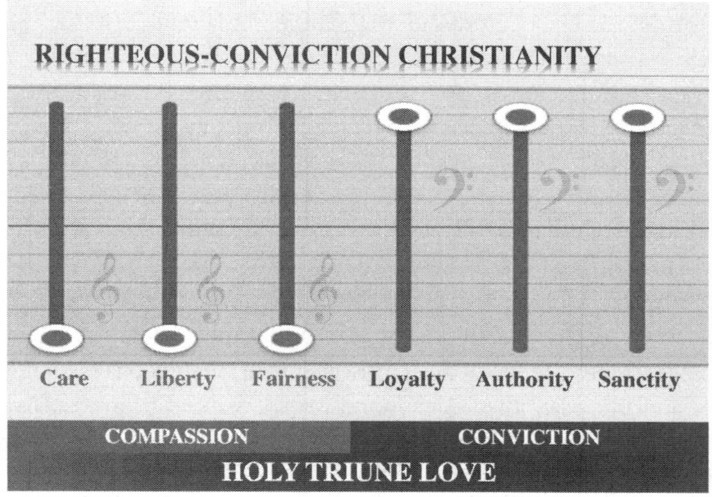

This book is an attempt to offer faithful sheet music to Christ-followers who long to sing a better song to our broken and needy world—a song of harmonious, compassionate conviction.

How to Turn up the Treble

In the following pages, we will explore ten tactics (one per chapter) designed to turn up the treble of compassion without sacrificing the bass of righteous conviction. Each "treble tactic" can be seen as a corrective to a corresponding bass-pounding fallacy. While these fallacies are rarely stated in explicit terms, they unfortunately are alive, well, and widespread throughout much of the Christian world. In fact, these fallacies escalate the incessant culture war drumbeat that makes peacemaking, bridge-building, and reconciliation in our contemporary milieu so very challenging.

With Haidt's three principles of moral psychology in mind, these ten treble tactics are nested within the following three broad strategies: I. *Engage the Elephant*, II. *Honor the Sacred*, and III. *Expand the Tribe*.

Part I: Engage the Elephant. When confronted with a cultural conflict, most of us launch into facts, logic, and reasoned persuasion—often with unbecoming intensity and snark. This opening section makes the case for building emotional, intuitive, and relational rapport instead. Chapter 1 illustrates the importance of befriending the behemoth before engaging the rider; chapter 2 explores why pachyderms lean toward humility, but away from pride; and chapter 3 discusses the different languages of the rider (arguments) and the elephant (story).

Part II: Honor the Sacred. Human beings rarely, if ever, deny their active moral intuitions. So if we want to persuade someone, we must identify and respect what that person considers sacred. With this in mind, chapter 4 discusses the virtues of viewing empathy as a skill that can be developed rather than a fixed trait that only some people possess. While most of the conflict we discuss in this book is between competing cultural tribes, sometimes intra-tribal tensions surface. Using the prism of Moral Foundations Theory, chapter 5 explores a long-standing theological conflict while also considering a strategy for promoting greater Christian unity. Chapter 6 considers how to honor and map the other side's moral matrix without compromising one's own convictions. As a case study, we will examine the question of standing or kneeling during the national anthem.

Part III: Expand the Tribe. Human beings are deeply tribal creatures. Great good and abhorrent evil have come from fanning the flames of tribalism. But who is my fellow tribe member? Is it possible to widen the circle and expand the tribe? This final section explores a Christian response to these questions. Chapter 7 focuses on the heart of God in light of the most challenging moral command ever uttered—love your enemy. Chapter 8 is a call to bring back exorcisms. Not exorcising demons, but exorcising *demonization*. Chapter 9 challenges us to focus on the ministry of reconciliation rather than self-serving reputation management. The final treble tactic in chapter 10 will encourage us to consider whether our online behavior is adding to the deafening drumbeat of division or turning up the treble of compassion.

Part I: **Engage the Elephant**

"If you want to change someone's mind . . . talk to the elephant first. If you ask people to believe something that violates their intuitions, they will devote their efforts to finding an escape hatch—a reason to doubt your argument or conclusion. They will almost always succeed."[1]

—JONATHAN HAIDT

1. Haidt, *Righteous Mind*, 50.

Chapter 1

Treble Tactic One: Befriend the Behemoth

Bass-Pounding Fallacy: Righteous Indignation Excuses Rude Rhetoric

"Dale Carnegie was one of the greatest elephant-whisperers of all time. In his classic book *How to Win Friends and Influence People*, Carnegie repeatedly urged readers to avoid direct confrontations. Instead he advised people to 'begin in a friendly way,' to 'smile,' to 'be a good listener,' and to 'never say "you're wrong."' The persuader's goal should be to convey respect, warmth, and an openness to dialogue before stating one's own case."[1]

—JONATHAN HAIDT

Do you remember the name of your high school librarian? I do. Her name was Helen Porter. As a librarian you have to be doing something right, or at least memorable, for former students to recall your name. If Helen was anything, she was memorable. Well into her sixties, she was quick, clever, dry, and quirky. Most importantly, she was the caretaker of the library's beloved mascot—a scruffy taxidermied owl by the name of Isaac.

While some students called Helen by her first name, she seldom returned the favor. Instead, she gave us nicknames. Mine was "Bursitis"—a twist on my surname. I was not super-thrilled with it. After all, adding an

1. Haidt, *Righteous Mind*, 48.

"itis" to a word is rarely a good thing (in this case: the inflammation of the bursa sac, a painful condition affecting the joints.).

Apparently, I was a pain in some part of Helen's anatomy because one day she imparted a particularly memorable kernel of wisdom that has stayed with me my entire adult life. With the erudite Isaac peering over her shoulder, she looked me square in the eye and said, "Bursitis, no one is completely worthless. At least you can serve as a bad example." Ouch. Thanks, Helen.

A Gator in Wildcat Clothing

While my beloved librarian was having a little fun at my pubescent expense, her nugget of wisdom is actually quite profound. It's true that sometimes we learn as much from cautionary tales as we do from inspirational ones. We will consider both good and bad examples in this chapter, starting with a misstep from my own life.

Several years ago, I gave an apologetics talk to the University of Kentucky InterVarsity Christian Fellowship chapter. I spoke on three of my favorite topics: C. S. Lewis's Lord, Liar, or Lunatic Trilemma; Blaise Pascal's Resurrection Trilemma (the disciples were either Deceived, Deceivers, or Correct); and Pascal's Wager.[2] This was a pretty thick slab of meat for these undergraduate students, so I thought it might be good to start off with a light appetizer. I decided to break the ice by wearing a bright blue Kentucky Wildcat pullover. I opened the talk with all of the usual niceties—"Thanks for inviting me, it's great to be here in Big Blue country . . ." You get the picture. Then, right before I moved into the heart of my talk, I ripped off the Wildcat jacket to reveal my true identity—an obnoxiously bright Pantone 172 Florida Gator orange polo shirt! As a former University of Florida employee, this stunt was intended to be a humorous warm-up to the evening. Instead, it unwittingly poured salt into a gaping wound the Gators had inflicted on the Wildcat football team just a few days earlier (the final score was 65–0). Needless to say, the temperature of the room remained frosty for the duration of the evening.

You might think this was a harmless faux pas, but Southeastern Conference fans take their football seriously. In fact, it is almost a religion. OK, for many, it is a religion. Athletic fanaticism, however, is hardly unique

2. For more on these arguments, see Lewis, *Mere Christianity*, 54–56, and Morris, *Making Sense*, 109–29 and 173–80.

to the southern part of the United States. A few years ago, a study was conducted in England, where soccer (real football according to my British friends) reigns supreme. Ardent Manchester United fans were asked to write an essay on the virtues of their team. The study participants were then told to walk to another building where someone would record their avid support on videotape. Along the way, however, each participant came upon a fallen jogger writhing in pain. In some cases, the injured person was wearing a Manchester United shirt; other times the jersey of their archrival, Liverpool. More than 90 percent helped the ManU jogger, while 70 percent ignored the injured Liverpudlian.[3] This Good Samaritan study illustrates the deeply ingrained tribalism that we all share and how it often expresses itself through our sports allegiances, which is one reason why I am allowed to criticize *my* own team, but not *yours*!

How to Become an Elephant Whisperer

So far this chapter has been a bit like a trip to the zoo. We have strolled past the bird, reptile, and cat habitats, but now we come to the star of the show, the elephant. Several years ago, Marquette University professor Michael Johnson took a memorable trip to one of the largest zoological properties in the United States—Disney's Animal Kingdom. While observing scientists studying elephants, Johnson was struck by a thought. As a computer engineer, he wondered what it would be like to study elephant communication patterns. This question led to the development of the Dr. Dolittle Project, which funded research of animal vocalizations. By utilizing speech-processing technology and methods, Johnson and his colleagues identified a repertoire of five distinct African elephant vocalizations.[4] "We can't hear a difference but the computer can," Johnson says. "Elephants often talk at a very low frequency, eight to 14 hertz. We hear it as a rumble, but it is actually a vocalization that they can hear just fine."[5]

This insight reinforces the first principle of moral psychology—*intuitions come first, strategic reasoning second.* While it might be comforting to imagine ourselves as purely rational beings with strategic reasoning firmly ensconced in the driver's seat, Jonathan Haidt believes this is a

3. Zaki, *War for Kindness*, 44–45.

4. The five different vocalizations include the croak, noisy rumble, rev, snort, and trumpet. See Clemins, "African Elephants."

5. Etter, "Listening," 15.

delusion. Instead, Haidt likens our strategic reasoning to a rider sitting atop an enormous intuitive elephant with a mind of its own. So rather than brilliantly shifting and steering a nimble sports car, it is more accurate to imagine our reason straddling the largest land mammal on the planet. Haidt observes: "When we see or hear about the things other people do, the elephant begins to lean immediately. The rider, who is always trying to anticipate the elephant's next move, begins looking around for a way to support such a move."[6]

Once we understand that intuition is more basic than strategic reasoning, then we can see why focusing on logic, arguments, and reasons as the sole or even primary means of persuasion is an ill-advised strategy. Logic, arguments, and reasons are the language of the rider, not the elephant. If elephants are antagonistic toward one another then rational strategies will backfire, often leading to stampedes rather than warmth. The first step then with people on the other side of an issue is to find a way to befriend the behemoth, to get elephants leaning toward each other. Intuitive elephants are constantly communicating with each other beneath the surface. The untrained rational rider might perceive this communication "as a rumble," as our pachyderm professor Michael Johnson puts it, but there is an ongoing intuitive exchange that our elephants "hear just fine."

Haidt cites Dale Carnegie as "one of the great elephant-whisperers of all time. In his classic book *How to Win Friends and Influence People*, Carnegie repeatedly urged readers to avoid direct confrontations. Instead, he advised people to 'begin in a friendly way,' to 'smile,' to 'be a good listener,' and to 'never say "you're wrong."' The persuader's goal should be to convey respect, warmth, and an openness to dialogue before stating one's own case."[7] Before launching into arguments, or even attempting humor at the other person's expense (mea culpa!), start by asking yourself these questions: Am I on the same frequency with my conversation partner? Is there an intuitive resonance? Are we in sync? If not, focus your energy on relationship cultivation rather than rider-centered persuasion. Otherwise, we are asking people to go against their elephant or "violate their intuitions," something people simply will not do. Instead, "they will devote their efforts to finding an escape hatch—a reason to doubt your argument or conclusion. They will almost always succeed."[8]

6. Haidt, *Righteous Mind*, 71.

7. Haidt, *Righteous Mind*, 48.

8. Haidt, *Righteous Mind*, 50.

Of course, all this talk about intuition does not mean that reasons and arguments are irrelevant. It simply means the elephant must be leaning in our direction *before* reasons and arguments will have leverage.

The Elephant in the Room

Christ-followers have a long history of pursuing persuasion . . . and for good reason. First Peter 3:15–16 tells us to "Always be prepared to give an answer to everyone who asks you to give the reason for the hope that you have. But do this with gentleness and respect, keeping a clear conscience, so that those who speak maliciously against your good behavior in Christ may be ashamed of their slander." This is the cornerstone apologetic text, frequently cited in support of a rational defense of the faith. After all, Peter is saying that each of us is called to give "answers" and "reasons" for our faith in Christ. That said, the text not only instructs us to offer a reasoned defense; we must do so in a winsome manner, with "gentleness" and "respect." In other words, Christian apologetics should be holistic, addressing both the high-road rider and the low-road elephant.

The evangelical movement should be commended for taking the cognitive dimension of this apologetic mandate seriously. During the past seventy-five years a wealth of apologetic resources has emerged. From the popular works of C. S. Lewis, Francis Schaeffer, Lee Strobel, and Os Guinness to the academic writings of Alvin Plantinga, William Lane Craig, J. P. Moreland, and Alister McGrath, there is no shortage of arguments to defend the Christian faith. Rider-focused apologetics is truly a great gift that should be treasured and celebrated.

That said, evangelicals have not always done so well with the second part of Peter's mandate—to engage the elephant with *gentleness* and *respect*. Instead, we have all too often embraced the bass-pounding fallacy that righteous indignation excuses rude rhetoric. John Stackhouse shares a bad example that would make my high school librarian proud. In *Humble Apologetics*, Stackhouse recounts the cautionary tale of a college student by the name of Bob, whose parachurch ministry had invited a famous Christian apologist (Stackhouse uses the pseudonym Dr. Ward) to speak on their secular campus.[9] When the much-anticipated evening arrived, Bob entered the venue with several nagging questions. What if Dr. Ward didn't live up to the hype? What if the questions from the

9. Stackhouse, *Humble Apologetics*, xiii–xvi.

skeptical audience twisted him in knots? What if their campus ministry's reputation was damaged beyond repair?

Bob's fears, however, were quickly laid to rest. The speaker, who had no less than six academic degrees and several acclaimed books to his credit, addressed the packed auditorium with confidence and ease. During the course of an hour, Dr. Ward made a strong case for the truth of the Christian worldview, its superiority to all other belief systems, and its unparalleled practical benefits.

Following Dr. Ward's address, the evening turned from monologue to dialogue. Bob tensed up once again. It is one thing to deliver a rehearsed speech, but something altogether different to answer hostile questions before a live audience. Each student question, however, floated over the proverbial plate like a lazy softball pitch that Dr. Ward effortlessly swatted beyond the fence. That is until the final questioner approached the microphone. He was an angry thirty-something graduate student "with a thick, black mop of hair matched by an unkempt black beard."[10] The graduate student unleashed a hard-edged, multi-part question that challenged not only the cogency of the Christian faith, but Dr. Ward's credibility, as well. Tension hung in the air as the audience anxiously anticipated a rejoinder from Dr. Ward. But instead of providing a respectful, careful response or inviting the questioner to discuss the complex question over a late-night beverage, Dr. Ward chose to pepper the student with a series of rapid-fire questions. Once it became clear that he could not respond to Dr. Ward without contradicting himself, the embarrassed student sheepishly responded, "I don't know." Dr. Ward acknowledged this unqualified surrender with a smug and beaming triumphant smile. The Christian emcee then invited the audience to thank Dr. Ward and the "room resounded with applause."

Bob was ecstatic! Dr. Ward had defended the gospel with uncompromising power and righteous conviction by thwarting the wily schemes of the rebellious student body. Bob rose to his feet and began to quietly sing, "Onward, Christian soldiers! Marching as to war." Then, as the large crowd exited the building, he overheard two female students talking. Moving closer, he heard one say to her friend, "I don't care if the son of a bitch *is* right. I still hate his guts."[11] Bob stopped dead in his tracks. Stunned, his euphoria slowly melted back into suffocating angst.

10. Stackhouse, *Humble Apologetics*, xv.

11. Stackhouse, *Humble Apologetics*, xvi.

What went wrong? Dr. Ward spoke with authority. He delivered his message with reverence and respect for biblical truth claims. He honored the righteous conviction intuitions of in-group loyalty, authority, and sanctity. In so doing, however, the pounding bass muted the treble of compassion, especially when he felt personally challenged. One can imagine Dr. Ward's internal dialogue: "Who is this cocky student to challenge my academic pedigree? I was writing books when he was still in diapers! How dare he!" In that moment, Dr. Ward took umbrage and succumbed to the fallacy we are seeking to correct in this chapter: the idea that righteous indignation gives us license to be rude. The consequences were swift and severe. By ignoring the compassion intuitions of care, liberty, and fairness, all of the good rider-focused content that was offered that evening failed to land as *righteous*. Instead, Dr. Ward was viewed as *self-righteous* ("I don't care if the son of a bitch *is* right, I still hate his guts"). All bass, no treble. What could have been a great night for the gospel was ruined by totally ignoring the elephant in the room.

In stark contrast to Dr. Ward's bad example, former *Moody Magazine* editor Jerry Jenkins recalls a time when Francis Schaeffer handled a similar question and answer session much differently. One of the most popular Christian apologists of the twentieth century, Schaeffer frequently addressed large crowds. After speaking to a group of around 4,000 people one night in Chicago, Schaeffer answered several questions. One questioner with cerebral palsy, however, struggled to clearly articulate his query. Many in the room grew impatient while Schaeffer dedicated several minutes to listening and clarifying the question. Schaeffer squeezed his eyes tightly shut to increase his concentration. He gently asked the questioner to repeat certain lines. Finally, with the content fully grasped, Schaeffer provided a careful, respectful, and gentle answer.[12] This patient and kind response no doubt charmed at least some of the elephants in the audience that night.

The Final Apologetic

Christ-followers should be on their best behavior when sharing the gospel with unbelievers (as Schaeffer demonstrated that night in Chicago), but we are also called to model unity, kindness, and love within the Christian fold. While Schaeffer offered many rider-focused arguments for the truth of the Christian faith during his lengthy apologetic ministry, he believed the final

12. Jenkins, "Letter to the editor," 8.

apologetic before the watching world is not the razor-sharp logic of arguments, but rather the love expressed between fellow believers. In *The Mark of the Christian*, Schaeffer wrote the following arresting words:

> In John 13 the point was that if an individual Christian does not show love toward other true Christians, the world has the right to judge that he is not a Christian. Here Jesus is stating something else which is much more cutting, much more profound: we cannot expect the world to believe the Father sent the Son, that Jesus' claims are true, and that Christianity is true, unless the world sees some reality of the oneness of true Christians.[13]

Did you get that? Schaeffer is saying that Jesus has given the world the right to judge the truth of the gospel on the basis of Christian unity. In other words, rider-focused truth claims are discredited when Christians fail to express love toward one another. So when the world sees Christians tearing each other apart, non-Christians have every right to question the truth of the gospel message. A sobering thought, indeed.

As I reflect upon the importance of charity and unity within the Christian family, my mind immediately goes to Brian McLaren, whom I mentioned in the introduction. My mind goes to McLaren because I have never seen any single Christian attacked more viciously by fellow believers. At the same time, I am not sure I have ever witnessed a persecuted believer respond with such grace. These contrasting examples would be a great master class on how *not* to treat fellow Christians with whom you disagree on the one hand; and how to exhibit Christian charity and kindness in the face of persecution on the other.

McLaren rose to prominence in the early years of the twenty-first century and at the pinnacle of his popularity was named one of *Time* magazine's most influential evangelicals in America.[14] Robert Webber called him the voice of the younger evangelicals[15] and Justin Taylor considered him the pastor of the postconservative movement.[16] Part of McLaren's appeal was his ability to put into words the angst many younger people were experiencing with modern expressions of Christianity.

While McLaren struck a chord with many millennials, his provocative proposals also came under fierce attack from some prominent evangelical

13. Schaeffer, *Mark of the Christian*, 189.

14. Van Biema, "Most Influential Evangelicals," 45.

15. Webber, *Younger Evangelicals*, 114.

16. Taylor, "Postconservative Evangelicalism," 18–26.

leaders. But his proposals weren't the only thing attacked. Many of his critics also engaged in scathing ad hominem arguments, bordering on libel and slander. One case occurred on the campus of a prominent theological seminary. During a chapel service, the seminary president and a panel of faculty members discussed McLaren's latest book. Over the course of the hour-long discussion, the president and panel confidently asserted that McLaren "rejects everything about Christianity," believes "God is ugly," is the "craftiest of the serpents of the field," "is following in the train of his father the devil," is "a wolf in sheep's clothing," is transparently "self-serving," and "offers a God with no moral demands."[17] This chapel-service conversation illustrates well the bass-pounding fallacy under consideration in this chapter. Much like Dr. Ward, the seminary president and faculty panel took umbrage at the doctrinal critique offered by McLaren's new book and the in-group loyalty intuitions kicked in. Instead of sticking to a scholarly assessment of the book, the president and panel proceeded to declare open season on McLaren's intentions and integrity—all without firsthand, personal knowledge of the author. The result: an hour-long jam session that was all bass, no treble. Again, what could have been an opportunity to model responsible academic engagement in a spirit of Christian charity was ruined by totally ignoring the elephant in the room.

The seminary panel's final critique point is that McLaren offers a God with no moral demands. I don't know about you, but I can't think of a morally demanding task that is more difficult than loving those who say mean-spirited things, especially when they don't know you personally. But McLaren has consistently refused to respond in kind. Instead of nurturing a jaded posture of suspicion and an attitude of retribution, he has adopted a spirit of generosity. On his sixtieth birthday, he blogged sixty reasons for being thankful. Here is number forty-five: "My critics have meant a lot to me. They helped me see how insecure I was; they kept me on my toes; they challenged me to think deeper and work harder, and they forced me to develop courage and confidence that I never would have developed otherwise. As one of my favorite prayers says, critics are really friends in disguise. How can I not be grateful for them?"[18]

This is just one example of McLaren's kindness and generosity. I interacted with McLaren through email and in several face-to-face interviews spanning a decade and could not have asked for a more gracious and

17. Mohler et al., "Panel Discussion."

18. McLaren, "60 gifts."

responsive dialogue partner. He answered every question with thoughtful and helpful candor. While he and I do not see eye to eye on every theological point, McLaren's second-mile form of Christianity has inspired me to become a more faithful Christ-follower. McLaren has consistently lived out Schaeffer's Final Apologetic.

At the end of the day, mean-spirited Christians do more damage to the cause of Christ than any attack leveled by non-believers. We ignore the elephant in the room at our own peril. At a time when so many evangelicals are mired in a can't-win culture war, we need to learn how to befriend the behemoth and reject the tempting fallacy that righteous indignation entitles us to rude rhetoric. And if we don't learn this lesson? Well, I guess we can at least serve as a bad example.

Chapter 2

Treble Tactic Two: Cultivate Humility

Bass-Pounding Fallacy: A Little Chutzpáh Never Hurt Anybody

"A whole lot of us go through life assuming that we are basically right, basically all the time, about basically everything: about our political and intellectual convictions, our religious and moral beliefs, our assessment of other people, our memories, our grasp of facts. As absurd as it sounds when we stop to think about it, our steady state seems to be one of unconsciously assuming that we are very close to omniscient."[1]

—KATHRYN SCHULZ

In 2019, Columbia Pictures released *Once Upon a Time in Hollywood*—a movie that went on to earn ten Oscar nominations. In this stylized love letter to his hometown, director Quentin Tarantino spared no expense in returning the Sunset Strip and other parts of Los Angeles to its 1969 neon-shimmering glory.

Early in the film, the audience is treated to an exhilarating ride along in Roman Polanski's vintage MG, as he and wife Sharon Tate breeze through the Hollywood Hills enroute to a star-studded party at the Playboy Mansion. As the open-air roadster glides to a halt in front of the regal estate, the camera follows Tate leaping into the arms of Steve McQueen,

1. Schulz, *Being Wrong*, 4.

then floating through a fluffle of bunnies before joining a gyrating throng of revelers on the grotto pool deck.[2]

I'm not sure if he arrived in a British sports car, but Christian apologist Lee Strobel once visited the Playboy Mansion. Instead of a lively pool party, however, Strobel was there to interview Hugh Hefner for the TV show *Faith Under Fire*. It would be the first public discussion of the Playboy mogul's religious beliefs. Wearing his iconic smoking jacket and burgundy pajamas, the seventy-eight-year-old Hefner did not disappoint. During the interview, Hefner calls the biblical notion of divinity "too childish." Instead, he understands *god* "as the beginning of it all and as a word for the great unknown." Organized religion is an exercise in fanciful hubris—"man's attempt to explain the inexplicable." To claim certain knowledge regarding the great mysteries and spiritual wonders of the universe would seem to endow religious believers with "almost God-like qualities." Instead, Hefner prefers humble agnosticism. That is until Strobel asks if he ever envies people with a deep religious faith. "Just the opposite," says Hefner. "I think I am a one-eyed man in a blind world. I think I see the world with remarkable rational clarity."[3] It is striking to observe Hefner's critique of religious hubris one moment, only to boldly claim for himself crystal-clear cycloptic vision the next. He is a one-eyed man in a blind world, yet impervious to his own chutzpáh.

Specks and Planks

While it might be tempting to don our ophthalmological scrubs and go digging around for the speck on Hefner's cornea, we should first acknowledge our own blind spots. In fact, the pantheon of infamous Christian planks includes medieval crusades, Native American genocide, South African apartheid, Civil War slavery, and the subjugation of women. All of the above were once justified with great conviction on biblical grounds. And all of the above are now repudiated with comparable conviction and biblical assurance. No doubt future Christians will look back upon our contemporary era with similar puzzlement concerning some of the causes and politicians current believers have chosen to support. Cautionary tales such as these should give us pause whenever the specter of absolute certainty wells up within us.

2. Tarantino, dir., *Once Upon a Time in Hollywood.*
3. Strobel, "Hefner Interview."

Whether playboy or puritan, we all tend to overestimate our ability to see the world as it really is. And we all tend to defend our beliefs with great zeal and tenacity as if our perceptions should be obvious to all. Kathryn Schulz, author of *Being Wrong*, captures this tendency to ascribe blindness to nearly everybody but ourselves:

> A whole lot of us go through life assuming that we are basically right, basically all the time, about basically everything: about our political and intellectual convictions, our religious and moral beliefs, our assessment of other people, our memories, our grasp of facts. As absurd as it sounds when we stop to think about it, our steady state seems to be one of unconsciously assuming that we are very close to omniscient.[4]

So why are hubris and swagger wired into our makeup? Why do we imagine ourselves as rational race car drivers skillfully maneuvering our personal MG through the hills, valleys, twists, and turns of life? Why are we convinced that our cognitive high beams illuminate the rational road before us with perfect clarity? Why are we so reluctant to admit when we are wrong? And what are the costs of failing to cultivate intellectual humility and a proper kind of confidence?

What She Said, What He Heard

My wife and I have joked for years that one day we will write a book entitled *What She Said, What He Heard*. Hardly a week goes by without adding another entry to our long list of humorous miscommunication blunders. Of course, we are not the only couple with this perennial challenge. Schulz starts her book with one such conversation between a husband and wife in Grand Central Station:

> **MAN:** You said pound cake.
>
> **WOMAN:** I didn't say pound cake, I said crumb cake.
>
> **MAN:** You said pound cake.
>
> **WOMAN:** Don't tell me what I said.
>
> **MAN:** You said pound cake.
>
> **WOMAN:** I said crumb cake.

4. Schulz, *Being Wrong*, 4.

MAN: I actually saw the crumb cake but I didn't get it because you said pound cake.

WOMAN: I said crumb cake.

MAN: Well, I heard pound cake.

WOMAN: Then you obviously weren't listening. Crumb cake doesn't even sound like pound cake.

MAN: Well, maybe you accidentally said pound cake.

WOMAN: I said crumb cake.[5]

Jonathan Haidt describes a mild domestic dispute of his own. While working in his home office one morning, his wife asked him to not leave dirty dishes on the kitchen counter where she prepares food for their child. Haidt recalls, "Her request was polite but its tone added a post-script: 'As I have asked you a hundred times before.'"[6] Without missing a beat, Haidt interjected "something about the baby having woken up at the same time that our elderly dog barked to ask for a walk and I'm sorry but I just put my breakfast dishes down wherever I could. In my family, caring for a hungry baby and an incontinent dog is a surefire excuse, so I was acquitted."[7] After successfully vindicating himself, he returned to writing about the first principle of moral psychology: *intuitions come first, strategic reasoning second*. Then, it hit him:

> There I was at my desk, writing about how people automatically fabricate justifications of their gut feelings, when suddenly I realized that I had just done the same thing with my wife. I disliked being criticized, and I had felt a flash of negativity by the time Jayne had gotten to her third word ("*Can you not . . .*"). Even before I knew why she was criticizing me, I knew I disagreed with her (because intuitions come first). The instant I knew the content of the criticism ("*. . . leave dirty dishes on the . . .*"), my inner lawyer went to work searching for an excuse (strategic reasoning second). It's true that I had eaten breakfast, given Max his first bottle, and let Andy out for his first walk, but these events had all happened at separate times. Only when my wife criticized me did I merge them into a composite image of a harried father with too few hands, and I created this fabrication by the time she had

5. Schulz, *Being Wrong*, ix.
6. Haidt, *Righteous Mind*, 52.
7. Haidt, *Righteous Mind*, 52.

> completed her one-sentence criticism *(". . . counter where I make baby food?")*. I then lied so quickly and convincingly that my wife and I both believed me.[8]

We all know what it feels like to be criticized. Just think back to the last time this happened to you. Be honest. Was your initial gut reaction to withhold judgment long enough to carefully review the evidence marshaled by your accuser as a good judge or scientist would do? Probably not. More than likely, your initial reaction was to launch into a defensive posture even before the charge was fully articulated. Instead of enlisting the services of an unbiased judge or careful scientist, our low-road elephant instantaneously calls upon the high-road strategic-reasoning rider to function as a defense attorney or public relations practitioner. This is why the rider rarely engages in *exploratory reasoning* to look for the actual truth in a situation, as a good scientist or judge would do. Instead, the rider employs *confirmatory reasoning* to pursue the evidence and arguments that support the preferences or convictions of our low-road elephant. This widespread problem is known as motivated reasoning or confirmation bias.[9]

Haidt simplifies the phenomenon of motivated reasoning by juxtaposing two words: *can* and *must*. When we *want* something to be true, we ask ourselves the following question: "*Can* I believe it?" We then search for reasons and evidence to support the desirable proposition. It doesn't take much, "a single piece of pseudo-evidence" will do the trick. We now have justification in case anyone challenges us. On the other hand, if we *don't* want to believe something, we ask ourselves, "*Must* I believe it?" Even a shred of counter-evidence will satisfy us. Haidt adds, "You only need one key to unlock the handcuffs of must."[10]

Cognitive neuroscientist Tali Sharot points out an additional problem known as the "boomerang effect." When we are presented with data and arguments that contradict our current beliefs, we not only dismiss the new piece of unwelcome evidence, we frequently develop new reasons and counterarguments never before considered. The upshot: unwelcome arguments and evidence reinforce confirmatory reasoning and greatly reduce the possibility of open-minded exploration of truth.[11]

8. Haidt, *Righteous Mind*, 54.

9. Haidt, *Righteous Mind*, 76–80.

10. Haidt, *Righteous Mind*, 84. Haidt credits social psychologist Tom Gilovich for this insight.

11. Sharot, *Influential Mind*, 17.

Why are we so susceptible to this kind of thinking? Why are we wired to function as lawyers and PR practitioners rather than judges and scientists? Haidt explains this quirk of human nature in evolutionary terms. The intuitive elephant is much older and more primal than our high-road rational capacities, as can be seen by the similar low-road neurocircuitry found in other primates. For most of our existence, the human species lived in a dangerous world in which immediate fight-or-flight responses were necessary for survival. This is why the amygdala is on a hair trigger.[12] The low-road intuitive elephant with its quick, automatic circuitry is well suited to this kind of high-risk environment, but over time humans developed the capacity for verbal communication and with this skill came strategic reasoning. Survival no longer depended solely upon gut reaction, but also upon the ability to persuade others that we should be viewed as socially competent and trustworthy partners. Consequently, Haidt believes the primary function of this relative newcomer to the game—the high-road rider—is to offer a rational defense for the low-road intuitive judgments of the elephant rather than to seek out the actual truth in every situation. In other words, reputation management tends to drive us to engage in confirmatory rather than exploratory reasoning, especially when personal interest is at stake.

Now, Haidt's two primary insights in this context—human beings feel before thinking and engage in post-hoc rationalization—do not necessarily hinge upon an evolutionary explanation. Perhaps we could attribute this quirk (the rider as lawyer and PR practitioner rather than objective judge and scientist) to our fallen nature.[13] As self-centered sinners, our selfishness and corruption frequently blind us from the truth. The fact that we rationalize so easily and so well is simply evidence of Jeremiah 17:9: "The heart is deceitful above all things and beyond cure. Who can understand it?" Perhaps the rider was divinely designed to pursue truth through exploratory reasoning, but the effects of the fall have produced confirmation-seeking advocates and spin doctors inside each and every one of us. Whatever the origin, there is little doubt that we make most decisions at the elephant level and are vulnerable to not only motivated reasoning but managing our reputations with unbridled swagger.

12. Timothy Jennings calls the amygdala, "the brain's 'alarm' center and the region associated with the emotions of fear and anxiety." See Jennings, *God-Shaped Brain*, 254.

13. It is beyond the scope of this book to weigh in on the controversy between theistic evolutionists and Intelligent Design advocates. For an interesting primer on this subject, see Stump, *Four Views*.

The Famous Chinese Character for Picnic Area

Let us return to Kathryn Schulz, who offers her own insights into our error-prone and rationalizing species. Schulz opens her 2011 TED Talk, "On Being Wrong," with a story.[14] She and a friend are traveling across the country through state parks and national forests. Somewhere in South Dakota, Schulz asks a question about something that has been bugging her for 2,000 miles: "What's up with the Chinese character I keep seeing by the side of the road?" Her friend stares at her blankly. Schulz clarifies, "You know, all the signs we keep seeing with the Chinese character on them?" Her friend continues to stare, then suddenly bursts into laughter . . . you mean "the famous Chinese character for picnic area?"[15]

Once the audience laughter subsides, Schulz asks the following question: "How does it feel to be wrong?" People in the front row respond: "dreadful" and "thumbs down." Schulz affirms the answers; but explains these are responses to a different question. They are answering the question, "How does it feel to *realize* you are wrong?" It is dreadful to *realize* you are wrong. Just *being* wrong doesn't feel like anything.[16]

Schulz illustrates the difference by invoking the famous Looney Tunes Road Runner cartoon. Nearly every episode ends with the Road Runner dashing off a cliff, followed closely by the inept Wile E. Coyote. This is not a problem for the Road Runner since birds can fly. At first, it doesn't seem like a problem for the suspended-in-mid-air coyote, either. That is until he *realizes* his predicament and plummets to his poof-of-dust demise. Schulz says when we are wrong about something, but don't yet realize it (or refuse to realize it), we are like the coyote. We just insist that we are right, which keeps us from looking down. It feels good. It feels safe. We feel like we are on solid ground, but we are actually floating in unsupported thin air. We are already wrong; we just aren't aware of it yet. Schulz now corrects something she said a moment before—"being wrong does feel like something; it feels like being *right*."[17]

Schulz tells another story. A woman undergoes surgery at one of the top teaching hospitals in the country. In the recovery room, she wakes up to discover the surgeon has operated on the wrong leg. When the hospital

14. Schulz, "On Being Wrong."
15. Schulz, "On Being Wrong."
16. Schulz, "On Being Wrong."
17. Schulz, "On Being Wrong."

releases an official statement, it reads, "For whatever reason, [the surgeon] simply *felt* he was on the correct side of the patient." The takeaway? "Trusting too much in the feeling of being on the correct side of *anything* can be very dangerous."[18]

This feeling of rightness is heightened by wrapping ourselves in the blanket of certainty. It feels warm, cozy, and safe, but provides a false sense of security. Not only that, it makes us look foolish or even dangerous—especially to those on the opposite side of an issue. If this is true, then unassailable certainty does not persuade opponents or charm pachyderms; instead, it serves as elephant repellant.

Now Schulz makes it clear that knowledge and certainty, while related, are not synonymous. "Certainty suggests something bigger and more forceful than knowledge. The great American satirist Ambrose Bierce defined it as 'being mistaken at the top of one's voice,' and it is this shouted-from-the-rooftops quality that makes certainty distinctive."[19] Certainty also possesses a double-edged quality. We are quick to condemn it in our opponents, while seldom able to perceive it in ourselves.

> The certainty of those with whom we disagree—whether the disagreement concerns who should run the country or who should run the dishwasher—never looks justified to us, and frequently looks odious. As often as not, we regard it as a sign of excessive emotional attachment to an idea, or an indicator of a narrow, fearful, or stubborn frame of mind. By contrast, we experience our own certainty as simply a side-effect of our rightness, justifiable because our cause is just. And, remarkably . . . we cannot transpose the scene. We cannot imagine, or do not care, that our own certainty, when seen from the outside, must look just as unbecoming and ill-grounded as the certainty we abhor in others.[20]

So why do we fail to own up to our mistakes, instead latching onto an unassailable sense of certainty so much of the time? Haidt has already offered us one reason: reputation management. Polishing our profile enhances our tribal status, while admitting failure leaves us vulnerable to exclusion, even expulsion from the tribe. Schulz offers two additional reasons. The first is related—the plague of *perfectionism*. We learn very early that the path to success is to avoid red ink, so marked-up assignments belong to

18. Schulz, "On Being Wrong."

19. Schulz, *Being Wrong*, 163.

20. Schulz, *Being Wrong*, 164.

kids who are "lazy, irresponsible dimwits." We are taught that mistakes and flaws go hand in hand, "so we just insist that we are right because it makes us feel smart and responsible and virtuous and safe." But, like the coyote in mid-air, this feeling is fool's gold. The second explanation is *error blindness*. Being wrong feels like being right because we lack an infallible internal guide that alerts us to mistakes. Reputation management, perfectionism, and error blindness are serious threats to our collective well-being and interpersonal relationships, because if you disagree with me then you must be either ignorant, stupid, or evil. As Schulz points out, "This attachment to our sense of rightness keeps us from preventing mistakes and causes us to treat others terribly."[21] This isn't exactly a great recipe for loving the person next door, but it is the perfect recipe for chutzpáh.

Chútzpah Versus *Chutzpáh*

The bass-pounding fallacy for this chapter is a little *chutzpáh* never hurt anybody, but what exactly does this mean? I have been using *chutzpah* in a fairly indiscriminate manner up to this point, but the time has come to offer a more careful definition. Let's turn to well-known author and speaker Malcolm Gladwell, who offers clarification in an episode of his podcast *Revisionist History*.[22]

Gladwell identifies two different kinds of *chutzpah*. Both mean "bold," but very different kinds of boldness—one virtuous; the other vicious. The first kind of *chutzpah* is *chútzpah*. It places the accent on the initial syllable and means "audacious" or "surprisingly courageous." It is the lone college student challenging a Tiananmen Square tank or the LDS Church advertising in *The Book of Mormon* playbill. *Chútzpah* is admirably daring.

The second kind of *chutzpah* is *chutzpáh*. The accent is on the latter syllable and is pronounced, "Whoofs-pá!" It means "shameless," speaking and acting without any self-awareness or regard for another person's feelings, perspective, or well-being. *Chutzpáh* is brazenly bold, void of conscience. It is tobacco companies knowing that cigarettes cause cancer or Ponzi schemers hoodwinking the elderly.

One word. Two meanings. And the two are often conflated.[23]

21. Schulz, "On Being Wrong."

22. Gladwell, "Chutzpah vs. Chutzpah."

23. Throughout the episode, Gladwell speaks to his Jewish neighbor who explains that Americans typically use the word *chútzpah* as a term of endearment, while Israelis

Gladwell illustrates the difference by contrasting two men from Brooklyn. One is the personification of *chútzpah*, the other *chutzpáh*. The first story takes us back to where this chapter began—the Hollywood Hills. Gladwell arrives at a 1960s-style house, perched above Tinsel Town—something straight out of *Once Upon a Time in Hollywood*. He is there to interview an elderly man who grew up in Brooklyn, but settled in Los Angeles seven decades ago. His name is Al Ruddy. After high school, Ruddy set his sights on the entertainment industry. Completely green, the Jewish Ruddy decides to write an outrageous television script about a concentration camp run by bumbling Nazis. Somehow, Ruddy lands a pitch meeting with legendary CBS CEO William S. Paley, who is also Jewish. Ruddy's agent kicks off the meeting by explaining the concept, but the CBS boss finds "the idea of Nazis doing comedy totally reprehensible." The frazzled agent turns to Ruddy, who has "never sold a thing in his life." Seizing upon this opportunity Ruddy leaps to his feet and acts out the whole pilot with larger-than-life mannerisms, including a bit about a Nazi guard who turns a blind eye to prisoner shenanigans: "I see nothing, I know nothing, I was not here, I did not even get up this morning!"[24] By the end of the pitch, Paley and the other executives in the room are doubled over in laughter. The head of CBS says, "I don't know if I can ever buy that show, but I just want to commend you. That's one of the funniest things I've ever heard."

The rest is history. Paley does buy the show. *Hogan's Heroes* runs for six seasons and wins two Emmys. A Jew pitching a show about a concentration camp managed by maladroit Nazis (some of whom would be played by Jewish actors) to a room full of Jewish TV executives just twenty years removed from the Holocaust . . . that's bold. That's daring. That's Tarantino-esque.[25] That's *chútzpah*.

Chutzpáh is a different story. A very different story. The Brooklynite in this account is Joseph Colombo, a well-known Mafia don. While Ruddy is making a name for himself on the West Coast, Colombo is back East creating the Italian American Civil Rights League. The goal of this new organization is to rebrand the image of Italian Americans and legitimize the work of Colombo and his associates. Colombo's strategy includes

generally employ *chutzpáh* as a term of derision.

24. For a highlight reel, see Des Hammond, "Sergeant Schultz."

25. Tarantino has a penchant for rewriting history in his films, including a graphic Jewish revenge scene in *Inglourious Basterds*. An homage to *Inglourious Basterds* can be found near the beginning of *Once Upon a Time in Hollywood* as well.

newspaper advertising and targeted campaigns against big brands like Alka Seltzer ("Mama Mia, that's a spicy meatball!") that allegedly stereotype Italians. He even hits the talk show circuit, including a guest appearance on the Dick Cavett Show. While this shameless crusade to sanitize the image of the Cosa Nostra families is advancing publicly, Colombo and his associates are privately up to their eyeballs in illicit Mafia maleficence. Bold, yes. Daring, yes. But this is not *chútzpah*, something to be admired. No, this is *chutzpáh*, brazenly bold without conscience.

Then, like something straight out of a Hollywood script, *chútzpah* meets *chutzpáh*. After *Hogan's Heroes*, Ruddy lands a job as an executive with Paramount Pictures. One of his first assignments is to produce a new movie about the mob. That's right, *The Godfather*. When Colombo gets word of the project, he is outraged. The real-life mafia don does everything within his power to grind production to a halt. Ruddy is stalked. His windshield broken. The studio experiences union problems, death threats, and bomb scares. Finally, Ruddy is dispatched to New York for a sit down with Colombo, "Brooklyn to Brooklyn." He invites Colombo to read the 155-page script. After struggling with the first few pages, Colombo gives up. As Gladwell puts it: "a Mafia boss isn't going to work his way through a 155-page script. The whole point of being a Mafia boss is that you don't have to read things that are 155 pages." After Colombo's associate, a fellow by the name of Caesar, also refuses to read it, the mob boss simply asks Ruddy to delete the word "Mafia" from the film. Ruddy gladly complies and the two shake hands. "From that moment on, all trouble with the movie ceased." Little did Colombo know that the word "Mafia" only appeared once in the entire script.

So *Chútzpah* defeats *Chutzpáh*. Gladwell summarizes the encounter eloquently: "*Chutzpáh* is a bunch of violent mobsters threatening to shut down a movie because it depicts them as violent mobsters. *Chútzpah* is tricking them because they are too lazy to read the script." One word. Two meanings. And the two are often conflated. Gladwell continues: "Over the years our moral vocabulary has become impoverished, which is a problem because you cannot make sense of things you cannot describe. And lumping together 'audacity' [chútzpah] and 'shamelessness' [chutzpáh] creates a loophole large enough to drive a tank through."[26]

26. Gladwell, "Chutzpah vs. Chutzpah."

David, the King of Chútzpah *and* Chutzpáh

The difference between chútzpah and chutzpáh is also well illustrated by two very different stories from the life of David. The first is when David is quite young. We all know the story: with great courage, boldness, and audacity, the physically overmatched and under-resourced shepherd boy slays the towering giant. In this story, we see the young David exuding chútzpah, remarkable courage and cunning.

We know the second story, as well. David is now king of Israel. After committing adultery with Uriah's wife, Bathsheba, David orders Uriah to the front line of a battle that guarantees his demise. In this story, we see the elder David's cup overflowing with chutzpáh—shameful and wanton disregard for Uriah's well-being.

The first kind of chutzpah (chútzpah) is virtuous; the second (chutzpáh) is vicious. The first is worthy of *commendation*; the second *condemnation*. The first grows out of a proper confidence; the second out of unbridled arrogance.

How about us? In our interaction with people on the other side of the cultural divide, do we ever conflate chútzpah and chutzpáh? Yes, there are times when we are called to daring acts of faith, like the young David. Yes, there are times when we must stand with Joshua and proclaim from the rooftops, "For me and my house, we will serve the Lord!" In these moments of courageous conviction, however, which kind of chutzpah do we project? Chutzpáh is not reserved for pornographers, adulterers, murderers, and mafia dons. Whenever we boldly proclaim our convictions without an ounce of humility, that's chutzpáh. Whenever we pompously ignore our own vulnerability to motivated reasoning, reputation management, perfectionism, and error blindness, that's chutzpáh. Whenever we act as if two of the key pillars of Christian anthropology—finitude and fallenness—don't apply to us, that's chutzpáh. Whenever we pretend that knowing the one who knows it all turns us into *know it alls*, that's chutzpáh. So maybe it is true that a little chutzpah never hurt anybody; just make sure you put the accent on the right syllable.

Chapter 3

Treble Tactic Three: Swap Stories

Bass-Pounding Fallacy: Arguments Persuade Pachyderms

> "People's minds will sync up in the presence of story, but the process relies heavily on there being some similarity between the storyteller and the listener. . . . The more the commonality between the storyteller and the listener, the more an MRI will show brains in sync."[1]
>
> —ALAN ALDA

In 1968, Werner Klemperer won the first of two Emmy Awards for his role as Colonial Wilhelm Klink in *Hogan's Heroes*. That year would also turn out to be the halfway point for the show's successful six-year run. CBS launched another program in 1968 that to this day is still going strong: *60 Minutes*. Alan Alda, who starred in *M*A*S*H* (yet another CBS blockbuster), explains part of the secret to the news program's enduring success. Alda recalls *60 Minutes*'s founder Don Hewitt sharing the following story: "When a producer would come into his office to pitch a segment, if they started telling him about an issue, or a law that needed to be changed, or a scam that was making the rounds, he would put up his hand to stop them, and he'd say, 'Tell me a story.'"[2]

Hewitt believed these four words were the secret sauce for *60 Minutes*. Yes, *60 Minutes* is a journalistic news program that deals with important and serious subject matter, but each "segment isn't a treatise on espionage,

1. Alda, *If I Understood You*, 178.
2. Alda, *If I Understood You*, 162.

it is a story about the fortunes of one particular spy; it isn't an analysis of corporate malfeasance, it tracks the misfortunes of a whistle-blower."[3] In other words, *60 Minutes* skillfully moves important issues from the abstract to the concrete, contextualizing facts in a story. Through the years, seasoned reporters such as Mike Wallace, Morley Safer, Ed Bradley, and Lesley Stahl have addressed the rider but only after engaging the elephant first. Jonathan Haidt explains the power of story to move people: "Reasoning matters, of course, particularly between people, and particularly when reasons trigger new intuitions. Elephants rule, but they are neither dumb nor despotic. Intuitions can be shaped by reasoning, especially when reasons are embedded in a friendly conversation or an emotionally compelling novel, movie, or news story."[4]

In chapter 1, we discussed the importance of gentleness, kindness, and good old-fashioned decency. If you want to persuade someone, it starts at the intuitive/emotional/relational level. In chapter 2, we considered the importance of intellectual humility. While we might know the One who is omniscient, we ourselves are not. Acting like a *know-it-all* with total disregard for the other person's opinion is chutzpáh—a sure-fire way to turn someone off. Elephants lean away from the proud; but toward the humble. In this chapter, we will learn that arguments and logic speak to the rider, while stories are the language of the elephant. And while both are important, if we want to persuade someone, we should start with story.

The Ubiquitous Appeal of Stories

Alan Alda continues to add to his long list of film credits. Well into his eighties, he recently appeared in the acclaimed movie *Marriage Story*, which was nominated for six Academy Awards. That said, Alda's primary passion in the latter part of his career has been helping scientists translate technical information into stories. Narrative is our fundamental way of understanding the world, but we too often traffic in dry facts rather than tantalizing tales. "Our lives are filled with stories," Alda says, "yet when we want to communicate something important to us, we often forget there's a story behind it."[5]

3. Alda, *If I Understood You*, 162.
4. Haidt, *Righteous Mind*, 71.
5. Alda, *If I Understood You*, 163.

A dinner party encounter illustrates this point. During the meal, an acquaintance asked Alda if he was working on any new projects. Without missing a beat, he responded, "I helped start the Center for Communicating Science and I spend most of my time helping scientists and doctors communicate better with the public and with policymakers, and in fact . . ."[6] Before completing his first sentence, he noticed his conversation partner's eyes glazing over. Alda later reflected upon his mistake. He teaches scientists how to communicate, yet he had so easily fallen into the trap of starting with facts instead of story. If he could return to that dinner party and do it all over again, he would have "told her instead about the young medical student who helped a woman actually understand her diagnosis, and even sat and cried with her. Then after my dinner partner asks me how in the world we had been able to help a young doctor learn to do that, I could tell her a couple of facts. Because now she wants to know. . . . The trouble with a lecture is that it answers questions that haven't been asked."[7]

When we stop to think about it, stories are everywhere. They are all around us, populating nearly every aspect of our shared public experience. Consider the following vignettes from five domains of life: politics, law, sports, entertainment, and religion.

Politics: Carson, Trump, and the Horse Needle. Neuroscientist Tali Sharot remembers exactly where she was the night of September 16, 2015. She was sitting on the couch watching the second Republican primary debate. She vividly remembers an encounter between candidates Ben Carson, a pediatric neurosurgeon, and Donald Trump, a real estate developer. The moderator asked Dr. Carson to address Mr. Trump's persistent assault on childhood vaccinations and his alleged claims that they can lead to autism. Carson matter-of-factly responded, "There have been numerous studies, and they have not demonstrated that there is any correlation between vaccinations and autism."[8] The moderator asked if Mr. Trump should cease making these claims. Carson continued, "I think he's an intelligent man and will make the correct decision after getting the real facts."[9]

Just then, candidate Trump interjected: "Autism has become an epidemic. . . . It has gotten totally out of control. . . . You take this little beautiful baby, and you pump—I mean, it looks just like it's meant for a horse, not for

6. Alda, *If I Understood You*, 169.

7. Alda, *If I Understood You*, 169.

8. Sharot, *Influential Mind*, 3.

9. Sharot, *Influential Mind*, 3.

a child. And we've had so many instances, people that work for me. Just the other day, two years old, two-and-a-half years old, a child, went to have the vaccine, and came back, and a week later got a tremendous fever, got very, very sick, now is autistic."[10]

As a neuroscientist and mother of small children, Sharot had read the relevant scientific literature and fully agreed with Carson. Yet, her response to Trump's vivid anecdotal story was "immediate and visceral. An image of a nurse inserting a horse-sized syringe into my tiny baby emerged inside my head and would not fade away."[11] Carson interjected, trying again to make the scientific case. Sharot, herself a respected member of the scientific community, still felt panicky. "Proof, shmoof," she thought to herself. "Dr. Carson could have cited a hundred studies, and it would have had no effect on the storm that erupted inside my head. I was absorbed by that stallion of a needle that was about to cause my child to get very, very ill."[12]

Ultimately, Sharot overcame her emotional reaction and reflected upon what had happened. "While Carson was targeting the 'cerebral' part of me, Trump was aiming at the rest of me."[13] In other words, Carson spoke to the rider, while Trump went straight for the emotional and intuitive elephant. Sharot intellectually sided with Carson, but he failed to extinguish the raging inferno that Trump had ignited inside her brain. Why? Because you can't douse emotional fires with dry facts. Sharot wonders "what would have happened if Dr. Carson had done a better job of addressing people's needs, desires, motivations, and emotions, rather than assuming that they would make a correct decision after receiving the facts."[14] In other words, what would have happened if he had embedded the facts in an emotionally compelling story.

Law: The Tale of Two Trials. In 1994, Orenthal James Simpson was acquitted of murdering his ex-wife Nicole Brown Simpson and Ronald Goldman. Some called it the trial of the century. It was filled with drama, suspense, disbelief, and memorable lines, including Johnnie Cochran's now iconic, "If it doesn't fit, you must acquit." Even though Simpson was acquitted in the criminal trial, the Goldman family filed a civil suit shortly thereafter. The outcome was much different the second time around—Simpson

10. Sharot, *Influential Mind*, 3–4.
11. Sharot, *Influential Mind*, 4.
12. Sharot, *Influential Mind*, 4.
13. Sharot, *Influential Mind*, 4–5.
14. Sharot, *Influential Mind*, 5.

was found guilty of wrongful death. While the burden of proof in a criminal case is beyond a reasonable doubt, a civil trial only requires the evidence to be more likely than not. Additionally, the accused is required to testify in a civil case, whereas in a criminal trial he or she can plead the fifth. Another important difference in this case was the photographic evidence showing Simpson wearing a pair of the exact same Bruno Magli shoes that had left bloody imprints at the crime scene.

That said, Dan Petrocelli, the Goldmans's attorney in the civil case, identified what he believed was the most critical difference between the two trials. In the criminal trial, lead prosecutors Marcia Clark and Christopher Darden made the mistake of focusing on the issue of domestic violence as a social topic, whereas Petrocelli told a coherent and comprehensive story of what happened in the Simpson-Brown relationship. In other words, the criminal team centered on an abstract issue, while the civil team focused on a concrete story. As Petrocelli puts it, jurors aren't moved by issues, they "decide cases based on the *story* of the case."[15]

Sports: Come Back to the Ballpark, Tom! I am currently writing this chapter in quarantine. While the loss of life and disruption to the economy have been devastating, sports fans like me have also felt the void of live athletic contests. The stoppage in play has forced fans to binge classic sporting events on YouTube, ESPN, and other sports channels. I have chosen to watch old baseball games. I know, some people find baseball about as exciting as watching grass grow, but if you know what to look for, every game has an overarching plot line with several subplots emerging as the story unfolds.

Sometimes, however, the plot thickens outside the lines. For instance, consider one of the most colorful players to ever play for the Cincinnati Reds: pitcher Tom Browning. Browning owns the only perfect game in Reds' history, but he has also been known to leave the ballpark during the middle of the game. Perhaps his most bizarre departure took place when the Reds were in Chicago one afternoon in 1993. In the top of the third inning Browning, in full uniform, snuck out of the dugout, walked across Sheffield Avenue, and found his way to the high point of an apartment building overlooking Wrigley Field. Browning later said this stunt was designed to loosen up his struggling teammates. Plus, he had always wanted to hang out with the rowdy Cub fans on the Wrigley rooftops.[16]

15. Goldman, "What's Your Son Worth?"

16. WCPO 9, "Reds add."

My favorite Browning getaway story, however, took place during the second game of the 1990 World Series. The underdog Reds were facing the heavily favored Oakland A's and the game was moving toward extra innings. As a starting pitcher, Browning wasn't scheduled to pitch until game three, but the length of the game had thinned the Reds' pitching options. If the game went much longer, Browning might need to be called into service. Only one problem: manager Lou Piniella could not locate his star southpaw. Unbeknownst to Piniella, Browning was driving his pregnant wife to the hospital. Piniella panicked. Long before cell phones, he called up to the radio booth and asked Reds announcer Marty Brennaman to make a public plea for Browning to return to the ballpark. Moments later, Fox color commentator Tim McCarver recounted the story to the TV audience, adding "I tell you I've heard of a lot of things happening in a baseball game, but I've never heard of that."[17] Fortunately, it all worked out in the end. The home team rallied to win in the bottom of the tenth, Browning was able to witness the birth of his child, and the Reds went on to sweep the A's in four games.

Entertainment: A Well-Told Story Is a Powerful Thing. At the 2020 Academy Awards, *The Neighbors' Window* won the Oscar for Best Live Action Short Film. In an homage to Hitchcock's *Rear Window*, this twenty-minute film tells the story of a harried thirty-something couple who develop an obsession with the carefree life their younger neighbors are leading in an adjacent apartment building. That is, until the neighbors' journey takes an unexpected turn. This cautionary tale reminds us that what we see from afar often looks very different up close.[18]

During his acceptance speech, director Marshall Curry dedicated the Oscar to his mother, "the best story-teller [he] has ever known." Curry's mother grew up on a peach farm in rural South Carolina. He remembers she always had a story on the tip of her tongue, whether it was "about some crazy thing that happened with her siblings when she was growing up or some weird dog she had seen or something the taxi driver had told her about his life that would break your heart." By watching his mother, Curry learned from a young age "that a well-told story is a powerful thing. It can change the way we see the world, and it can help us notice and care about other people. And maybe love each other a little bit more."[19]

17. WCPO 9, "Where's Browning?"

18. Curry, "The Neighbors' Window." Midway through the film, late-night parties turn into late-night caretaking as the young husband develops terminal cancer.

19. ABC, "Marshall Curry Accepts Oscar."

The same night *American Factory* won the Oscar for Best Documentary Feature. This film chronicles the cross-cultural challenges of turning a shuttered Midwest automobile factory into a Chinese-run glass plant. *American Factory* was the first film produced by Barack and Michelle Obama's production company, Higher Ground. In an interview about the film, the former first lady said they selected this project because "it's not an editorial." Instead, the directors "let people tell their own story." While explaining the purpose of their new production company, the former president explained why story is central to the mission of Higher Ground: "A good story is a good story. Whether it is a documentary or a scripted story that helps people understand something they didn't understand before, we want to see if we can give voice to that."[20]

Religion: Stories Wake Us Up. Imagine you are sitting in church one Sunday morning and the preacher is droning on and on about something completely mind-numbing. You are bored out of your mind. You discreetly scan through social media when out of the blue the preacher says, "Let me tell you a story." What do you do? Your eyes lift and you place your phone on the pew. Stories grab our attention; a good story holds it.

Krista Tippett understands the power of a good story. In 2013, President Obama awarded Tippett with a National Humanities Medal for her work. As the host of the PBS radio program and podcast *On Being*, Tippett often explores how spirituality and story conjoin to create a more compassionate world. In a 2010 TED Talk, Tippett observed, "Compassion is unleashed in wider and wider circles by signs and stories, never by statistics and strategies. We need those things too, but we are also bumping up against their limits."[21] Tippett has interviewed many scientific and religious leaders, including Jonathan Haidt and Brian McLaren. In her 2014 interview with McLaren, he reminded the listening audience that "we Christians have a story [and] we are probably at our worst when we present our faith as a *system* rather than a *story*."[22] In other words, McLaren tells us that systems resonate with riders, while stories connect with the intuitive elephant. This is one reason McLaren prefers reading the Bible as an overarching story from Genesis to Revelation, rather than as a systematic book of doctrines.[23]

20. Netflix Film Club, "American Factory."
21. Tippett, "Reconnecting with Compassion."
22. Tippett, "On Being with McLaren."
23. McLaren, *New Kind of Christianity*, 33–97.

Perhaps more than any recent Christian writer, C. S. Lewis understood the subversive power of story as a vehicle for communicating the gospel. Lewis explained it like this: "But supposing that by casting all these things into an imaginary world, stripping them of their stained-glass and Sunday school associations, one could make them for the first time appear in their real potency? Could not one thus steal past those watchful dragons?"[24] These comments resonate nicely with the sentiment of his good friend and colleague J. R. R. Tolkien, who once suggested that slipping into an imaginary world "shocks us more fully awake than we are for most of our lives."[25]

Once Upon a Time

This human fascination with stories can be traced all the way back to the crib. As the host of the PBS show *The Human Spark*, Alan Alda traveled to Yale University's Infant Cognition Center to observe some baby science. The lab explores what infants understand about their physical and social world by exposing young children to a variety of puppet shows. In one show, three bunnies wearing different colored shirts are introduced. A ball appears. Two of the bunnies playfully share the ball, rolling it back and forth. The third rabbit, however, steals the ball and disappears. After watching this sequence several times, the child is given a chance to select between the cooperative bunny and the mean one. Over 80 percent of the time, infants and toddlers select the cooperative puppet.[26]

In another experiment, the child watches three different shapes interact on an incline. All have press-on googly eyes to give the shapes the appearance of personality. The red circle tries to scale the hill, but cannot do it on its own. Then a yellow triangle assists the circle up the hill. Finally, a blue square appears at the top of the hill and aggressively pushes the circle back down the slope. After watching the show six to eight times, children are given the chance to select between the helpful and mean puppets. Again, infants overwhelmingly select the cooperative shape.[27]

While the primary purpose of these experiments is to determine whether or not babies come into the world with a sense of morality (the

24. Lewis, "Fairy Stories," 37.

25. Duriez, *C. S. Lewis Handbook*, 203–4.

26. *New York Times*, "Right from Wrong?"

27. Alda, *If I Understood You*, 163–64.

answer appears to be yes),[28] science communication professor Graham Chedd has a different takeaway from the experience. Alda recalls,

> Graham came away from the shoot wondering if there wasn't something else happening in the child's mind. He said, "I interpreted it, in addition, as meaning that the baby is able to put a story to it, is able to interpret what was going on as a story . . . That shape is trying to get up the hill, and this other shape is trying to push it down, and this one's trying to push it up." There's a little story that forms in the baby's mind to interpret what she or he is seeing. . . . All through childhood, that's what you do: "Once upon a time . . ." It's all stories.[29]

Karen Wynn, director of Yale's Infant Cognition Center, agrees with Chedd's assessment: "In order to sense a meaning—good or bad—to the actions, there has to be a narrative . . . Babies are following events and understanding them in *context*." In other words, infants aren't just making moral judgments in a vacuum. They are assessing right and wrong within the flow of a story.

So, what makes for a good story? Aristotle believed a good story must include a beginning, middle, and end. He thought the beginning needs to include the introduction of the protagonist and a goal. During the first part, the story should be told in such a way that pity is evoked. During the middle of the story, dramatic action emerges as the protagonist faces some sort of obstacle. This elicits fear or at least tension in the audience. Finally, the end of the story should offer a sense of resolution with the achievement or denial of the goal. Aristotle thought this resolution brings about a kind of catharsis or release of the built-up tension.[30]

When speaking to groups, Alda often illustrates the importance of suspense in the following way. He asks for a volunteer to carry an empty water glass across the stage. The audience usually laughs because walking across a stage with an empty glass in your hands isn't the most riveting thing to watch. Then Alda fills the glass with water all the way to the top. The volunteer is now told to carry the glass across the stage again, only

28. As already discussed in this book, humans come into the world with a broad range of moral intuitions. Does this point to a moral designer of the universe or is this phenomenon best explained naturalistically? Justin Barrett, a psychologist at Fuller Graduate School, supports the former proposition, while Paul Bloom, a Yale psychologist, defends the latter. See Barrett, *Born Believers*, and Bloom, *Descartes' Baby*.

29. Alda, *If I Understood You*, 164–65.

30. Alda, *If I Understood You*, 171–72.

this time if she spills even one drop her entire village will die. Of course, no one believes there is an actual village at stake in this exercise, but the entire audience is still spellbound. Alda notes, "If even a bead of water runs down the side of the glass, you can hear them gasp." The takeaway from this exercise? "We can identify with someone who has a goal, but we *root* for someone with both a goal and an obstacle."[31] He adds, "It's not dramatic to carry an empty glass. We have to fill it to the brim."[32]

Brains in Sync

Julia Reichart, one of the directors of *American Factory*, explains how she and husband/co-director Steven Bognar approach each documentary. "What we always try to do is see everyone's point of view and [remember] that everybody has their reasons," says Reichart. "When you go to all these different kinds of places there's two things that you do. One is you try to be yourself. And the other is you try to connect. And you listen, and you don't go in with an idea of what [the story is] supposed to be about."[33]

Stephen Covey points out the scarcity of this kind of active, engaged listening: "Most people do not listen with the intent to understand; they listen with the intent to reply. They're either speaking or preparing to speak."[34] I don't know about you, but this statement hits home. I am often guilty of this sin. Instead of carefully and actively listening so that I can understand my conversation partner, too often I am thinking about what I am going to say next to advance my own argument and puff up my own ego. James 1:19 reminds us to "be quick to listen, slow to speak and slow to become angry." Unfortunately, in our very divided culture, we too often flip the script. We are quick to become angry, quick to speak, and slow to listen (if we listen at all).

We've already seen how Francis Schaeffer could charm elephants with gentleness and respect. Another hallmark of his ministry was active, compassionate listening. Schaeffer was fond of saying, "If I only have one hour to spend with someone, I will spend the first fifty-five minutes listening, and the final five providing an answer." Schaeffer's love and concern for

31. Alda, *If I Understood You*, 172.
32. Alda, *If I Understood You*, 177.
33. Netflix Film Club, "American Factory."
34. Covey, *Highly Effective People*, 239.

people from all walks of life is what many friends and co-laborers remember most about him.[35]

Schaeffer also worked hard at finding common ground with his conversation partners. He was a remarkable autodidact, reading across a wide variety of disciplines—from art to zoology. This range of knowledge helped Schaeffer find common ground with nearly every person he encountered. The importance of common ground is identified in another episode of *The Human Spark*. This time, Alda traveled to Princeton University, where he reported on a research project that placed subjects into MRI machines and then studied the degree to which the brains between storytellers and listeners would synchronize. What he found was "people's minds will sync up in the presence of story, but the process relies heavily on there being some similarity between the storyteller and the listener. . . . The more the commonality between the storyteller and the listener, the more an MRI will show brains in sync."[36] What this tells us is that story is important, but even more important is a sense of connection and commonality between the storyteller and the listener. Stories aren't neutral. Rapport between the storyteller and listener is essential for the story to have maximum impact.

Leaving My Father's Faith

In my Humanities Philosophy class we cover the major arguments for Christian Theism, including the cosmological, teleological, and moral arguments. We also consider counterevidence, such as the argument from evil—if God is all-powerful and perfectly loving, why is there apparent non-redemptive pain, suffering, and evil in the world? We interact with famous skeptics from the past such as David Hume and Bertrand Russell, as well as the four horsemen of Neo-Atheism—Richard Dawkins, Daniel Dennett, Sam Harris, and Christopher Hitchens. Many of my students are shocked to discover that the New Atheists view religion as a worldwide pandemic in desperate need of a cure.

That said, we also interact with atheists who hold very different views toward religion. Haidt, for instance, believes that religion provides an important social function by binding individuals into moral teams that can contribute positive goods to society. Exposure to different types

35. Burson and Walls, *Lewis and Schaeffer*, 47–48.

36. Alda, *If I Understood You*, 178.

of atheists and agnostics challenges the tendency to paint all unbelievers with the same brush.[37]

Narrative is an excellent tool for humanizing people on the other side of any issue, including the theist/atheist chasm. That's why I show my students the film *Leaving My Father's Faith*. This documentary tells the story of Tony and Bart Campolo. Tony is a well-known evangelical professor, author, and speaker, whose ministry has ranged from social justice advocacy to providing spiritual counsel to President Clinton. Much like his father, Bart is a dynamic speaker who spent more than thirty years doing urban ministry before he de-converted around the age of fifty. Today, Bart serves as a secular-humanist chaplain at the University of Cincinnati. The film includes face-to-face conversations between father and son, as well as a series of email exchanges. It is within the narrative flow of this conversation that we learn of Bart's journey in and out of the Christian faith, the real-life issues that prompted this shift, and Tony's response to his son's defection.

Bart begins his story with a fast-food conversion account. As he puts it, "Some people go to churches with gothic arches and Roman arches, I had the golden arches. I became a McChristian."[38] At the age of sixteen, Tony sent Bart to Camden, New Jersey, where he helped lead a church day camp. Bart says he doesn't remember a lot about that first summer other than it was "pure chaos. For four hours each day it felt like all I did was yell 'No!,' 'Stop,' and 'Be quiet!' . . . Instead, what stands out in my memory are the precious, sparkling little boys and girls I fell in love with that summer, and the incredible confusion I felt as I began to realize what they were up against."[39]

This confusion crystallized in the life of Shonda, who as a nine-year-old was gang raped by four men. When Shonda asked her Sunday school teacher why God did not intercede and make the men stop, her teacher spoke about divine *sovereignty* and assured the little girl that God must have had a good reason for allowing it to happen. Bart could hardly blame Shonda for not trusting a heavenly father who either couldn't or wouldn't stop such a brutal attack. God's inability or unwillingness to save Shonda from this unspeakable cruelty was the first step in Bart's loss of faith.

37. For an excellent talk on the problem of stereotyping, see Adichie, "Danger of a Single Story."

38. Wright, dir., *Leaving My Father's Faith*. All of the quotations in the remainder of this chapter are from this film unless otherwise noted.

39. Campolo and Campolo, *Why I Left, Why I Stayed*, 13.

This shift got Bart thinking about the Christian doctrine of *salvation*. How could a perfectly loving God damn an emotionally and physically abused little girl for not believing in him? Bart's gut told him that if God is truly good then Shonda would be in heaven whether she believed in Jesus or not. Consequently, he became a universalist and wrote articles defending his new position. Bart recalls fellow Christians attacking him as a heretic: "They thought I was trying to mess with their faith; I was just trying to hold onto my own."

The next step in Bart's destabilization came when he realized two of his college roommates were gay. One of his roommates wanted to discuss his sexual orientation with Bart, but was afraid the conversation would ruin their friendship. When he finally broached the subject, Bart responded with genuine concern and curiosity: "Wow, that must be so hard, what's that like?" His roommate turned to him with a smile and said, "I think we're going to be able to stay friends." Through real-life encounters with members of the LGBTQ community, Bart came to the conclusion that *Scripture* was wrong on the issue of *sexuality*, at least homosexuality.

As Bart was losing confidence in Scripture, he was also losing faith in prayer or *supplication*—the act of making requests known to God. While in Camden, Bart had witnessed all kinds of pain and suffering, but he "saw God answer prayer precisely as often as if there was no God." If God is good, surely he would eagerly answer the prayers of the sick, the hungry, the marginalized. Doesn't the Bible say we have not because we ask not?

Losing faith in prayer led to the final step in Bart's deconversion story. He gave up belief in the *supernatural*. A bike accident left him with a severe concussion. When he finally started to recover, Bart realized "my identity, my personality is in my brain. You smash my brain against a tree, I will change. . . . I know this sounds crazy, but for the first time in my life it dawned on me that when I died and my brain broke down that I would be gone." The film pictures Bart's faith as a Jenga tower. Every time he shifted his thinking on a key doctrine, a block would fall from the tower. First it was *sovereignty*, then it was *salvation*. Over time, the removal of the *sexuality*, *Scripture*, *supplication*, and *supernatural* blocks toppled his tower for good.

Bart told his parents of his departure from the faith after a festive Thanksgiving meal. A very full Tony recalls the indigestion the conversation caused: "it was like somebody put a knife in my stomach. . . . I lost not just a son to the faith, I lost a colleague from a movement." Bart's mother,

Peggy, helped Tony gain some perspective that evening before they went to bed. She said, "Stop to think about it for a moment. Your son is a good husband, a faithful husband. His wife adores him, he adores her. They've got two children, they dote on them and those children love them intensely. . . . He's doing good for people all over. Now, that he doesn't use the word 'Christian' is not a negation of all of that."

Peggy helped Tony view the glass as half full rather than half empty. Bart left Christian ministry and eventually became a secular humanist chaplain with the goal of helping non-religious students find meaning and purpose in life. He describes a recent student encounter this way: "The other day I talked to a college kid who was going to waste his life making rich people richer and by the end of the conversation the kid was talking about using his gifts and abilities to feed hungry people in the third world. And if my dad can go, 'That's kingdom work!' Terrific."

With a renewed appreciation for *this* life ("For me, to live as though there is no God is to take *this* life much more seriously"), Bart articulates an eloquent secular humanist purpose statement:

> What I'd like to do is I'd like to live until I die. Really live. A big part of what I consider to be my ministry in the world is to tell a story of how we live for just a little bit of time and then we die and are gone forever. But that we're part of a larger story, kind of the epic of all nature. That life is not meaningful intrinsically, but that we can make meaning within our lives. That life has no meaning, but there can be a lot of meaning within life. And that the reason to create meaning is that's what will cause you the greatest amount of happiness and well-being. And that's what will cause the greatest amount of happiness and well-being for everyone you care about. . . . I've become convinced that the best way to make the most of life is by loving people and by pursuing goodness with all your heart.

When Tony reflects upon Bart's secular humanist ministry, he wonders if his son isn't more faithful to the call to Christian discipleship than he is: "I say to myself, when the chips are really down, he's no longer a believer but he sure looks like a disciple to me. . . . When it comes to doing it on a face-to-face level, I think my son is more of a disciple than I am." Tony goes on to identify Bart as an "anonymous Christian." He believes Bart is doing what Jesus called his disciples to do, but he is not explicitly "doing it in his name. Of such people Jesus said, 'If they're not against us, they're for us.'"

While Bart offers several intellectual reasons for his shift to secular humanism, Tony believes his son ultimately slipped away because he stopped communing with fellow believers. As a sociologist, he believes Bart entered the faith through hanging around Christians and eventually his loss of faith "was not so much an intellectual process as it was a matter of leaving a fellowship, a community of fellow believers. Leaving the Christian faith is the result of disengaging from that plausibility structure and getting sucked into the dominant culture, which is secular."

Near the end of the film, Tony offers viewers a word of caution. He makes it clear that the world isn't split into neat black and white categories of "believers" and "unbelievers." He admits to his own intellectual and emotional struggles. He says, "I'm a believer with times of doubt. I would hope and pray that you [Bart] are a doubter who from time to time says, 'maybe these things are true. Maybe my father's right after all.'"

The film concludes without clean and neat resolution. As Christians, we would prefer seeing a beautiful prodigal son moment as the screen fades to black, but unfortunately that isn't the way many real-life stories play out. One of the reasons Tony agreed to this public exchange with his son is because he "hopes [his] arguments will model for other Christians a way to keep talking with our non-believing loved ones that is entirely loving and respectful without compromising the gospel."[40] I believe he succeeds in striking a harmonious balance of treble and bass.

After watching the film, my students participate in a conversation about what they have witnessed. They often note how helpful it is to see abstract arguments embedded in a story, within the flow of real lives. They also note how encouraging it is to see the story of a father and son who have such different worldviews, yet continue to show deep respect and love for each other. Many appreciate seeing an atheist or agnostic person who is sacrificially trying to make the world a better place. Others like how Bart doesn't try to convert believers to unbelief, but rather encourages them to love people and pursue goodness with all their heart. The final takeaway for many students is the invaluable lesson of this chapter: to have any hope of swaying elephants, you have to swap stories.

40. Campolo and Campolo, *Why I Left, Why I Stayed*, 5.

Part II: **Honor the Sacred**

"If you want to *understand* another group, *follow the sacredness*. As a first step, think about the six moral foundations, and try to figure out which one or two are carrying the most weight in a particular controversy. And if you really want to open your mind, open your heart first."[1]

—JONATHAN HAIDT

1. Haidt, *Righteous Mind*, 312.

Chapter 4

Treble Tactic Four: Build Empathic Muscle

Bass-Pounding Fallacy: Understanding the Other Is Treason

"Being a psychologist studying empathy today is like being a climatologist studying the polar ice: Each year we discover more about how valuable it is, just as it recedes all around us."[1]

—JAMIL ZAKI

Joker is one of the most intriguing movies in recent memory. Nominated for eleven Academy Awards, the film tells the story of Arthur Fleck, who grows up to become Gotham's chief villain and Batman's archnemesis. In this gritty and gripping character study, we learn that Arthur has experienced a lifetime of mental, emotional, and physical abuse. His heartbreaking backstory includes a delusional mother, violent stepfather, backstabbing co-workers, incessant bullying, abject poverty, and mental illness.

Arthur tries to make his way in the world as a clown by day and aspiring comic by night. In one counseling session, the camera focuses on a journal entry. The scribblings scream for help: "I just hope my death makes more sense than my life."[2] In another session Arthur is on the verge of a breakthrough, but his counselor is tone deaf: "You don't listen, do you? I don't think you

1. Zaki, *War for Kindness*, 10.

2. Phillips, dir., *Joker*.

ever really hear me. You just ask the same questions every week: How's your job, do you have any negative thoughts? All I have are negative thoughts."[3] The session ends with Arthur learning that Gotham is cutting social services, including access to his counseling and medications.

As the film accelerates toward its dramatic conclusion, Arthur's life and actions spiral out of control. He fights back on the subway, killing three inebriated Wall Street bullies.[4] With a new sense of empowerment and purpose, he seeks revenge on others who have wronged him. He becomes a symbol for the disenfranchised, an agent of chaos and carnage.

In the film's climactic scene, Arthur appears on Murray Franklin's late-night talk show. Light banter turns heavy when he confesses to the subway killings. Arthur is now full Joker, the transformation complete. A stunned Franklin asks Joker why he committed the crime:

> **JOKER:** I killed those guys because they were awful. Everybody is awful these days. It's enough to make anyone crazy. . . . Why is everybody so upset about these guys? If it was me dying on the sidewalk, you'd walk right over me. . . . Everybody just yells and screams at each other. Nobody's civil anymore. Nobody thinks what it's like to be the other guy.
>
> **MURRAY:** I tell you this, not everyone is awful.
>
> **JOKER:** You're awful, Murray. Playing my video, inviting me on the show. You just wanted to make fun of me. You're just like the rest of them.
>
> **MURRAY:** You don't know the first thing about me, pal. Look what happened because of what you did. What it led to. There are riots out there, two policemen are in critical condition. . . . Someone was killed today because of what you did.
>
> **JOKER:** How about another joke, Murray? What do you get when you cross a mentally ill loner with a society that abandons him and treats him like trash? I'll tell you what you get, you get what you ****ing deserve.[5]

Arthur suddenly pulls out his gun and shoots Franklin on live TV.

One of the most intriguing aspects of this film is how it elicits wildly divergent responses. Even among Christians. One Facebook friend (full

3. Phillips, dir., *Joker*.
4. Phillips, dir., *Joker*.
5. Phillips, dir., *Joker*.

disclosure, my daughter) posted: "Saw Joker this afternoon and all I want is to be his friend."[6] This post didn't surprise me, because Ashley has always focused on the marginalized, the bullied, the ones who are excluded. But other Christians align more with the following *Breakpoint* podcast headline: "A Meme of Mass Violence: 'Joker' and the Rise of 'Demonic Antiheroes.'"[7] Christians in this camp are sounding an alarm that this movie glorifies violence and humanizes a dangerous villain.

Why has *Joker* elicited such polar opposite responses from equally committed Christ-followers? Moral Foundations Theory offers some insight. The first response focuses on the *compassion* intuitions. Arthur is someone with mental health issues who was bullied and lost access to counseling and medication. While not condoning destructive behavior, this perspective understands the constellation of factors that turned Arthur into the Joker. It is easy to see how someone with strong care and fairness intuitions might focus on the pain Arthur had to endure. The second response centers on the *conviction* intuitions. Joker is a nihilistic sociopath who generates widespread chaos, terror, and bloodshed as the film unfolds. It is equally easy to see how someone with heightened in-group loyalty, authority, and sanctity intuitions would view Joker as a threat to the stability of society. Moral Foundations Theory helps us see some measure of truth in both perspectives.

In the next three chapters, we will learn how to honor the other person's sacred intuitions. As Jonathan Haidt suggests, "If you want to *understand* another group, *follow the sacredness*. As a first step, think about the six moral foundations, and try to figure out which one or two are carrying the most weight in a particular controversy. And if you really want to open your mind, open your heart first."[8]

The Empathy Deficit

Jamil Zaki is a professor of psychology at Stanford University, where he also directs the university's social neuroscience laboratory. As a child, Jamil grew up bouncing back and forth between his mother's and father's homes. His parents split up when he was eight, but the divorce wasn't finalized until he was twelve.

6. A. Burson, "Saw Joker this afternoon."
7. Stonestreet, "A Meme of Mass Violence."
8. Haidt, *Righteous Mind*, 312.

His mother and father met at Washington State University, both beneficiaries of generous international student scholarships. This sense of commonality forged an initial bond. Over time, however, a myriad of differences tore them apart. Mom was Peruvian; Dad Pakistani. Mom was "full of warmth and nerves," placing family above everything else. Dad, on the other hand, prioritized "intellect and ambition." Jamil recalls, "Where he came from, the student who scored highest on an exam would end up in college. The student who scored second highest would end up on the streets."[9]

As a single child, Jamil "was the only bridge between their worlds." While the glue of his parents' relationship dissolved, he somehow maintained a bond with both. "I learned to tune myself to their different emotional frequencies. . . . Empathy saved me, but not because it came easily. My parents' divorce was like an empathy gym for me, forcing me to work at care and understanding. And that experience of stretching myself and the benefits that it caused is part of why I study what I do."[10]

Zaki's childhood prepared him for such a time as this; empathy is on the decline, and has been for a while now. In a 2006 commencement speech to the Northwestern University graduating class, Senator Barack Obama observed: "There's a lot of talk in this country about the federal deficit, but I think we should talk more about our empathy deficit. . . . We live in a culture that discourages empathy. A culture that too often tells us our principal goal in life is to be rich, thin, young, famous, safe, and entertained. A culture where those in power too often encourage these selfish impulses."[11] Obama's statement is supported by the data. Psychologists studying empathy over the past several decades note a steep decline with the typical person in 2009 showing less empathy than 75 percent of the population in 1979.[12] Zaki offers the following ironic quip: "Being a psychologist studying empathy today is like being a climatologist studying the polar ice: Each year we discover more about how valuable it is, just as it recedes all around us."[13]

Many people point to technology and increasing political polarization as two reasons for this decline,[14] but even when empathy is present it rarely extends beyond those closest to us. This is biologically understandable

9. Zaki, "Building Empathy."

10. Zaki, "Building Empathy."

11. Zaki, *War for Kindness*, 9–10.

12. Zaki, *War for Kindness*, 8.

13. Zaki, *War for Kindness*, 10.

14. Haidt and Abrams, "The Top 10 Reasons."

given how empathy moves us to circle the wagons around family and friends, especially in the face of a perceived threat. (Be honest: How many of us were handing out packs of toilet paper to random strangers during the pandemic?)[15] While caring for our inner circle is a good thing, parochial empathy can also produce fissures. Zaki explains how easy it is to create an us versus them mentality:

> People effortlessly carve the world into insiders and outsiders. Divisions between groups can be biological (old versus young), traditional (Real Madrid versus Barcelona), momentary (one pickup basketball team versus another), or even made up. Assemble a group of strangers, give half of them blue armbands and the other half red ones, and they will build new prejudices on the fly, judging their fellow reds (or blues) as kinder, more attractive, and more capable than the sinister blues (or reds) on the other side. Boundaries between insiders and outsiders destroy virtually every type of empathy scientists can measure.[16]

Harvard psychologist Mina Cikara notes that conflict not only intensifies the situation, it can flip empathy completely on its head. When this happens we don't merely tune out the other side, we actually begin to enjoy their suffering. This phenomenon is called *schadenfreude*. Her studies of subjects in New York and Boston demonstrate that Yankee and Red Sox fans savor the misfortunes of their rivals, even when they lose to other teams.[17] They feel the other's pain; not as anguish, but as euphoria. As an Ohio State football fan, I must confess that I have succumbed to *schadenfreude* on more than one occasion, and the satisfaction intensifies each year that Ohio State extends its winning streak over the Michigan Wolverines![18]

Not only do we relish our rival's pain, we feel a tinge of betrayal when someone from the home team fraternizes with the other side. Several years ago, ESPN tapped into this impulse when the network created a college football promotional spot that featured two students smooching and whispering sweet nothings. As the camera slowly pulled away, their true identities became clear with the male student wearing an Ohio State sweatshirt

15. Fortunately, there are exceptions to the rule—like this guy: *Good Morning America*, "This man left hand sanitizer."

16. Zaki, *War for Kindness*, 56.

17. Cikara, "Us Versus Them."

18. At the time of this writing, Ohio State has defeated Michigan eight years in a row. And, yes, I am aware of the irony of sharing this heartless flaw in the midst of a chapter promoting empathy. Another bad example moment for me.

and the co-ed sporting Michigan attire. The following words drove home the point: "Without sports, this wouldn't be disgusting."[19]

Unlocking Empathy

OK, we have an empathy problem; but, can we do anything about it? The answer depends on how we understand the nature of this incredibly important resource. Let's consider two competing views.

Down through history, the dominant perspective has considered empathy an inherited, hardwired trait. Either you have it or you don't. Zaki labels this view the Roddenberry Hypothesis. Gene Roddenberry, that is—the creator of *Star Trek: The Next Generation*. On one end of the empathic spectrum "we have the USS *Enterprise*'s ship's counselor Deanna Troi, known throughout the galaxy for her empathy; she catches other people's feelings and can read their minds. On the other side, we have the android Data, who doesn't feel emotions himself and can't tell what other people are feeling either."[20] The rest of us fall somewhere between these two extremes. This view considers empathy a *trait*, similar to a person's adult height. Traits are pretty much determined for us. Advocates for this perspective are *fixists*. While we all have a set point and range for empathy, fixists focus on the set point and ask how empathic a person *is*.[21]

Emerging research, however, is suggesting that empathy is more like a *skill* that can be developed. People in this camp are *mobilists*, focusing on ranges rather than set points. Instead of asking the static question of how empathic a person *is*, they ask how empathic a person can *become*.[22] This view likens empathy to a muscle that will either grow or atrophy depending on how much it is exercised. Just as work-out machines focus on various muscle groups, targeted compassion exercises can build different types of empathic muscle.[23] As we previously learned, Zaki's childhood was like an empathy gym, generating greater compassion and understanding through hard emotional labor. His adult research has confirmed that he is not unique; we all have the capacity to improve our empathic physique.

19. AnnArborIsAW****, "Ohio State-Michigan."
20. Zaki, "Building Empathy."
21. Zaki, *War for Kindness*, 22.
22. Zaki, *War for Kindness*, 22.
23. Zaki, *War for Kindness*, 46–47.

> Different circumstances can affect our empathy in different ways. A hateful political climate can atrophy it while managing two very different parents can grow it. And we can grow our empathy on purpose through practice. You make decisions about whether or not to practice empathy all the time: Will you cross the street to avoid a homeless person or pay attention to their pain? Will you dismiss someone who disagrees with you or try to figure out why they feel the way they do? When we practice engaging over and over again, we build an empathy that is deeper, broader, and more muscular.[24]

This debate between fixists and mobilists is hardly theoretical. Zaki's research shows that mind-set matters: Those who *believe* they can grow their empathy (mobilists) actually exert more effort and produce greater empathic results, while those who don't (fixists) tend to exhibit parochial empathy at best. Zaki summarizes the findings of one of his studies:

> New fixists empathized lazily, for instance with people who looked or thought like them, but not with outsiders. New mobilists, by contrast, empathized even with people who were different from them racially or politically. . . . New fixists and new mobilists pledged equal amounts of time [in the study] when helping was easy, but mobilists volunteered more than twice as many hours than fixists when more was required. Situations that normally turn people away no longer fazed them.[25]

This new mobilist view of empathy is promising. If our ability to empathize isn't hardwired and predetermined, then we can all do something about our current empathy crisis. But what exactly do we mean when we talk about empathy? While a frequent topic of conversation, it's actual meaning is often like an alluring and elusive butterfly, enticing from a distance but difficult to grasp the closer we get to it. As Zaki points out, "Most of us think we know what 'empathy' is, yet we often mean different things when we use it."[26] Despite decades of debate, however, most empathy researchers now agree on the main contours of a definition. Zaki describes empathy as an "umbrella term" that involves three separate yet related processes: *sharing*, *thinking*, and *caring*.

Nested under the notion of *sharing* is *emotional empathy*—the ability to vicariously enter into another person's feelings and experiences. Imagine

24. Zaki, "Building Empathy."

25. Zaki, *War for Kindness*, 31.

26. Zaki, *War for Kindness*, 178.

your friend has been waiting to hear whether or not he has been admitted to graduate school. The letter finally arrives. He opens it and collapses to the ground. If you are a good friend, you will likely mirror his body language, perhaps shedding a tear yourself.[27] "Experience sharing is widespread—people 'catch' one another's facial expressions, bodily stress, and moods, both negative and positive," writes Zaki. "Our brains respond to each other's pain and pleasure as though we were experiencing those states ourselves."[28] This "leading-edge" dimension of empathy is reflexive, taking place at the elephant level. The more connected we are to someone, the more likely we will experience emotional empathy.

Nested under the notion of *thinking* is *cognitive empathy*—the ability to reflect upon what another person is feeling. As you share your friend's sense of rejection and disappointment, you create a mental map of what's going on inside his head. You try to gauge his level of distress. You imagine the thoughts and questions that are racing through his mind. "You think like a detective, gathering evidence about his behavior and situation to deduce how he feels." This type of empathy takes place at the rider level and includes things like the ability to mentalize; it's "an everyday form of mind reading."[29]

Nested under the notion of *caring* is *empathic concern*—compassionately addressing another person's need. Zaki points out, "If while your friend weeps, all you do is sit back, feel bad, and think about him, you're a less-than-stellar pal."[30] This is the pay-off dimension of empathy. As James 2:15–16 tells us, "Suppose a brother or a sister is without clothes and daily food. If one of you says to them, 'Go in peace; keep warm and well fed,' but does nothing about their physical needs, what good is it?" In other words, what good is emotional and cognitive empathy without empathic concern? Feeling another person's pain is not enough; we need to help alleviate it if we have the power to do so.

Now, these dimensions of empathy can relate to one another in various ways: a mother might not understand why her baby is crying, but she *feels* her child's pain and is motivated to do something about it. Emergency room personnel might feel the anguish of their patients, but in order

27. For the fascinating story of how scientists discovered mirror neurons in Macaque monkeys, see Goleman, *Social Intelligence*, 40–44.

28. Zaki, *War for Kindness*, 179.

29. Zaki, *War for Kindness*, 180.

30. Zaki, *War for Kindness*, 180.

to think clearly and act quickly they must learn how to modulate their emotions. Many people on the autism spectrum struggle with cognitive empathy or knowing what is going on in the other person's mind, but they can still share and care about the feelings of others.[31] Psychopaths have the opposite profile: they can tell what others are feeling, but they are unaffected by their pain.[32]

Sharing, *thinking*, and *caring* each promote kindness in their own way. Primatologist Frans de Waal describes the interrelationship between these empathic dimensions using a "Russian Doll" analogy. Zaki explains:

> As he sees it, the primitive process of experience sharing is at the core—turning someone else's pain into our own creates an impulse to stop it. Newer, more complex forms of empathy are layered on top of that, generating broader sorts of kindness. Through mentalizing, we develop a fine-grained picture of not just what someone else feels, but why they feel it, and—more important—what might make them feel better. This spurs a deeper concern, a response focused not only on our own discomfort but truly on someone else. The global kindness Peter Singer describes in *The Expanding Circle*[33] is a further extension of concern—pointed not at any one individual, but at people as a whole.[34]

Identifying which dimension is most relevant in any given situation can help us devise targeted strategies for rebuilding empathy. Mentalizing might effectively put us in the shoes of a homeless person, whose life experiences we might never have contemplated. This might happen through "perspective-taking exercises or virtual reality." In tribal confrontations, we might focus intensely on our opponent but not on what is best for them. We might even enter into *schadenfreude*. "Contact, and especially friendships across group lines, can change that." For professionals facing a high degree of burnout due to excessive emotional empathy, contemplative techniques can move people toward the more objective kind of compassion—empathic

31. For a discussion of Simon Baron-Cohen's autism research and two dimensions of cognitive style (systemizing and empathizing), see Haidt, *Righteous Mind*, 116–21.

32. Zaki, *War for Kindness*, 181.

33. Singer, *Expanding Circle*.

34. Zaki, *War for Kindness*, 181.

concern.[35] The first step, however, is becoming conversant with these different dimensions of empathy.[36]

Empathy Leaders

While we are facing an empathy crisis, there is hope. Empathy leaders are emerging in different walks of life, finding creative and inspiring ways to generate compassion in their respective spheres of influence. They are displaying a willingness to try something different, to fight for empathy . . . that's bold. That's audacious. That's virtuous. Consider three empathy leaders from different sectors of society who are overflowing with chútzpah.

Guardians Over Warriors. Sue Rahr grew up as the sole girl with six brothers. She knew what it was like to play rough and settle disputes with testosterone. In one of her first encounters as a police officer, a drunk man punched her in the face. In a matter of seconds, she wrestled him to the ground. Rahr was no slouch; she could take care of herself. But after thirty-three years on the force with stints in every unit—including formative years in internal affairs—she came to the conclusion that too many police officers were leading with violence and intimidation rather than using force as a last resort. That's why, when she was promoted to executive director of the Washington State Criminal Justice Training Commission (CJTC), everything changed.

When Rahr took over at the CJTC, there was a "military-boot-camp atmosphere." In one of the training classrooms a poster "warned recruits that 'officers killed in the line of duty use less force than their peers.'"[37] Now, a new sign appears above the academy's entrance: IN THESE HALLS, TRAINING THE GUARDIANS OF DEMOCRACY. Instead of leading with

35. Paul Bloom is a critic of emotional empathy and advocates for dry, rational empathic concern instead. He writes, "It is because of [emotional] empathy that citizens of a country can be transfixed by a girl stuck in a well and largely indifferent to climate change. It is because of empathy that we often enact savage laws or enter into terrible wars; our feeling for the suffering of the few leads to the disastrous consequences for the many. A reasoned, even counterempathic analysis of moral obligation and likely consequences is a better guide to planning the future than the gut wrench of empathy." Bloom, *Against Empathy*, 127. While I am sympathetic to Bloom's concerns, we need both the high- and low-road forms of cognition involved when it comes to empathy: the head and the gut. In other words, there are ways to achieve greater rider involvement without calling for elephant game-hunting.

36. Zaki, *War for Kindness*, 182.

37. Kindy, "Creating Guardians, Calming Warriors."

intimidation, cadets are now taught to LEED: LISTEN AND EXPLAIN WITH EQUITY AND DIGNITY. This message reinforces a seismic shift from warrior domination to guardian responsibility.[38]

The atmosphere has changed at CJTC. Instead of incessant saluting and strict top-down stratification, Rahr has instituted a more open atmosphere. "We don't need cops to salute," says Rahr. "We need cops to talk." Cadets still spend plenty of time learning how to wield their weapons; but now they also take classes on "emotional intelligence, 'heart math,' racial bias, and mental illness."[39] Their hands-on training includes significant time participating in simulations, where they can practice "managing volatile situations" with empathic skill rather than brute force. In other words, a police academy empathy gym.

While old-school law enforcement still views empathy "as a weakness or catering to political correctness," Rahr argues that it protects everyone when volatile situations arise. "Police officers deal with people in crisis, and having your trauma acknowledged lowers the tension. Listening is a de-escalation strategy."[40] Research is showing that guardian graduates are displaying greater empathy and care than officers that went through warrior training.[41] In 2015, President Obama appointed Rahr to the Task Force on 21st-Century Policing. Her influence was felt in the final report, which read: "Law enforcement culture should embrace a guardian—rather than a warrior—mindset." As Zaki notes, "In a dark moment for American policing, [Rahr] has cast a light."[42]

Changing Lives through Literature. This is a story of two embittered Bobs. Our first Bob—Bob Waxler—is an English professor at the University of Massachusetts-Dartmouth. He had a beef with the increasing marginalization of literature at his school. The second Bob—Bob Kane—is a Massachusetts District Court judge. He was frustrated with the alarming rate of recidivism in his courtroom. One day during a friendly tennis match, the two Bobs hatched a daring solution to their two problems. They would launch a book club for convicts. If the experiment worked, Bob the professor

38. Zaki, *War for Kindness*, 128.

39. Zaki, *War for Kindness*, 129.

40. Zaki, *War for Kindness*, 130.

41. Zaki, *War for Kindness*, 131. In one study, 300 Seattle police officers took LEED training. After several months, the research revealed the guardian-trained officers "used force 30 percent less often than their peers."

42. Zaki, "Building Empathy."

would demonstrate the power of story to change lives; while Bob the judge would reduce the number of reoffending criminals.

Book club invitations were extended to convicts with "long rap sheets and a high risk of reoffending."[43] For faithful engagement, participants would receive a reduced prison sentence. Not everyone was enthused. Few prisoners were literary buffs and university administrators were concerned about prisoners coming to campus. Nevertheless, the project moved forward. The first class had "eight students with 142 convictions among them, including several violent crimes."[44] During that first session, Waxler told one member of the group that he seemed a bit tense. The guy responded, "You're the guy who looks tense, Professor!"[45]

They discussed novels such as *The Old Man and the Sea* and *Bastard Out of Carolina*, "stories of risk, loss, and redemption."[46] They read material that gave inmates opportunities to use their moral imagination and put themselves in the shoes of the characters. In one story, a group of friends inadvertently "interrupt a couple mid-romance, leading to a brutal fistfight. Things escalate quickly: The three teens potentially (but not clearly) attempt sexual assault and end up hiding out in the fetid pond while their car is trashed for retaliation." The reading group is riveted. Waxler raises the question, "Were these guys bad guys or could this have happened to anyone?" This leads into a discussion about moral ambiguity and how one bad decision can lead to a lifetime of regret. As the classroom empties, one prisoner confides to Waxler: "This story is really my story."[47]

During several months of reading and discussion, participants were given a new lens through which to view themselves. Many had been labeled "bad guys" their whole lives. "Fiction revealed that underneath every crime is a person: flawed but still deserving dignity."[48] Many of the stories showed characters breaking the cycle of bad choices. It opened up new possibilities, rather than a future of hopelessness. In short, The Changing Lives Book Club became an empathy gym for the participants.

After completing the program, the two Bobs held a graduation ceremony in Kane's courtroom. In the presence of family and friends, graduates

43. Zaki, *War for Kindness*, 88.
44. Zaki, *War for Kindness*, 88.
45. Zaki, *War for Kindness*, 88.
46. Zaki, *War for Kindness*, 88.
47. Zaki, *War for Kindness*, 89.
48. Zaki, *War for Kindness*, 89.

beamed as they received diplomas and books. "The celebration recast them as people with insight and opportunity, in the same room where they had been condemned just months before."[49]

Research shows this program works. When contrasting those who went through the program with comparable men on probation, 45 percent of probationers in the comparison group reoffended, while less than 20 percent of the book club participants reoffended. Even those who reoffended often committed a lesser crime. Waxler credits the book club empathy gym: "I like to believe . . . they have a little more respect for human beings, and have to think twice before hitting another person." Changing Lives book clubs have since spread to several other states, including California, New York, and Texas. They are even starting to spring up in England.[50]

A Radical Experiment in Empathy. As a university professor, I personally know the power of a good story. Sam Richards, a professor of sociology at Penn State University, is skilled at helping his students harness their moral imagination for the purpose of generating empathy. Imagine sitting in on one of his lectures. We take a seat in the back row just as Richards asks his students to envision what it would be like if 100 years ago China had come to the United States and found the valuable resource of coal. The Chinese leaders built alliances with American politicians and began to export coal back to China to power their cities. To protect their financial interests, the Chinese stationed troops in Appalachia and posted Asian symbols and signs to intimidate and subjugate the populace. As Chinese wealth grew, the American quality of life plummeted.

After painting this picture, Richards asks, "Can you imagine walking out of this building and seeing a tank sitting out there or a truck full of soldiers? Just imagine what you would feel because you know why they are here. If you can, that's empathy. You've left your shoes and you've stood in mine."[51] Then Richards pivots and asks his audience to imagine what it would be like to walk in the shoes of an ordinary Arab Muslim living in Iraq. You just want a better life for yourself and your family, but you are struggling. You are under siege from outside incursions into your land because of oil. You watch TV and read newspapers and see Americans who are rich and happy, all because your resource is powering their lavish lifestyles. This might not be true, but it is what you see. And you see

49. Zaki, *War for Kindness*, 90.

50. Zaki, *War for Kindness*, 91.

51. Richards, "A radical experiment."

American leaders praying to the Christian God, asking their God to bless this crusade. "These two wars, the ten years of sanctions, the eight years of occupation, the insurgency that has been unleashed on your people, the hundreds of thousands of civilian deaths because of oil. You can't help but think that. You talk about it. It's in the forefront of your mind always . . . Everyone in your country has been touched by the violence, the bloodshed, the pain, the horror."[52]

Richards then projects a picture of two Iraqi men who have been captured by US soldiers after an attack on their unit. First, he asks the audience to step into the shoes of the American soldiers. "Can you feel their rage? You just want to take these guys and wring their necks." But then comes the real radical experiment in empathy. He asks us to put ourselves in the shoes of the captured Iraqi men.

> Are they brutal killers or patriotic defenders? Which one? Can you feel *their* anger, *their* fear, *their* rage at what has happened in *their* country? Can you imagine that maybe one of them in the morning bent down to their child and hugged their child and said, "Dear, I will be back later. I am going out to defend your freedom, your lives." Can you imagine that? You see, that's empathy. That's also understanding.[53]

Richards concludes his presentation by explaining why he chose such an emotionally charged, volatile subject for this lecture. He tells his students that we are allowed to hate "these people with every fiber of our being. And if I can get you to step into their shoes and walk an inch, one tiny inch, then imagine what kind of sociological analysis you can do in all other aspects of your life. . . . I am not saying I support the terrorists in Iraq, but as a sociologist I am saying that I understand. And now, maybe you do too."[54]

A God of Compassion

Why should Christ-followers care about empathy? Quite simply, it is at the center of the gospel story. The Christian God is not distant and removed from creation. The second person of the Trinity took on human form and entered into this world of pain, struggle, and heartache. Hebrews 4:15–16

52. Richards, "A radical experiment."
53. Richards, "A radical experiment."
54. Richards, "A radical experiment."

reminds us that "we do not have a high priest who is unable to empathize with our weaknesses, but we have one who has been tempted in every way, just as we are—yet he did not sin. Let us then approach God's throne of grace with confidence, so that we may receive mercy and find grace to help us in our time of need." The God of the Christian story is a God who possesses and models all three empathic dimensions: *emotional empathy* (feels our pain), *cognitive empathy* (understands our pain), and *empathic concern* (is moved to do something about it). I don't know about you, but this provides me tremendous confidence and comfort during times of suffering and difficulty. It also challenges and inspires me to chip away at our current empathy crisis by working on my own empathic physique.

During the turbulent foment of the 1960s, Francis Schaeffer challenged fellow Christians to reject a posture of superiority and cultivate empathy. In his classic book *The God Who Is There*, Schaeffer issued this clarion call:

> Dare we laugh at such things? Dare we feel superior when we view their tortured expressions in their art? Christians should stop laughing and take such men seriously. Then we shall have the right to speak again to our generation. These men are dying while they live; yet where is our compassion for them? There is nothing more ugly than a Christian orthodoxy without understanding or without compassion.[55]

Schaeffer is right—a hard heart is nothing to joke about. This last line, originally penned more than fifty years ago, is especially poignant today: "There is nothing more ugly than a Christian orthodoxy without understanding or without compassion." Trying to understand the other is not treason; it is an attempt to live out the second greatest commandment—to love our neighbors as ourselves. To cast Schaeffer's sentiment into the imagery of *All about the Bass*, we might say: "There is nothing more ugly than drowning out the treble of compassion with the pounding bass of conviction." We can check all the right boxes, affirm all the correct beliefs, but if our orthodoxy does not move us to real-life empathy, we are like that annoying tricked-out car with the amped-up bass that shakes the shutters as it slowly bounces past our house. All bass, no treble.

55. Schaeffer, *God Who Is There*, 34.

Chapter 5

Treble Tactic Five: Spot Theological Specialties

Bass-Pounding Fallacy: Doctrinal Precision Trumps Christian Unity

> "When I encounter what looks like a deep theological difference, I try to remind myself to ask what specialization might be at work in the other person's way of viewing things, and how I might learn from it."[1]
>
> —RICHARD J. MOUW

A few years ago, my wife and I took a memorable vacation to the Ligurian coast of Northern Italy. We stayed in the quaint harbor town of Rapallo, where Friedrich Nietzsche wrote part of his famous book *Thus Spoke Zarathustra*. Nietzsche was known for walking long distances while working out his philosophy.[2] During the winter of 1882–83, he roamed the breathtaking Italian countryside from Rapallo to Santa Margherita to Portofino.

Our journey took us along the same stunning path. The purpose of our trip, however, was not to follow in the footsteps of this enigmatic atheist, but rather to walk the trail of a lesser-known skeptic—ten-year-old Calvin Becker. Calvin is the fictitious narrator of one of my favorite

1. Mouw, *Las Vegas Airport*, 121.

2. For more on Nietzsche's affinity for working while walking, see Gros, *Philosophy of Walking*.

novels, *Portofino*.[3] Written by Frank Schaeffer, the son of Francis Schaeffer, this delightful tale is both hilarious and touching (think Christian *Wonder Years*). It tells the story of an American missionary family and their annual trek from the snowcapped Swiss Alps to the picturesque shores of the Italian Riviera. Each chapter is loaded with accounts of the precocious Calvin getting into all sorts of mischief. Schaeffer's ability to bring Calvin's seaside escapades to life with such exquisite skill is what inspired us to experience Portofino for ourselves.[4] We were not disappointed.

As we walked along the path from Santa Margherita to Portofino, we recalled some of Calvin's shenanigans. Here's one of our favorites: the family is eating dinner on the final night of their vacation and Calvin's sisters are upset because it rained all day. Mrs. Becker chastises them for not giving thanks in all things, but Reverend Becker turns it into a teaching moment about the sovereignty of God. During this impromptu devotional, one of Calvin's sisters, Rachel, speculates, "You mean if I had gone out to the point, I might have had a cramp or something and drowned, and God knew it so He made it rain to save me?" While Mom and Dad affirm Rachel's spiritual insight, the older sister, Janet, whispers an alternative scenario: "Or might have been raped." This comment sparks a series of angry exchanges and opens the door for the opportunistic Calvin to get Janet into trouble: "Mommy, what's 'rape'?"[5] After his inquiry is ignored for the third time, Calvin describes the meltdown:

> Then Janet made a big mistake, or rather God did because He's sovereign. Dad had said many times how the great Reformation hero, Calvin, showed us we are in a state of Total Depravity and so is our free will so we really can't even think with our fallen minds or choose to do good things because we are so depraved. So God made her say, "I only asked!" Then God made Dad throw down his napkin and say, "That's it!"[6]

After Janet is sent to her room, Calvin performs a saltshaker experiment. He wonders if shaking the container in fits and spurts will confound God's plan. Salt flies everywhere and fills Calvin's hair. The father's wrath suddenly

3. Schaeffer, *Portofino*, 128–29. While a work of fiction, the story is loosely based on several of Frank's childhood experiences.

4. Schaeffer was kind enough to give us some personal tips as we retraced Calvin's footsteps.

5. Schaeffer, *Portofino*, 128–29.

6. Schaeffer, *Portofino*, 129–30.

shifts to his only son. When asked why in the world he poured salt all over himself, Calvin blurts out, "God made me do it!"[7]

While Calvin is sitting in his room awaiting his corporal punishment for blasphemy, he ponders his father's Reformed teaching on predestination and free will. He wonders why his father would punish him if God has determined all things and humans cannot really choose otherwise. Calvin remembers his father saying that free will really just means that we are "free to recognize God's plan."[8] Little Calvin is confounded.

In the end, Calvin receives a stay of execution on the condition that he will never again attribute his sin to divine causation. He exchanges hugs and kisses with his father. The warmth of the moment, however, is interrupted by a nagging thought: "I wondered if God had known he would change his mind and not spank me and if this was part of the plan."[9]

This humorous vignette unites two of my favorite topics: Italy and Calvinism. As a philosophy and theology professor at a Christian university, I've had the privilege of introducing the age-old Calvinism-Arminianism controversy to thousands of students over the years. Each semester, after explaining the finer details of free will and determinism and wrestling with the core teaching of these theological systems, we make it personal. I ask for one Calvinist and one Arminian volunteer to participate in a conversation in front of the class. Instead of a heated debate, it is an opportunity for the class to hear the stories of fellow classmates who take this subject matter seriously. It never fails to be one of the great learning experiences of the semester.

This chapter is designed to have a similar feel. Instead of digging into the finer systematic points of this debate, we will examine Calvinism and Arminianism through the prism of Moral Foundations Theory.[10] While most of this book focuses on turning up the treble toward those outside the Christian tribe, treating fellow believers with gentleness and respect is essential, as well—something that has not always happened when it comes to doctrinal disputes. As mentioned in chapter 1, the Final Apologetic according to Francis Schaeffer is Christian unity and the love that

7. Schaeffer, *Portofino*, 131.

8. Schaeffer, *Portofino*, 132.

9. Schaeffer, *Portofino*, 132. A version of this Calvin Becker saltshaker recounting originally appeared in my co-authored book, *C. S. Lewis and Francis Schaeffer*, 83–84.

10. For a good introduction to this subject matter, see Walls and Dongell, *Why I am Not a Calvinist*, and Peterson and Williams, *Why I am Not an Arminian*.

flows between fellow believers. This chapter will explore how unity can be promoted in the midst of our theological differences. At the same time, we will discuss why it is so critical to communicate in both delivery and content a version of the gospel message that honors the full range of our God-given moral intuitions.

In chapter 3, we learned that the first three blocks that toppled Bart Campolo's tower of faith were sovereignty, salvation, and Scripture—three topics central to the Calvinism-Arminianism dispute, as well. Bart and Tony wrote a book called *Why I Left, Why I Stayed*—a title that also fits nicely with the structure of this chapter. In what follows, we will focus primarily on the stories of two men who have wrestled deeply with the subjects of sovereignty, salvation, and Scripture, in general, and the difficult doctrine of unconditional election, in particular. The first is Austin Fischer, who chose to *leave* Calvinism behind, while the second is Richard Mouw, who chose to *stay* and promote a more compassionate brand of Calvinism.

Austin Fischer: Why I Left

A Blind Date with John Piper: In *Young, Restless, No Longer Reformed*, author and pastor Austin Fischer explains his entry into and exodus out of Calvinism. His story began on "a blind date with John Piper."[11] As a teenager Fischer was already a Christian, but felt something was missing. He went to his youth pastor, who recommended Piper's book *Desiring God*. He quickly learned that Piper was one of the leading voices for a Reformed renewal movement known as Neo-Calvinism.[12] By reading Piper, Fischer learned that God isn't concerned with the American Dream or our self-centered satisfaction. Instead, "God cares about God and wants me to care about God." Fischer quickly tuned into "the animating impulse of Neo-Calvinism: It's all about God's glory." From first to last, the Christian story is all about God; but here's the really good news for humanity: "God is most glorified in us when we are most satisfied in him." In other words, God's glory and our satisfaction are not at odds, and the only way to achieve satisfaction in this life (and the next) is to seek God with all that we've got. Fischer enthusiastically recalls his initial reaction to Piper's words: "Living a life for the glory of God is the most joyful, exciting, and

11. Fischer, *No Longer Reformed*, 7.

12. For a good introduction to the New Calvinism, see Hansen, *Young, Restless, Reformed*. For a recent update, see Hansen, "Still Young, Restless, and Reformed?"

compelling thing you can do with the fleeting existence you're given on earth."[13] The blind date with Piper had gone well. Fischer had found what he was looking for: an intellectually serious, muscular form of faith. A faith he could put a ring on. Or so he thought.

The Cost of Calvinism: Thus began Fischer's theological deconstruction. Everything he had believed about his Christian faith was now called into question. It was both exhilarating and painful. Fischer remembers, "I knew I was awash in Christianity that had little to do with Jesus and a lot to do with me—my comfort, my security, my stuff, my appeased conscience, my mansion in heaven. I knew I needed a new God and was confident John Piper was introducing me to him."[14] As invigorated as he was by this new God-centered theology, Fischer couldn't shake an uneasy feeling and began to realize the cost of this wedding ring would be high.

Like many people when they first begin courting Calvinism, Fischer suffered from sticker shock. The price would include rejecting one's *intuitive* belief in free will[15] and embracing a God who is the "all-determining reality" of everything that comes to pass, including the eternal destiny of each person. In other words, the doctrine of unconditional election. Once the implications began to sink in, Fischer asked, "'So you're telling me that God has already determined everyone who will be in heaven and hell?' This big, ugly question is what anyone who wrestles with Calvinism must square off with sooner or later, and it was a tough question for me to get a handle on. How was that fair?"[16] When he raised this question, fellow Calvinists said you don't want *fair*, because we are all sinners who deserve

13. Fischer, *No Longer Reformed*, 8.

14. Fischer, *No Longer Reformed*, 9.

15. It is important to recognize that most Calvinists do not reject human freedom, but instead of affirming an intuitive libertarian notion of freedom (we are free when we have two or more live options available) as Arminians do, Calvinists typically affirm a highly counterintuitive form of freedom known as compatibilism (we are free when we do what we want to do, even though our thoughts, desires, and actions have been determined for us). According to most Reformed philosophers, a compatibilistic notion of freedom is necessary to hold together the central Calvinist claims of total, unconditional divine determinism and human moral responsibility. This chapter will not evaluate the cogency of either of these forms of freedom. What is relevant here is to recognize that the Arminian view of freedom is highly intuitive and readily activates our *liberty* intuition, while the Calvinist view is highly counterintuitive and does not. For more on why Calvinism requires compatibilism, see Feinberg, "God, Freedom and Evil," 465. For a good introduction to the topic of free will and determinism, see Timpe, *Free Will*.

16. Fischer, *No Longer Reformed*, 9.

hell. What you want instead is *grace*. This answer didn't fully appease Fischer; after all, if God is the all-encompassing determinator of reality then that must include the predetermination of all the sins that will send the non-elect to hell. How is that just?

The biggest hurdle for Fischer, however, was the notion of divine love: "Perhaps our problem with the idea that God has unconditionally predetermined who to save and who to condemn is that it doesn't seem loving, and the Bible certainly tells us God is loving."[17] When Fischer continued to voice his discomfort with the bass-pounding doctrine of unconditional election, he was told by Calvinist comrades to lean into concepts like *divine mystery* and *transcendence*: "God exists on a completely different plane, shrouded in the veil of divine mystery," he was told. "God is not like us. And this means that we cannot simply project onto God all the virtues we find desirable as humans. We cannot assume that God's love, justice, and goodness match up perfectly with our notions of love, justice, and goodness."[18] In other words, Fischer was told to suppress his deepest and most certain moral intuitions when it comes to things like love, free will, and justice. The Calvinist story was saying that God's ways are not only higher than our ways, but completely contrary when it comes to these topics. God's transcendence and mysterious moral compass are not only beyond our comprehension, they flip our sense of morality on its head.

The TULIP Tiger: The deeper Fischer moved into Calvinism, the more intuitive turmoil he felt. While his *conviction* intuitions were fully engaged by the Calvinist account of a majestic sovereign king (authority) doing all things for his own righteous glory (sanctity), including the selection of the elect for heaven (in-group loyalty), his *compassion* intuitions were deeply offended. His care, liberty, and fairness intuitions were violated by this exclusive story of in-grouping and out-grouping, elect and non-elect.[19] It didn't land right, this story of disproportionate favor. What kind of perfect

17. Fischer, *No Longer Reformed*, 10.

18. Fischer, *No Longer Reformed*, 10–11.

19. It could be argued that the Calvinist story not only activates the conviction intuitions, but the compassion intuitions (with the exception of liberty), as well, when talking about God's love and grace for the undeserving elect. But when the narrative expands to include discussion of the non-elect, it isn't difficult to see how the bass takes over and mutes the treble. The same point can be made about Piper's doctrine of Christian Hedonism discussed a few pages back. The notion that God is most glorified in us when we are most satisfied in him applies to the elect alone, because in the Calvinist view God is most glorified in the damnation of the non-elect, a state that does not produce any kind of satisfaction for the reprobate.

parent would act this way? How could this be loving? Even more unsettling, it is a story of a God who has predestined the unfavored others to commit the very sins that will send them to hell forever—all for the sake of his divine glory. Fischer soon discovered that his intuitive elephant was divided; and a schizophrenic pachyderm is hard to handle.

But, for the time being, Fischer had larger problems: there was another big-game animal on the loose in search of prey. Piper explains this metaphor by recounting how the sovereign King of creation hunted him down:

> So when I went to college and began to hear people give a framework to this [Calvinism], I revolted against the sovereignty of God . . . When I arrived at Fuller Seminary, I took a class on systematic theology with James Morgan . . . and another with Dan Fuller on hermeneutics. And coming from both sides—theology and exegesis—I was feeling myself absolutely cornered by all the evidences of God's sovereignty in the Bible . . . I would put my face in my hands in my room, and I would just cry because my world was coming apart. I just couldn't figure anything out . . . But at the end of James Morgan's theology class, I wrote in a blue book: "Romans 9 is like a tiger going around devouring free-willers like me." And it did.[20]

Fischer had the same tiger on his tail, and like Piper, finally gave in. Like many others who have come kicking and screaming into the fold, Fischer submitted to a Calvinist reading of Scripture. "I didn't feel as though the Bible left me any option."[21]

The Little Girl in the Red Coat: While Fischer "had been a reluctant convert to Calvinism . . . any move away from it would not come easy."[22] During his undergraduate years he remained solid in his allegiance despite challenges from various professors. By the time he was in seminary, however, his caged elephant started making some noise. Fischer recalls a Calvinist theologian speaking to one of his classes. A fellow student asked the theologian why God *causes* terrible suffering. The theologian did not have an answer, but "believed God would make it up to them in some way." While Fischer appreciated the humility and sincerity of the response, he couldn't avoid a follow-up question: "How will God make it

20. Piper, "Interview with John Piper," 220–21.

21. Fischer, *No Longer Reformed*, 11.

22. Fischer, *No Longer Reformed*, 19.

up to the reprobate?"[23] The guest theologian paused and answered, "You know, there are certain things that I just don't know but am willing to live with. And that's one of them."[24] Fischer bristled.

Fischer had heard this response before. One of his Calvinist friends, when pushed on the reprobate, says it is a necessary part of the Calvinist story, but he doesn't think about it all the time. "Subsequently, he thinks I make too big a deal out of them. . . . Why let them disrupt everything else? Why dwell on them? And to that I can only answer—because you can't forget the little girl in the red coat."[25]

"The little girl in the red coat" refers to a scene from *Schindler's List*. Director Steven Spielberg shot this film in black and white, except for a little Jewish girl whose red jacket distinguishes her from the monochromatic surroundings. As Nazis are rounding up some of the town's Jewish families and executing others in the street, the little girl in the red coat is shown weaving through the chaos. She is terrified, confused, alone. We see the unspeakable carnage unfolding from a distant hilltop, where the hero of the film, Oskar Schindler, watches in horror. He can't take his eyes off the little girl in the red coat. You sense his heart and mind; his compassion is palpable. The child escapes harm in this scene, but later in the film Schindler walks by a pile of bodies and is crushed when he spots the little girl in the red coat stacked among the dead.

This powerful scene released Fischer's caged elephant, which was now trumpeting for all to hear. While God might make everything right for the elect in heaven, how about the unconditionally damned? Fischer finally admitted to himself that Calvinism had no satisfying answer.

> The book of Exodus is kick-started when an oppressed group of slaves cry out in agony, and God hears them. . . . Their God is a God who sees oppressive suffering and hears cries of agony—their God is a God who can't forget the little girl in the red coat. . . . The point here is simple. There is no suffering like that of the damned, no oppression like that of the reprobate, so if you're a Calvinist, you don't have permission to look away. You don't get to treat them like a finer point of eschatology that need not be dwelt on because God teaches us to pay *the most attention to people like this*. If you're going to be a Calvinist, you don't get to forget the reprobate and shame on you if you do. I fought off my desire to look away and

23. "Reprobate" is another word for the "non-elect."

24. Fischer, *No Longer Reformed*, 25.

25. Fischer, *No Longer Reformed*, 25–26.

> forced myself to hear their cries. I forced myself to remember the little girl in the red coat and reconcile how a good God creates her so he can damn her.[26]

Young, Restless, No Longer Reformed: Fischer eventually left Calvinism and opted for a form of Arminianism known as Freewill Theism,[27] which he found both biblically and intuitively appealing. He could no longer live a schizophrenic existence—affirming his *conviction* intuitions of in-group loyalty, authority, and sanctity, while simultaneously denying his *compassion* intuitions of care, liberty, and fairness. Calvinism had forced him to "call things 'good,' when they could only be considered the most morally repugnant atrocities imaginable, perpetrated by the Creator himself."[28] Every Calvinist attempt to explain God's impeccable character came up short. No analogy came close. God's ways were not only higher, they were completely opposite. For Fischer, this became the "fundamental turning point: I could no longer make any sense of the core Christian beliefs in God's love, justice, and goodness. I could no longer deceive myself into thinking I knew what I meant when I said God was good. I realized the only thing I could say about God was that he did everything for his glory. Seriously—that was it."[29] For Fischer, the Calvinist God was a Nietzschean will-to-power deity—all bass, no treble.

Richard Mouw: Why I Stayed

A Softer, More Tender TULIP: In the 1979 film *Hardcore*, a desperate father from Grand Rapids (Jake) travels the country in search of his runaway teenage daughter. In Las Vegas, Jake meets a teenage prostitute named Niki. As the two wait to board a flight to Los Angeles, the conversation deepens. Niki wonders if Jake's anger and negativity are rooted in his religion, leading to a discussion of Jake's belief in the Calvinist TULIP:

> **NIKI:** What the crap?

26. Fischer, *No Longer Reformed*, 26. Some readers might rightly ask the question: How do we know the little girl's eternal destiny? Does a Calvinist view require the belief that a little Jewish girl is necessarily among the unconditionally non-elect? It is a fair question and I suspect many Calvinists would not include this little girl, who died prior to the age of accountability, necessarily among the reprobate.

27. For a good introduction to this type of theology, see Basinger, *Freewill Theism*.

28. Fischer, *No Longer Reformed*, 26.

29. Fischer, *No Longer Reformed*, 27.

JAKE: It's an acronym. It comes from the Canons of Dordt. Every letter stands for a different belief, like—Are you sure you want to hear this?

NIKI: Yeah, yeah. Please go on. I'm a Venusian myself.

JAKE: Well, **T** stands for "total depravity": all men through original sin are totally evil and incapable of good. All my works are as filthy rags in the sight of the Lord.

NIKI: That's what the Venusians call negative moral attitudes.

JAKE: Be that as it may, **U** stands for "unconditional election": God has chosen a certain number of people to be saved, the elect, and he's chosen them from the beginning of time. **L** is for "limited atonement": only a limited number of people will be atoned and go to heaven. **I** is for "irresistible grace": God's grace cannot be resisted or denied. And **P** is for "perseverance of the saints": once you're in grace, you cannot fall from the numbers of the elect. That's it.

NIKI: Before you can become saved, God already knows who you are?

JAKE: Oh yes, he'd have to. That's predestination. I mean, if God is omniscient, if he already knows everything—and he wouldn't be God if he didn't—then he must have known, even before the creation of the world, the names of those who would be saved.

NIKI: Well, then, it's all worked out, huh? It's fixed.

JAKE: More or less.

NIKI: I thought I was ****ed up.

JAKE: Well, I admit it's a little confusing when you look at it from the outside. You have to try to look at it from the inside.[30]

Richard Mouw opens with the above scene in his book *Calvinism in the Las Vegas Airport*. While he does not recommend the film for "spiritual edification," Mouw has a personal connection. The film's director, Paul Schrader, is a former Calvin College professor, where Mouw taught

30. Quoted by Mouw, *Las Vegas Airport*, 12–13. Theologically careful readers will note that Jake has conflated predestination with foreknowledge in this exchange. Classical Calvinism claims that God knows the future because he unconditionally and unilaterally causes it to happen. Arminianism, on the other hand, claims that God's predestining will is informed by his knowledge of human choices that have yet to be made.

philosophy for many years. Much of the movie was also filmed in the Los Angeles area, where Mouw would later serve as the president of Fuller Theological Seminary.

The main reason, however, that Mouw includes this scene is to hold it up as a bad example. As a Calvinist, he believes "the TULIP doctrines are a summary—the right one, as I view things—of the way God goes about saving people. But TULIP is not something that is designed to attract a person to Christianity in the first place."[31] Consequently, he believes Jake should have taken a different approach with Niki. He should have started by listening to Niki's story, which might have included things like child abuse, risky behavior, trust issues, and "an inability to accept genuine love." There was also a moment in the conversation when Jake could have asked Niki about her own "Venusian" religion in order to locate some common ground. "Instead of hitting Niki directly with the 'high Calvinism' of the TULIP doctrines, I would rather have her hear a compassionate word," suggests Mouw. "If I'm right about Niki, she did not need a theology lesson. She needed a God who spoke to her in soft and tender tones."[32] In the language we have been using in this book, it appears Jake made two mistakes: first, he started with the rider, and second, when he did address the elephant he focused exclusively on the pachyderm's conviction intuitions. Instead, Jake should have engaged the elephant first and done so "in soft and tender tones"—activating the pachyderm's compassion intuitions.

Mouw seems to side with Jake on one point, however: the Calvinist TULIP is "confusing when you look at it from the outside. You have to try to look at it from the inside." Mouw admits, "when stated bluntly, [the TULIP doctrines] have a harsh feel about them. To articulate them 'with gentleness and respect' takes some effort."[33] In other words, discussion of the TULIP should be reserved for converts, those who are inside the fold. If Niki were to be converted, Mouw hopes "she would eventually come to understand the basic issues at stake in the TULIP doctrines," but this might require some updated and modified language.[34] If Mouw could speak to a converted Niki, he would talk about the *human condition* instead of total depravity; *divine selectiveness* instead of unconditional election; *a mission accomplished* rather than limited atonement; a *pursuing God* instead of

31. Mouw, *Las Vegas Airport*, 106–7.

32. Mouw, *Las Vegas Airport*, 108.

33. Mouw, *Las Vegas Airport*, 14.

34. Mouw, *Las Vegas Airport*, 15.

irresistible grace; and *divine faithfulness* rather than perseverance of the saints. This updated language not only makes these doctrines more accessible, but it offers a more positive frame. It also attempts to activate the *care* foundation, because this reframing emphasizes God's active, faithful, and certain pursuit of his chosen sheep.

A Journey toward Convicted Civility: All of the above are attempts to shift away from a bass-pounding, hardcore brand of theology to a "kinder, gentler Calvinism."[35] That said, the mild-mannered Mouw has no problem kicking his comrades in the pants if he feels they need a lesson in civility. In the following reproof, Mouw makes it clear that the Calvinist movement needs to turn up the treble in many areas of life, including the treatment of those outside the Calvinist fold. He even wonders if the Calvinist sheet music could benefit from a new arrangement.

> One area, for example, where I believe Calvinism has been embarrassingly weak is in ethics . . . Calvinists have certainly not stood out in the Christian community as especially pure people when it comes to the way they behave. They have frequently been intolerant, sometimes to the point of taking *abusive* and violent action toward people with whom they have disagreed. They have often promoted racist policies. And the fact that they have often defended these things by appealing directly to Calvinist teachings suggests that at least something in these patterns may be due to some weaknesses in the Calvinist perspective itself. On such matters, it seems clear to me that Calvinists ought to repent and admit to the larger Christian community that we have much to learn from others—from Mennonites, from black members of South African Pentecostal churches, from the followers of Saint Francis, and many others.[36]

Mouw's quest for a satisfying social ethic began during the turbulent sixties. While a young seminary student, he realized his social justice sensibilities were out of step with many in his tradition. This came into focus one weekend when he was sent to preach at a Dutch-American church. While in town he was hosted by a church elder and his wife. Following dinner the elder read from the Bible. Upon finishing, the man told Mouw that the passage they just read "reminded him of Heidelberg One, adding that it is wonderful for a person to be able to say, 'My only comfort in life and death is that I am not my own.'"

35. Mouw, *Las Vegas Airport*, 98.

36. Mouw, *Las Vegas Airport*, 114–15.

They then retired to the living room to watch the evening news. The main story focused on a civil rights march that was being led by Martin Luther King, Jr. Mouw remembers his "host grew agitated, and he walked over to turn off the TV set, telling me he couldn't stand to hear 'all of this stuff about the colored people and their complaints.'" Mouw respectfully disagreed, defending Dr. King's cause. This disagreement led to an intense exchange. Mouw recalls, "At one point [the elder] pounded his fist on the coffee table and shouted, 'I don't want those people moving into my neighborhood! What I have I got on my own, and no one is going to take it away from me!'" Mouw diffused the situation, but later the irony sunk in: "The person who had shouted that what he possessed he had gotten on his own and no one could take it away from him had only minutes before told me that his only comfort in life and death was that he was not his own. That lesson stayed with me."[37] He vowed to help fellow Calvinists do better.

As the radical sixties gave way to the early seventies, Mouw penned his first book, entitled *Political Evangelism*. It focused on the need for evangelical social engagement and encouraged Christians to take responsibility for the cultural common good. By the early eighties, Christians were responding to that call in droves. Behind the leadership of Jerry Falwell and others, a political alliance was forged with the Republican party. While Mouw was pleased to see Christians engaged in the public square, he was less enthusiastic about the Moral Majority's agenda. That's when he decided "it wasn't enough for evangelicals to just get involved, we need the right kind of theology."[38] This led to constructive dialogue between Mouw, the staunch Calvinist, and more progressive Christians such as John Howard Yoder, Ron Sider, and Jim Wallis. As the drumbeat of the culture war increased, however, Mouw could not help but notice that evangelicals were getting "into the incivility of the larger culture. We embarrassed ourselves in the ways in which we talked about faith and public life."[39]

As the late eighties faded into the decade of the nineties, Mouw realized it wasn't enough to just get involved and to clarify your theology, "we have to cultivate the right spirit." Around this time, he picked up a book by Martin Marty entitled *By Way of Response*.[40] The simple brilliance of the following two sentences hit Mouw like a bolt of lightning: "One of the big

37. Mouw, *Las Vegas Airport*, 106.

38. Mouw, "Convicted Civility."

39. Mouw, "Convicted Civility."

40. Marty, *Response*.

problems in the world today is that people who have strong convictions aren't very civil and people who are civil often don't have very strong convictions. And what we really need is convicted civility."[41] Marty's language captures perfectly what we have been discussing in this book. People with strong convictions who aren't civil are all bass, no treble. People who are civil without strong convictions are all treble, no bass. Convicted civility strikes the right balance.

The last three decades of Mouw's ministry have been characterized by convicted civility, including a commitment to robust inter-faith dialogue. Mouw recommends Christians enter into these conversations keeping three guiding principles in mind: 1. Talk about Jesus as the opportunity arises, 2. maintain a learner's attitude, and 3. be willing to work together for the common good. Additionally, we should explain the other person's beliefs in a way they would endorse and avoid comparing our best exemplars with the other side's worst.

Mouw offers the following cautionary tale. After spending a few days in interreligious dialogue on the campus of Brigham Young University, he attended a militantly aggressive anti-Mormon Christian talk. Following the lecture, Mouw thanked the speaker for making some important points, but also encouraged him to do additional research because he knew his Mormon friends would object to how some of their beliefs were portrayed. The speaker did not care for the advice. Mouw recalls:

> He got very angry and said, "You intellectuals, you always have to come up with all these nice distinctions and these nuances and all the rest. We don't have time for that. We're in a battle for the truth and we've got to win the battle!" And I thought afterward, isn't it ironic that for the sake of the truth we're willing to tell untruths—[And to do it] in the service of the One who said, "I am the way, the truth and the life." The fact is if we care about the truth, we need to be sure we are telling the truth.[42]

Common Grace: We've now considered several commendable attempts to turn up the Calvinist treble, but Mouw is well aware of the difficulty involved. In fact, he believes the doctrine of unconditional election presents a unique challenge for Calvinists. Mouw eloquently explains the theological and practical hurdle:

41. Mouw, "Convicted Civility."

42. Mouw, "Common Good."

> I am a Calvinist, and we Calvinists have our own special theological forces at work in emphasizing a lack of commonness with other human beings. The one that first comes to mind is the classic Calvinist insistence that the human race is divided into two categories: the elect and the non-elect. To be sure, other evangelicals—as well as other groups adhering to historic Christian teachings—posit a fundamental duality in this regard. But the common division between, say, the "saved" and the "lost" does not necessarily promote the rigidity that may appear to be endemic to Calvinism. A Wesleyan can preach without any theological confusion about the doctrinal boundaries of Wesleyanism, that Christians should nurture "a heart for the lost." Unsaved people can be viewed, from that perspective, as having lost their way, as experiencing predicaments that are of their own making. For a Calvinist to advocate the nurturing of "a heart for the reprobate" does not have the same spiritual or theological feel to it. If one's eternal destiny is decided by God's eternal decrees rather than our own free choices—and this is a standard expression of a Calvinist-type logic—then why should we have a "heart" for those for whom God himself has no "heart"?[43]

We learned earlier that Austin Fischer left Calvinism because he couldn't stop thinking about the little Jewish girl in the red coat and the God who created her so he could damn her. Fischer's compassion intuitions rejected such divine hardness of heart. In his autobiographical memoir, *Adventures in Evangelical Civility*, Mouw likewise assesses Calvinism in light of the horrors of the Holocaust. But instead of pondering how one can bow the knee to the God of Calvinism, he asks a different question: "Why should we have a 'heart' for those for whom God himself has no 'heart?'" In other words, could our love possibly exceed God's love?

Mouw considers two Calvinist responses to this question in light of a chilling scene from William Schirer's book *The Rise and Fall of the Third Reich:*

> In the new batch of Jews lined up at the edge of the pit is a little Jewish boy, about ten years old. As the Nazis wait, cold, callous, even enjoying what they are about to do, cigarettes dangling out of their mouths, the little boy, not comprehending, but fearful, clings to his father. Looking down on his son's anxious face, the helpless father tries to comfort his child. In a moment, father and son will go down into the huge grave, atop a mass of dead bodies to be shot.[44]

43. Mouw, *Adventures*, 214–15.

44. Quoted in Mouw, *Adventures*, 215.

The first response comes from David Engelsma, an emeritus professor at Reformed Protestant Seminary. A long-time critic of Mouw "for basing [his] theology on feelings [rather] than on Reformed orthodoxy," Engelsma admits that he is occasionally "inclined to agonize over a particular case of suffering in the life of the non-Christian, [but] he realizes the need to hold that tendency in check by reminding himself of his Calvinist convictions."[45] Now, these comments were made specifically in reference to the above horrific scene. In order to suppress any natural feelings of empathy, Engelsma is saying he intentionally ruminates on his Calvinist conviction that "the suffering of the reprobate wicked outside of Jesus Christ does not break the heart of God, for God acts through these despicable murderers and evildoers [the Nazis] to punish the ungodly [the Jews] in righteousness."[46] Engelsma's answer to Mouw's question? No, we shouldn't have a "heart" for those for whom God himself has no "heart."

This is a shocking statement and worth reflecting upon carefully. Engelsma says that he is occasionally tempted to feel empathy for suffering people whom he views as non-elect. In a moment of weakness (as he would put it) he is tempted to feel sorry for Jewish parents and children, who were not only being murdered by the Nazis, but emotionally and psychologically tortured prior to their deaths. But then he catches himself and uses his Calvinist convictions to mute his compassion for the non-elect because his version of Calvinism tells him that God does not have a heart for the non-elect and if God does not feel badly for them, then, as a good Calvinist, he shouldn't either.

The other Calvinist response we will consider comes from Mouw himself, who is greatly distressed by Engelsma's comments. In fact, he finds Engelsma's statements both "theologically wrong and morally offensive." While he understands the logic, he strongly condemns allowing the doctrine of unconditional election and reprobation to take command of one's practical and emotional life in this way. To see empathy as impious and hardness as holy is a morally toxic cocktail. Instead of following Engelsma's logic, Mouw believes Calvinists should "nurture a compassion for [the non-elect] in their sufferings, because of the doctrine of common grace, which teaches us that God himself has this attitude of favor toward those whom he has not elected."[47] Mouw encourages fellow Calvinists to

45. Mouw, *Adventures*, 215.

46. Mouw, *Adventures*, 215.

47. Mouw, *Adventures*, 216.

lean into this doctrine of common grace when interacting with those who hold different beliefs.

Now, it is fair to ask whose position (Engelsma or Mouw) is more consistent with the rider-focused logic of five-point Calvinism? I will let you draw your own conclusions. That said, there is no doubt that Mouw's brand of Calvinism leads to better practical and social outcomes. Jamil Zaki tells us that "disengagement builds emotional calluses. For decades, the psychologist Ervin Staub has studied individuals who kill during the war or genocide. He finds that they turn off their empathy, 'reducing [their] concern for the welfare of those [they] harm or allow to suffer.'"[48] We cannot end this section without siding strongly with Mouw: No matter our theological tradition, we must do whatever it takes to cultivate an empathic heart and never use our theological convictions as a tool to mute our compassion intuitions. Intentionally building emotional calluses on the basis of our theological convictions is not only deeply disturbing, but utterly contrary to Christ's command to love our enemies—something we will explore in greater detail in chapter 7.

Honor Sacred Specializations

As a former Calvinist myself, and current Wesleyan, it should come as no surprise that I track with Austin Fischer's theology. If Scripture and moral intuition both emanate from God, then they should cohere at a fundamental level. As the author of this book, however, and someone actively pursuing compassionate conviction, I also see great value in Richard Mouw's kinder, gentler brand of Calvinism and commitment to convicted civility. Fischer and Mouw should both be commended for turning up the treble in their own respective ways. There are many lessons we could glean from the stories of these two men. However, I'd like to conclude this chapter by discussing the importance of showing convicted civility toward fellow Christians.

As mentioned in the introduction to this chapter, I always close my Calvinism-Arminianism unit by facilitating a student-to-student conversation in front of the class. We cover a lot of ground in this hour-long discussion. I ask the Calvinist student questions like, "Why should we pray, share our faith, or do mission work if God has already unconditionally determined everything, including the eternal destiny of each person?" I

48. Zaki, *War for Kindness*, 25.

ask the Arminian student questions like, "If it is possible to lose your salvation, how do you feel secure in your personal relationship with God?" Students in the audience get in on the fun with queries of their own, some sounding oddly similar to the musings of the precocious Calvin Becker (minus the salty hairdo)!

I always conclude the hour with the following question: "I know you have theological differences, but what do you respect or admire most about the opposing view?" I am consistently pleased to hear generous responses like, "I appreciate how Calvinists are willing to go against their own intuitions or feelings to honor biblical authority" and "I like how Arminians talk so much about God's love for all people."

These comments remind me of Mouw's discussion of theological specialization: "When I encounter what looks like a deep theological difference, I try to remind myself to ask what specialization might be at work in the other person's way of viewing things, and how I might learn from it."[49] Just as medical doctors have their different areas of expertise, theological traditions have sacred specializations. Each sacred specialization—divine sovereignty for the Calvinist and divine character for the Arminian—activates a different cluster of venerable intuitions. As Haidt reminds us: "If you want to *understand* another group, *follow the sacredness*. . . . Think about the six moral foundations, and try to figure out which one or two are carrying the most weight in a particular controversy."[50] Without ignoring deficiencies, Calvinists and Arminians would both do well to begin by recognizing the intuitions activated by the other side's sacred specialization.

Haidt also explains how our tribal nature in the political sphere makes it constitutionally impossible for conservatives and liberals to see the whole picture. Consequently, both have something important to contribute to a healthy political life—the yin-yang balance of conservation and progress.[51] Is it possible that both sides of the Calvinism-Arminianism theological debate are likewise constitutionally incapable of seeing the whole picture? Can we make such a suggestion without fear of being called a traitor by our own side? Can we enter into a more generous conversation without compromising our own theological convictions?

Adopting an elephant-friendly yin-yang attitude would also pave the way for more productive rider-focused dialogue. When entering into

49. Mouw, *Las Vegas Airport*, 121.

50. Haidt, *Righteous Mind*, 312.

51. Haidt, *Righteous Mind*, 294–98.

theological conversation, Calvinists and Arminians would do well to follow Mouw's inter-religious dialogue principles: Each side should listen to learn, work together for the common cause of Christ, never put your best up against their worst, and represent the other side in a way they would recognize. Developing these habits of heart and mind with fellow believers would prepare us for a more generous public witness; so when we do get out of the saltshaker and enter the world, our message will be seasoned with the zest of authentic convicted civility.[52]

52. Kudos to you if you caught this callout to Rebecca Manley Pippert's classic bestseller, *Out of the Saltshaker*.

Chapter 6

Treble Tactic Six: Map the Moral Matrix

Bass-Pounding Fallacy: We Own All of the Moral High Ground

> "We all have a sacred story in us—a story that gives us meaning and purpose and how we organize our lives. If you know someone, if you've talked to them face-to-face, if you can forge a connection, you may not agree with them on everything but there's some common ground to be found and you can move forward."[1]
>
> —BARACK OBAMA

A week after the world watched George Floyd take his final breath under the knee of a white Minneapolis police officer, New Orleans Saints quarterback Drew Brees was asked to comment on the prospect of NFL players resuming their well-documented kneeling protests. His response was unflinching:

> I will never agree with anybody disrespecting the flag of the United States of America or our country. Let me just tell you what I see or what I feel when the national anthem is played and when I look at the flag of the United States. I envision my two grandfathers who fought for this country during World War II—one in the Army and one in the Marine Corps. Both risking their lives

1. Netflix Film Club, "American Factory."

> to protect our country and to try to make our country and this world a better place.[2]

The backlash from the sports world was swift and severe. As one reporter put it, "Just like that, the issue was grabbed from behind and tossed back, horse-collar tackle style, into the headache-inducing argument that erupted three years ago."[3] LeBron James tweeted, "WOW MAN!! . . . You literally still don't understand why Kap was kneeling on one knee?? Has absolute nothing to do with the disrespect of [flag emoji] and our soldiers (men and women) who keep our land free."[4] Former NFL wide receiver Eric Jennings said, "Two words come to mind: callous and selfish."[5] Through tears, Saints teammate Malcolm Jenkins posted an emotionally raw video: "Drew Brees, if you don't understand how hurtful, how insensitive your comments are, you are part of the problem. . . . And it's unfortunate because I considered you a friend. I looked up to you. You're someone I had a great deal of respect for. But sometimes you should shut the **** up."[6]

Hours after Brees made his controversial statement, CNN personality Don Lemon dedicated an extended segment to the topic. One of his guests, former NFL player Benjamin Watson, said that he wasn't surprised by Brees's convictions, but his tone and timing were off: "He definitely could have answered that question much better and in a much more compassionate way. . . . especially this week, it was tough to hear." Lemon, a Louisiana native, offered his own perspective, "My family are die-hard Saints fans and every single person in my family is disappointed by Drew Brees's comments today and thinks he is completely out of touch with what is happening—and can't believe he is falling for the talking points of President Trump, who is comparing this to disrespect for the flag when this has nothing to do with the flag."[7]

By the following morning, Brees had issued a heartfelt apology: "In an attempt to talk about respect, unity, and solidarity centered around the American flag and the national anthem, I made comments that were insensitive and completely missed the mark on the issues we are facing right now as a country. They lacked awareness and any type of compassion

2. Brees, "Kneeling protests."
3. Brewer, "Saddest kind of wrong."
4. James, Twitter.
5. Jennings, "Greg Jennings explains."
6. Jenkins, "Malcolm Jenkins."
7. CNN, "Backlash."

or empathy." He went on to express his commitment to the cause of racial equality through learning, listening, and serving as an ally for equal rights. "I will never know what it's like to be a black man or raise black children in America but I will work every day to put myself in those shoes and fight for what is right."[8]

While many gladly accepted his apology, not everyone was quick to forgive, including two African American sports commentators. Hall of Fame tight end Shannon Sharpe said the apology was "meaningless because the guys know he spoke his heart the very first time around." Sharpe then encouraged Brees to retire because his black teammates "will never look at him the same."[9] Maria Taylor on ESPN's *First Take* offered her own impassioned commentary: "My patience left my body when I watched George Floyd take his last breath. So if that didn't affect you and make you reassess the way you're going to address a question that includes racial injustice in our country after you watched that man die in the middle of the street, something's off."[10]

As I viewed countless videos, posts, and articles, one recurring question emerged: How could a respected person of character with a fifteen-year track record of serving the diverse New Orleans community be so tone deaf? Lemon put it well: "I don't understand how Drew Brees, who has done so many good things in the past, especially the money he donated during COVID-19 . . . I don't understand what he's not getting about this particular issue."[11]

I hear this a lot when discussing divisive material in my classes. Whether it is abortion, gun control, immigration, or LGBT marriage equality, students often say, "I just don't understand how a seemingly normal person could believe such and such . . ." As Kathryn Schulz pointed out in chapter 2, the typical answer to this question is one of three options: they are either *ignorant*, *stupid*, or *evil*. But Moral Foundations Theory can show us a fourth possibility: perhaps the other side has a different moral focus. As we've previously learned, morality binds and blinds. Moral teams circle around a unifying sacred value, then are blinded to the unifying sacred value of the other team. In these debates, we often wrongly assume that our team owns all of the moral high ground. This chapter will explore how

8. CNN, "Backlash."
9. Skip and Shannon, "Skip and Shannon react."
10. ESPN, "Passionate message."
11. CNN, "Backlash."

mapping the moral matrix of both sides can go a long way toward fostering understanding and respectful civil discourse.

Suspicion Versus Charity

In the aftermath of Floyd's death, when nerves were frayed and tensions high, it is easy to understand why so many piled on the Saints' quarterback—and did so without fear of a roughing-the-passer penalty.[12] Instead, Brees was the one who was justifiably flagged for not scanning the whole field more carefully before speaking. To his credit, he apologized and acknowledged how his comments "completely missed the mark." But now that the dust has settled, it appears fair to ask if his insensitive remarks could have been processed more productively. Jerry Brewer, an African American sports columnist for *The Washington Post*, offers the following advice:

> But there is a larger lesson to take from the Brees controversy. For those who want this chilling time to transform from a moment to a movement, Brees is exactly the kind of person who needs to be admonished—but also reached. He was wrong Wednesday, yet on the whole, he is fundamentally kind. . . . [In fact,] take all of him into account, and Drew Brees is among the most exceptional human beings in sports. If we agreed on criteria and a system to rank humanity, there is a chance he could finish No. 1. From his multifaceted efforts to revitalize New Orleans post-Katrina to his $5 million commitment to feed the needy in Louisiana during the pandemic, Brees epitomizes the character, benevolence and grace that people seek in a sports role model. . . . His critics need to have the emotional stamina to do more than tear him apart. They can expand his mind.[13]

This tribal impulse to rip the other side to shreds is widespread in our day and fosters the tendency to assume the worst in our opponents. We live in a call-out culture that gives us points for slamming our opponents to the turf, but doesn't reward us for helping them back up. Across the ideological spectrum, we view those on the opposing side with *suspicion*. Our elephant is already leaning in the opposite direction, so we are disinclined to give them

12. Maria Taylor made this specific point when she said, "All I can do is let you reveal yourself and countless people are doing that right now. And for the first time ever, they are reaping some kind of consequence that does not have any retaliation for me or for the people who are calling them out." ESPN, "Passionate message."

13 Brewer, "Saddest kind of wrong."

the benefit of the doubt. To use a different metaphor, it's like wearing dark shades through which every comment is viewed with cynical askance.

As people who are called to love our enemies, however, Christ-followers are commanded to wear a different set of glasses. Instead of a lens of suspicion, we are called to *charity*. Rather than assuming the worst of the other person's heart, mind, and intentions, we should cultivate an attitude of generosity that extends the benefit of the doubt. Why is this the correct pair of glasses for the Christian to wear? Because the second commandment tells us so. We are to treat others the way we want to be treated. If we don't like people misjudging our motives and rushing to judgment about our intentions, then we must avoid doing the same thing. A posture of charity is not only a higher ethic, it is also more likely to foster civility, understanding, and cooperation as we seek to create a more just and generous country for all—especially for those who are currently competing on an uneven playing field.

Moral Foundations Theory—Honoring the Sacred Center

When discussing his production company, Higher Ground, former President Barack Obama once said, "We all have a sacred story in us—a story that gives us meaning and purpose and how we organize our lives. If you know someone, if you've talked to them face-to-face, if you can forge a connection, you may not agree with them on everything but there's some common ground to be found and you can move forward."[14]

In the previous chapter, we explored the importance of Christians locating the sacred theological specialty of fellow Christians. By identifying and honoring what our fellow believer holds dear, we can approach our differences with increased grace and in the long run experience more productive rider-to-rider conversations concerning our theological differences. The same holds true for cultural divides like the one confronting us in this chapter. We need to identify the story the other side holds dear, then connect the dots between their central sacred value and active moral intuitions. Remember, people won't deny their active moral intuitions, so if you want to enter into meaningful dialogue and even persuasion, it starts by honoring the other person's elephant. Moral Foundations Theory can be a powerful tool in this regard.

14. Netflix Film Club, "American Factory."

As we've already learned, Moral Foundations Theory grew out of extensive cross-cultural research conducted by Jonathan Haidt and his colleagues. Haidt grew up in a culturally Jewish home in New York and studied philosophy at Yale. His graduate work at the University of Pennsylvania focused on evolutionary psychology, which often intersected with cultural anthropology. Haidt found that when he read psychologists and anthropologists, however, it was like they were from different planets (psychologists are from Mars, anthropologists from Venus?). The work of Richard Shweder, a University of Chicago cultural psychologist, provided the "Rosetta stone" or integration point.[15]

Haidt was especially interested in Shweder's extensive research in India, which demonstrated that moral diversity could not be reduced to issues of harm and fairness like many Western moral philosophers and psychologists argue. Rather, *individualistic* cultures—which emphasize rights and freedoms at the personal level—operate out of the ethic of autonomy, whereas *sociocentric* cultures—which emphasize hierarchy, structure, order, and stability—operate out of the ethics of community and divinity.[16]

Upon graduating from Penn with his doctorate, Haidt spent two years studying with Shweder as a post-doctoral fellow. His time at the University of Chicago included a three-month emersion experience in India. While his doctoral work had included research in Brazil, this cross-cultural experience in India provided deeper exposure to the ethics of community and divinity. During the first few weeks on the subcontinent, however, Haidt was flooded with "feelings of shock and dissonance." He recalls it like this:

> I dined with men whose wives silently served us and then retreated to the kitchen, not speaking to me the entire evening. I was told to be stricter with my servants, and to stop thanking them for serving me. I watched people bathe in and cook with visibly polluted water that was held to be sacred. In short, I was immersed in a sex-segregated, hierarchically stratified, devoutly religious society, and I was committed to understanding it on its own terms, not on mine.[17]

By the end of the three months, Haidt indeed began to understand Indian culture in a new way. Prior to the trip, he understood the ethics

15. Haidt, *Righteous Mind*, 14.
16. Haidt, *Righteous Mind*, 14–15.
17. Haidt, *Righteous Mind*, 101–2.

of community and divinity *intellectually*, but he could now viscerally *feel* them. This experience was Haidt's personal empathy gym, growing both his cognitive and emotional empathy. Without ignoring the potential abhorrent side of the ethics of community and divinity, which can lead to abuses of power and suppression, Haidt for the first time saw "beauty in a moral code that emphasizes duty, respect for one's elders, service to the group, and a negation of the self's desires."[18] He began to *feel* "positive essences emanating from some objects." A national flag was no longer "just a piece of cloth," particular books should be revered, and dead bodies deserve respect.[19] Haidt had previously theorized that the human mind "automatically perceives a kind of vertical dimension of social space," with the divine at the top and the demonic down below.[20] But he had now experienced and *felt* this vertical dimension for himself. During his time in India, he encountered few Americans. But when he settled into his seat on the return flight to Chicago, Haidt recalls hearing "a loud voice with an American accent saying, 'Look, you tell him that this is the compartment over *my* seat, and I have a *right* to use it.' I cringed."[21]

Haidt's Indian excursion solidified his commitment to pluralism. Rather than affirming a universal, one-size-fits-all morality on the one hand or an anything-goes relativism on the other, he came to embrace the belief that a finite number of moral modules can be arranged in various ways depending upon social and cultural considerations.

It is clear how Haidt's experience with Shweder provided the seedbed for Moral Foundations Theory. The ethic of autonomy is connected to the compassion cluster of care, liberty, and fairness, while the ethics of community and divinity resonate with the conviction intuitions of in-group loyalty, authority, and sanctity. Once his research crystallized, Haidt began to see how it applied to the political divide within the United States.

> Liberals have a three-foundation morality, whereas conservatives use all six. Liberal moral matrices rest on the Care/harm, Liberty/oppression, and Fairness/cheating foundations, although liberals are often willing to trade away fairness (as proportionality) when it conflicts with compassion or with their desire to fight oppression. Conservative morality rests on all six foundations, although

18. Haidt, *Righteous Mind*, 102.
19. Haidt, *Righteous Mind*, 105.
20. Haidt, *Righteous Mind*, 105.
21. Haidt, *Righteous Mind*, 102.

> conservatives are more willing than liberals to sacrifice Care and let some people get hurt in order to achieve their many other moral objectives.[22]

Haidt goes on to identify the most sacred value for both sides of the ideological spectrum. The conservative moral matrix centers on the "[preservation of] the institutions and traditions that sustain a moral community," while the most sacred value for the liberal moral matrix is "care for victims of oppression."[23]

Competing Quarterbacks and Sacred Values

We are now in a position to evaluate the opposing *kneeling* and *standing* narratives in light of Moral Foundations Theory. When I use this activity in class, I say to my students: "You probably have an opinion (maybe even a strong one) about this particular controversy, but I would encourage you to temporarily put your personal opinion aside and climb up to the balcony so we can gain a more objective perspective on this controversial topic." As we all know, temporarily setting our personal convictions aside is an important strategy for understanding opposing viewpoints. I then remind my students that there is a key difference between *understanding* and *condoning* the other person's view.

So imagine yourself as a student in this class. Climb up to the balcony. For the time being, set your personal convictions aside for the purpose of understanding both perspectives. Follow Haidt's example. Although his cross-cultural experience was disorienting at first, he resisted his self-righteous impulse to judge his hosts and instead committed himself to understanding Indian culture on its own terms, not his. For this exercise to work, we must do the same: commit ourselves to understanding both sides of the standing/kneeling controversy on their terms, not ours. I know this might feel like compromise or weakness, but nothing could be further from the truth. To understand the other side's sacred center, it takes tremendous self-control and *emotional stamina*—as Jerry Brewer put it. In short, it requires both cognitive and emotional empathy.

Colin Kaepernick and the Kneeling Narrative: Colin Kaepernick started this protest in August 2016 when he was a quarterback for the San Francisco

22. Haidt, *Righteous Mind*, 184.

23. Haidt, *Righteous Mind*, 297–306.

49ers. He began by sitting on the bench during the national anthem, but a week later shifted to kneeling after a Green Beret told him it would be more respectful. Following his first protest, reporters surrounded Kaepernick's locker and asked him to explain his actions:

> Ultimately it is to bring awareness and make people realize what's really going on in this country. There are a lot of things going on that are unjust [that] people aren't being held accountable for. And that's something that needs to change . . . This country stands for freedom, liberty, justice for all. And it's not happening for all right now. It's something I've seen, I've felt, something I wasn't quite sure how to deal with originally and it is something that's evolved . . . These aren't new situations. This isn't new ground. These are things that have gone on in this country for years and years and have never been addressed. And they need to be. Yes, I will continue to sit. I'm going to continue to stand with the people that are being oppressed. To me this is something that has to change. When there's significant change and I feel like that flag represents what it's supposed to represent and this country is representing people the way that it's supposed to, I'll stand.[24]

Kaepernick, who is biracial and was raised by white parents, began his protest at a time when young black men were five times more likely to be killed by a police officer in the United States than white men of the same age and nine times more likely than any other kind of American.[25] His protest started in the middle of a decade that had already seen the deaths of Tamir Rice, Michael Brown, Walter Scott, Freddie Gray, and Eric Garner, whose final words in 2014 were the same as George Floyd's: "I can't breathe."[26] During the last decade, countless other black men (and women) have died as a result of police brutality, yet little meaningful change to the criminal justice system has resulted.[27] Those who honor the kneeling narrative do so with a broken heart, sense of desperation, and fear for the lives of their loved ones. For those who take a knee, this is not an ideological debate; it is literally a matter of life and death.

When considering the *kneeling* narrative in light of our compassion and conviction intuitions, the first thing that pops out is how perfectly this

24. KTVU, "Kaepernick explains."

25. Swaine et al., "Young black men killed."

26. *The New York Times* reports seventy cases in which black men were killed after uttering these words. See Baker et al., "Three Words."

27. For example, see Demby, "Decade of Watching."

perspective aligns with the chief value of the liberal moral matrix: "care for victims of oppression." For those who resonate with the kneeling narrative, the *care/harm* intuition is not only activated but turned up full volume. The *liberty/oppression* intuition is also engaged by the way police brutality infringes upon the individual freedoms of minorities. This narrative argues that the flag should represent the rights and well-being of all Americans, but there is widespread racial injustice in this country. In short, we have an inequitable situation, so the *fairness/cheating* intuition is triggered. So we see all three compassion intuitions deeply engaged.

As we consider the conviction intuitions, we notice that Kaepernick uses his platform to speak for the voiceless members of his community. He is showing allegiance to his tribe when he takes a knee, so the *in-group loyalty/betrayal* foundation is honored. The Black Lives Matter movement is a challenge to the establishment, to the existing power structures of law and order, so it isn't clear that the *authority/subversion* foundation is easily engaged. That said, one way the authority intuition can be activated for people on this side is by appealing to the moral authority of great civil rights leaders of the past like Martin Luther King, Jr. Kaepernick and others in this movement believe that society is stratified to value some lives over others. This stratification is inherently degrading to minorities. Consequently, the *sanctity/degradation* intuition can be engaged in this manner.

It is clear that a broad range of moral intuitions are activated by this narrative, with a heavy premium placed on the compassion foundations. When folks are operating from a deep and wide base of moral intuitions, there is no way to argue them out of their position. We must begin by honoring the sacred, which in this case is "care for the oppressed."

Drew Brees and the Standing Narrative: Following practice one day in December 2017, reporters gathered around Drew Brees's locker. Instead of discussing the upcoming game against the Tampa Bay Buccaneers, they asked Brees about his grandfather Ray Akins, who had passed away the day before. With moist eyes and beaming pride, Brees honored his grandpa with a beautiful, near-flawless off-the-cuff, five-minute tribute. His profound pride and deep respect were palpable. The entire tribute is worth reading:

> He was probably one of the most incredible people you would ever meet. They just don't make them like that anymore, honestly. He was ninety-two years old. He lived an unbelievable life. He taught me so much about life, about respecting others, about

caring for others, about discipline, about hard work. Obviously, he was a football coach for thirty-eight years, so there was plenty of ball being coached along the way but more so than that just spending time with him, watching him and my grandmother—the way that they modeled for us what a relationship is supposed to look like. They were married sixty-six, sixty-seven years. I mean, pretty remarkable.

He was a guy who grew up [with] very humble means in Brady, Texas, which is like if you look at a map of Texas is the dead center of Texas. His dad was a straw boss, basically like a sharecropper on a big property. Grew up in a house with a dirt floor, no running water, no electricity, have to take the mules to the well to go get water maybe once a week. Basically have to hunt, kill, grow whatever you ate. Road a horse to school. So when people have this impression of what Texas is and what it's like, that was my grandpa.

When he turned eighteen years old, he graduated from high school and took a train down to San Antonio with some other boys from his high school and they enlisted in the Marine Corps. There was about a hundred guys there when they got there. They ran them through a battery of physical tests and psychological tests and they chose ten of them. You ten have qualified to have the opportunity to become a Marine and go serve your country. So he took the train out to San Diego, went through Marine Corps boot camp, shipped over to Guadalcanal for more training, then was there for the invasion of Okinawa, Japan, April 1, 1945—First Marine Division, First Battalion, First Regiment special weapons company. What he endured over there, I heard a lot about that over the years from him. He was very proud of being a Marine. That was something he took so much pride in. While it was hard to talk about the war for a long time, I think he reached a point where he felt there were so many lessons from it and it was a way to honor the guys he served with, too. He had 153 men in his special weapons company and he was one of three to survive. That just tells you how brutal that fighting was over there.[28]

He played college football at Southwest Texas University from 1946–1950. He had the opportunity to go play center for the Chicago Bears in 1950. They were going to pay him $500 a month, so he was going to make $6,000 for the year. Instead of that, he decided to become the athletic director of a 1-A high school in south Texas called Goldthwaite, where he was going to be the head football coach and athletic director. So times have changed a little

28. To hear Ray Akins recount war stories in his own words, see Akins, "Segment 1."

> bit. That was the start of his coaching career. He was a coach, athletic director, and teacher for thirty-eight years.
>
> He retired in 1988 to New Baden, Texas, to his property he had bought out there in 1960. He basically did all the work out there on that land. He had about a hundred head of cattle. That's what he loved. He loved being out there, working on fences and feeding the cows and checking on the heifers and doing all that stuff. And that's the stuff I got to do with him, as well. Me and my brother and the rest of the family. Lots of good times. Lots of good moments. He came and watched a lot of football games. He was an incredible man. I have a ton of memories and his legacy will live on forever in his family. Those are all of the things I want to instill in my kids, too.[29]

The above tribute is important backstory if we are going to try to understand Drew Brees and so many other people who support the standing narrative. With the life of Ray Akins in mind, let's return to the controversial comments uttered by the Saints quarterback in June 2020. Only this time, let's look at his entire statement:

> Well, I will never agree with anybody disrespecting the flag of the United States of America or our country. Let me just tell you what I see or what I feel when the national anthem is played and when I look at the flag of the United States. I envision my two grandfathers who fought for this country during World War II—one in the Army and one in the Marine Corps, both risking their lives to protect our country and to try to make our country and this world a better place. So every time I stand with my hand over my heart looking at that flag and singing the national anthem, that's what I think about. And in many cases, it brings me to tears thinking about all that has been sacrificed, not just those in the military but for that matter those throughout the civil rights movements of the sixties. And all that has been endured by so many people up until this point. And is everything right with our country right now? No, it's not. We still have a long way to go. But I think what you do by standing there and showing respect to the flag with your hand over your heart, it shows unity. It shows that we are all in this together, we can all do better, and we are all part of the solution.[30]

Brees begins with a strong statement. He says he "will never agree with anybody disrespecting the flag." He then immediately explains why. The

29. Brees, "Brees beams."

30. Brees, "Kneeling protests."

reason he would never agree with those who kneel during the anthem is because in his gut it *feels* like an act of betrayal toward his grandfathers. His love and respect for his grandfathers is so strong, he often wells up as the anthem is played. His sense of family loyalty, pride, and appreciation for their bravery is so deeply woven into the fiber of his being, he can't imagine hurting them by not honoring the sacred symbols of this country.

It is clear that the sacred center for Brees and others who have similar stories perfectly aligns with the chief value of the conservative moral matrix: "[preservation of] the institutions and traditions that sustain a moral community." Standing together for the national anthem and honoring the flag are acts of tribal solidarity. It is a tradition that dates back more than a century. These rituals are expressions of loyalty, honor, and reverence to our country, its leaders, our shared patriotic values, and those who have made and continue to make our current freedoms and democratic way of life possible. This includes respect for all of our guardian institutions, including law enforcement. To those on the standing side of this debate, refusing to honor the anthem and flag feels like a kick in the gut, a desecration of our shared sacred symbols. In fact, for those on this side of the debate, not standing to honor the flag and anthem feels sacrilegious. It is a visceral violation of what Americans hold dear, conveying deep disrespect toward those who risk their lives to make our freedoms possible.

The *standing* narrative activates a deep sense of fidelity to our country and those who serve with valor. It strongly engages the *in-group loyalty/betrayal* foundation. The American flag is a sacred patriotic symbol, engaging the *sanctity/degradation* intuition. Standing for the anthem demonstrates our submission to a higher, more noble shared purpose, activating the *authority/subversion* intuition. It is clear the conviction intuitions are turned up full force by this narrative.

But the compassion intuitions are engaged, as well. Remember, Haidt's research shows that the conservative moral matrix tends to be wide, building upon all six foundations. The *care/harm* module is activated because this narrative focuses on the pain that refusing to stand for the national anthem causes military and law enforcement families, especially those who might have lost a loved one in the line of duty. The *liberty/oppression* narrative is engaged, because the standing story focuses on how military and law enforcement personnel put their lives on the line to safeguard the freedoms we enjoy in this country. Finally, this narrative engages the *fairness/cheating* intuition because our military and police are trained to enforce the law, which means punishing lawbreakers. In this moral matrix, people should get what they deserve and be held accountable for their actions.

People in the standing camp would no doubt resonate with Haidt's experience in India when he described his newfound ability to recognize "beauty in a moral code that emphasizes duty, respect for one's elders, and service to the group" while *feeling* "positive essences emanating from some objects," including the national flag. While the standing narrative activates all six intuitions, the accent is on the conviction side of the equation. As we pointed out with the kneeling narrative, when folks are operating from a deep and wide base of moral intuitions, there is no way to argue them out of their position. We must begin by honoring what they find sacred, which in this case focuses on the dignity and "[preservation of] the institutions and traditions that sustain [our] moral community."

The Obama Bridge

After the class begins to see and understand the moral matrices on both sides, I always conclude this session by showing a video of then President Obama, who addressed this controversy in front of a military audience a month after Kaepernick's protest began.

> I believe that us honoring our flag and our anthem is part of what binds us together as a nation. And I think that for me, for my family, for those who work in the White House, we recognize what it means to us, but also what it means to the men and women who are fighting on our behalf. But I also always try to remind folks that part of what makes this country special is that we respect people's rights to have a different opinion. And to make different decisions about how they want to express their concerns. And the test of our fidelity to our Constitution, to freedom of speech, to our Bill of Rights is not when it's easy, but when it's hard. We fight sometimes so that people can do things that we disagree with. But that's what freedom means in this country.
>
> And so my hope would be that as this debate surfaces, we're always reminding ourselves that in a democracy like ours there are going to be a lot of folks who do stuff that we just don't agree with. But as long as they are doing it within the law, then we can voice our opinion objecting to it but it's also their right. It's also important for us to recognize that sometimes out of these controversies, we start getting into a conversation and I want everybody to listen to each other. I want Mr. Kaepernick and others who are on a

> knee, I want them to listen to the pain that may cause somebody who for example had a spouse or a child killed in combat and why it hurts them to see somebody not standing. But I also want people to think about the pain that he may be expressing about somebody whose lost a loved one who they think was unfairly shot.
>
> One of the things I always say about American democracy is it can be frustrating, but it's the best system we've got. And the only way we make it work is to see each other, listen to each other, try to be respectful of each other, not just go into separate corners. I do hope that anybody who is trying to express any political view of any sort understands that they do so under the blanket of protection of our men and women in uniform and that appreciation of that sacrifice is never lost.[31]

After watching the video, I ask the class what they thought President Obama did well. Students offer a variety of observations:

- he addressed the elephant first;
- he spoke in calm and measured tones;
- he opened and closed by honoring his military audience;
- he engaged both conviction and compassion intuitions;
- he used language that his immediate audience would understand: "we *fight* sometimes so people can do things we might disagree with";
- he encouraged both emotional and cognitive empathy; and
- he honored the sacred values of both sides.

This is an impressive list to glean from one relatively short video, and all of the above observations are spot on. I would also note the similarities to the convicted civility advice given by Richard Mouw in the previous chapter, who encourages people to listen to learn, work together for the common good, never put your best up against their worst,[32] and represent the other side in a manner in which they would recognize. Mapping the moral matrix like we've done in this chapter can lower the temperature and help us see that one side rarely possesses all of the moral high ground.

31. CNN, "Obama discusses."

32. The reader will notice that I have not used extreme exemplars, whose harsh rhetoric does nothing but divide and drive people deeper into their own corners. For one example, see G4ViralVideos, "Trump Tells NFL Owners."

Softening the Sharpe Rebuke

As noted at the beginning of this chapter, Brees's controversial comments struck many people as terribly insensitive and completely tone deaf—all bass, no treble. Even his apology felt hollow to some, including ESPN's Maria Taylor, whose heartfelt words expressed the lingering nagging suspicions of this camp:

> Let me be clear. I don't know what resides in his heart, but I know what should reside in your heart is empathy and I don't believe that you have to be trolled and dragged through Twitter and Instagram in order to change your mind and realize that what you said was intolerant and/or could be considered insensitive later. If you had been educated and forced to confront the issues and as I said had empathy in your heart, then you would have known the black experience is not easy, especially when 70 percent of your league is African-American.[33]

One of the strongest rebukes, however, came from Shannon Sharpe, who, as we read earlier, suggested that Brees hang up his cleats since his black teammates would never look at him the same. In response to this stinging critique, Brees contacted Sharpe. The two proceeded to engage in a thirty-minute conversation. "It took a lot of courage for him to reach out to me," said Sharpe. "A lot of people when you criticize them, [they say] I'm done with you. I have nothing to say to you. But it took a lot for him . . . because my criticism was harsh. There's no doubt about that."[34] Sharpe offers a peek inside the exchange:

> Drew said, "I think you know I have a good heart and that I've immersed myself in New Orleans since I arrived here. So for fifteen years I have been a pillar in the community and I don't want one bad mistake, one slip-up to ruin everything that I've built. I said, "Drew, what you have to understand is that for one second we didn't want you to be Drew Brees. We wanted you to be one of us. We wanted you to feel like what if that was *your* brother? If that was *your* uncle? If that was *your* father? You're still a married father. You're still a doting dad. But for one second you were black. How would you feel?" And I said, "Drew, when you said [your grandfathers] fought for the military, you do understand that not only were they fighting in a foreign land for freedoms

33. ESPN, "Passionate message."
34. Skip and Shannon, "Phone conversation."

> over there, but they were also fighting for freedoms back home. Like the freedom and the pride that you feel when you stand for that flag. Everybody does not feel that same sense of pride because they haven't been afforded some of the same opportunities that you and your ancestors have been afforded." Drew said, "I understand that . . . talking to a lot of my teammates, I can see the hurt that they felt."
>
> After talking to him, I could feel [his] pain. And I am not a guy who is easily forgiving. You got to show me. . . . I don't believe him saying what he said should be the end of Drew Brees. I believe he deserves an opportunity for redemption, because he's been too good in that community to let this one slip-up undo fifteen years of great service. And that's what I told him. I said, "Drew, I'll be here . . . I'm in your corner because I believe you can do this. I believe you could help us get to where we ultimately need to be."[35]

Sharpe's recounting of the conversation makes it clear that the two men employed many of the principles suggested by President Obama. The conversation included careful listening, mutual respect, and a growing sense of empathy. It's heartening to see a committed Christ-follower like Brees display the courage and humility to reach out to such a staunch critic. It's equally inspiring to see Sharpe take the advice of Jerry Brewer, who challenged critics to muster the emotional stamina to do more than tear Brees to shreds, but help *expand* his mind, as well.

Expansion seems to be the right way to think about this situation. Brees did not lack empathy; he just needed to expand it. He began to realize how he could honor the concerns of the kneeling protestors without dishonoring his grandfathers. Brees is not stupid, ignorant, or evil; he just needed to find a way to expand the tribe, which is the topic we will explore in the remainder of this book.

35. Skip and Shannon, "Phone conversation."

Part III: **Expand the Tribe**

"The more you emphasize common goals or interests, shared fate, and common humanity, the more they will see one another as fellow human beings, treat one another well, and come to appreciate one another's contributions to the community. Pauli Murray expressed the power of this principle when she wrote,'When my brothers try to draw a circle to exclude me, I shall draw a larger circle to include them.'"[1]

—GREG LUKIANOFF AND JONATHAN HAIDT

1. Lukianoff and Haidt, *Coddling*, 260.

Chapter 7

Treble Tactic Seven: Love Your Enemy

Bass-Pounding Fallacy: God Plays Favorites

"How do we create and imagine a circle of compassion, and then imagine nobody standing outside that circle?"[1]

—FATHER GREGORY BOYLE

One of the great joys of my job is taking students to Oxford, England. After an overnight flight from Chicago O'Hare to London Heathrow, we board a double-decker bus for the ninety-minute trip to High Street. As we get off the bus and gather the luggage, my wife has a standard line that she shares with our students: "Smelling the Oxford air raises everyone's IQ by twenty points!" Always good for a laugh.

I don't know about the air, but I never tire of the views—especially the dreamy Oxford spires. We are transported back in time as we bounce our luggage over the ancient cobblestone streets past the iconic Radcliffe Camera, Bodleian Library, and Bridge of Sighs.

Making our way up Broad Street toward our hotel, we pass the Christopher Wren-designed Sheldonian Theatre on the left and Blackwell's Bookshop on the right. After depositing our luggage, we return to Blackwell's—one of the most iconic bookstores in the world. As we wind our way

1. Boyle, "Compassion and Kinship."

through this four-level labyrinth, it's easy to imagine some of the great Oxford minds signing copies of their monographs.

Two Oxford authors who have conducted Blackwell book signings are Richard Dawkins and C. S. Lewis. At first blush, one might think these two men have little in common. Dawkins is the most famous atheist in the world today, while Lewis remains arguably the most famous Christian writer—nearly sixty years following his death. A closer look, however, reveals a couple of points of interesting resonance. Despite publishing successful academic works in their respective fields—evolutionary biology (Dawkins) and medieval and Renaissance literature (Lewis)—both earned a broader reputation for writing popular books *outside* their primary areas of expertise. Additionally, both were Oxford atheists for several years, each struggling with an issue known as the problem of exclusivity—the claim that one religion is true while all the rest are false.

The problem of exclusivity confronted Dawkins at the tender age of nine when his mother "pointed out that there were lots and lots of religions." The young Dawkins surmised that any claim to exclusive religious truth must be poppycock: "It was immediately clear to me there was no obvious reason why the [religion] I was brought up in was the correct one."[2]

Lewis had his own pivotal moment at the age of nine—his mother died of cancer. The devastation of his mother's death was followed by years of torturous boarding school experiences, a ruthlessly logical atheist tutor, and the horrors of World War I. While he spent his early years in a Christian home, all of the above solidified Lewis's atheism by the time he became a fixture at Oxford. Eventually, however, it dawned on Lewis that his favorite authors all shared one thing in common: a religious view of the world. By his early thirties, Lewis finally gave in "and admitted that God was God, and knelt and prayed; perhaps, that night, the most dejected and reluctant convert in all England."[3]

The above describes Lewis's conversion to Theism, but he wasn't yet a Christian. The final hurdle was the problem of exclusivity. While Dawkins viewed this problem as a decisive nail in the coffin of *all* religions, Oxford colleagues J. R. R. Tolkien and Hugo Dyson offered Lewis a different perspective. As the three men strolled along Addison's Walk one night, they discussed a more inclusive way of thinking about Christianity and other

2. Dawkins, "Conversation with Sweeney."

3. Lewis, *Surprised by Joy*, 228–29. For a brief overview of Lewis's formative experiences, see Burson and Walls, *Lewis and Schaeffer*, 23–34.

religions. One need not claim that Christianity is the only expression of truth and all other religions entirely false. Instead, they argued that Christianity is the *fullest* expression of divine revelation and whatever is true, good, and beautiful in other religions is "consummated and perfected" in the Christian story.[4] This perspective satisfied Lewis's longing to honor both the inclusive character of God and the unique claims of Christ. In an odd twist, the very issue that drove Dawkins away from the Christian faith catalyzed Lewis's return.

We are now moving into the third part of this book: Expand the Tribe. The bass-pounding fallacy in need of correction in this chapter is the notion that God plays favorites. As we saw in chapter 5, our theological assumptions about the nature and extent of God's favor can work their way into our attitudes and relationships, priming us for a more or less inclusive or exclusive orientation toward the world. In this chapter, we will explore the physiological and social implications of embracing a theology that fails to accurately reflect the fullness of God's favor. This is especially important in light of our deeply embedded tribalism. While it is unlikely that we can change our tribal nature, we do have the capacity, with God's help, to expand the circle. This starts by recognizing the inclusive heart of God, who loves all people without discrimination and desires the flourishing of every single person, not just members of a certain tribe.

Matthew 5: Be Complete, Not Perfect

I always begin my Humanities Philosophy course by discussing Matthew 5:43–48. In this provocative passage from the Sermon on the Mount, Jesus delivers the most demanding moral command ever uttered: love your enemy.

> You have heard that it was said, "Love your neighbor and hate your enemy." But I tell you, love your enemies and pray for those who persecute you, that you may be children of your Father in heaven. He causes his sun to rise on the evil and the good, and sends rain on the righteous and the unrighteous. If you love those who love you, what reward will you get? Are not even the tax collectors doing that? And if you greet only your own people, what are you doing more than others? Do not even pagans do that? Be perfect, therefore, as your heavenly Father is perfect.

4. Lewis, "Christian Apologetics," 102.

After reading this passage, I share with my students my own struggle to understand this confounding command. When I was a young Christian in my college days, this passage really confused me. How in the world am I supposed to be perfect as my heavenly Father is perfect? God is infinite; I am finite. God is holy; I am a sinner. God possesses all great-making qualities to the highest possible degree; I am flawed in many ways. Perfection? Seriously?

Some biblical expositors have suggested that Jesus didn't mean it literally. He was simply pointing out our inability to live up to God's perfect standard. Others focus on imputed righteousness—the idea that Christ's perfect sacrifice covers the forgiven believer. Still others use this passage to highlight common grace; that God gives temporal blessings to all. While one can find varying degrees of support for these concepts elsewhere in Scripture, none of these theories captures the full meaning of this passage. I remained puzzled.

That is until I went to seminary, where I learned New Testament Greek. In an advanced exegesis class, I conducted a study of the Greek word *teleios*—the word that is translated in the above passage as *perfect*. I concluded that rendering *teleios* as *perfect* fails to adequately capture what Jesus had in mind. Not only does it fall short; it actually stirs up a very different meaning altogether—something like getting 100 percent on your philosophy exam!

This, however, was not the message Jesus was conveying to his original audience. Instead of *perfect*, a more accurate rendering of *teleios* is *complete*. Rather than demanding an exacting, legalistic form of works-righteousness, Jesus tells his original agrarian audience that God blesses *all* people with rain and sun—both necessary ingredients to grow crops and sustain life. If God is not stingy with his blessings and favor, then we must follow his lead. We must cultivate a love for the righteous and unrighteous, family and enemy, in-group as well as out-group. Therefore, we should strive to communicate in word and deed a Christian story that does justice to the radically inclusive nature of God's love. While this does not mean that all people will necessarily experience reconciliation with God, it does mean that God desires the ultimate flourishing of every single person.

After establishing the meaning of Matthew 5:43–48, we move into a three-part assignment that will weave throughout the course. The first part of the assignment is for every student to identify their "other," the kind of person they find particularly difficult to understand. For this assignment, I tell them to focus on someone who is on the other side of a moral/religious/social issue, not just someone with a personality trait or habit that rubs them the wrong way. For instance, this could be someone who holds a different perspective on religion, gender equality, abortion, immigration, global warming, race relations, or what constitutes patriotism.

The second part of this Matthew 5 assignment is to go online and take a ninety-minute self-guided assessment called "The Open Mind App." Produced by Heterodox Academy, this interactive activity explains the three principles of moral psychology that we learned in the introduction to this book.[5] The third part of the Matthew 5 assignment comes at the end of the semester after students have been exposed to the ten treble tactics we are currently exploring. This final assignment is to write an "Understanding My Other" paper that explains how they will begin to try to understand and build a bridge to the person they identified in the first part of the Matthew 5 assignment. Time and again, I am inspired by the creativity and courage displayed by so many students in their quest to practice the Jesus ethic. I could share many student stories, but I will offer just one.

Sophia's Choice

Sophia came to me after class one day and asked if we could talk for a few minutes. "What's on your mind," I asked? She told me that she was having a problem with another student. The student in question was white, male, politically conservative, intelligent, and motivated to challenge what he perceived to be growing political correctness on our campus. As someone who had been raised in a diverse environment, Sophia struggled with his ideology. Even more, she was deeply bothered by social media posts targeted at "social justice warriors." She was coming to me today because some of her friends said this student respected me as a professor. When she first heard this, she thought to herself, "That doesn't sound like the Dr. Burson I've seen in class." Nevertheless, she wondered if I could help her better understand this fellow student who had slowly but surely become her "other."

By this stage in the class, we had covered several of the treble tactics. She was acquainted with the importance of speaking to the elephant first and actively listening to the other person's story, so I said, "If you really want to understand where he is coming from I think you should invite him to lunch or coffee and just listen to his story. Don't say anything, just listen

5. See Lukianoff and Haidt, *Coddling*, 248.

with curiosity. My guess is if you treat him with dignity, he will return the favor. I know it's going to be super hard, but that's my advice." Sophia wasn't thrilled with the prospect of humbly listening to someone who had deeply offended many of her peers, but she would think it over.

Over the next few weeks, I didn't hear anything from Sophia. Then the pandemic hit and we scrambled to transition the course online for the final six weeks of the semester. As the class came to a close, it was time for students to submit their "Understanding My Other" papers—the third and final part in the Matthew 5 assignment. I was especially curious to read Sophia's paper, given our conversation earlier in the semester. I wasn't disappointed. With her permission, I am pleased to share it with you:

> At the beginning of the semester, I described my "other" as males who objectify women. However, during the school year, as I kept meeting new people, I realized another "other" that has affected me are people whose ideology revolve around white supremacy. Growing up in a diverse area, then moving into a culture like IWU [Indiana Wesleyan University], which is primarily white, has been a significant shift for me. I am very passionate about helping those who are marginalized, whether that is by their race, sex, or social class. During this second semester, I've had a hard time dealing with people who make small-minded assumptions about people of different races and socioeconomic backgrounds based on stereotypes. These conversations that I was having with others developed anger within me. It got to the point where I was disgusted by being white and started to white shame others. This class, however, has helped me through the treble tactics to have civil conversations with others who may have different ideological perspectives. And with those conversations, it has helped me not group other white people from IWU based on stereotypes and claiming they are ignorant.
>
> These conversations have definitely toned down my pride and made me understand people for who they are. With that, they have shown me that most people's intentions aren't to marginalize or group people. I have developed a lot more compassion toward people who make assumptions of other ethnicities. During the Treble Tactic Nine: Pursue Reconciliation activity, we watched a Ted Talk by Daryl Davis. He showed by his example of reaching out to the KKK leader what it means to have true compassion on another. His approach to developing an understanding of his "other" motivated me to do the same.

> I set up a time to talk to my "other." I made sure my approach was one of willingness so that I could get to know who he was. Because of this approach his response was a lot friendlier compared to the times other people had talked to him. This *friend* has strong ideological views that conflict with the views of a lot of people at school. Most kids on campus and on social media just blow up in his face stating how he is wrong. I realized that approach brings no change. That is why I was determined to get to know him as a person first. And through that, I learned a lot about him: from his likes to the hardships he has endured over the years. After we talked about some personal interests and stories, I asked him about his ideological views and why he came to his position. No, I do not agree with his ideological perspective, but I now understand how he came to some of his beliefs.
>
> The Ted Talk in the Treble Tactic Ten activity raised something critical to think about—the shaming world of social media. My *friend* has been bashed, cyberbullied, and threatened for his beliefs. Through our conversations, I was able to see some active moral intuitions that I assumed he wouldn't have based on his social media appearance. These intuitions include *care* and *fairness*, which became clear to me after learning about some of his life experiences.
>
> This interaction has definitely taught me how to be more understanding and loving to my fellow neighbors. Though I get frustrated with statements that I hear on campus sometimes, I don't have the authorization to judge or stereotype. Instead, I will use it as a learning opportunity. Every person has a story, and because of that, they have hardships, and as Christians, our first job is to love. Judging, blaming, and shaming will get us nowhere, and we are living in a progressive culture that supports these mechanisms to bring awareness to the injustices happening today. I have been a part of this [call-out] culture when it comes to people like my *friend*, who makes bold statements about racial and socioeconomic issues; however, this approach doesn't bring the change that is so desperately needed. An attitude of humbling yourself and being able to learn from our "other" does.

Sophia means "wisdom" in Greek and she definitely lived up to her name in this exercise. In fact, I have inducted Sophia into my Matthew 5 Hall of Fame! Here are five takeaways from her paper:

1. Sophia chose to go a different route with her "other." Instead of perpetuating the destructive call-out culture, she met one on one and listened to his story with respect and humility.
2. Like Jonathan Haidt in India, Sophia chose to understand her "other" on his terms, not hers. And she did so without compromising her own social justice convictions.
3. In the final section of her paper, Sophia shifted from calling this student her *other* to her *friend*. Engaging the elephant first softened Sophia's attitude, which mellowed her conversation partner, as well.
4. Because she went into the conversation with an open mind, Sophia was able to identify some of her friend's active moral intuitions and locate his sacred values. By doing so, she gained greater insight into his moral vision.
5. By the end of the encounter, the fellow student had moved from evil enemy to human being with a life narrative behind his brash ideological persona. This shift in perspective enabled Sophia to empathize with her new friend, who has been bullied and bashed on social media.

Sophia mentioned Daryl Davis. For now, I will just say that Daryl is also in my Matthew 5 Hall of Fame. But you will have to wait until chapter 9 to read his story.

The Tribal Brain

As we have already learned, "the human mind is prepared for tribalism."[6] But if us vs. them thinking leads to exclusion, why are we designed this way? Perhaps most obviously, this kind of thinking promotes individual and group survival. The authors of *Blindspot*—Mahzarin Banaji and Anthony Greenwald—tell us that humans come into the world primed to attach to the familiar.

> Studies confirm that the tendency to prefer members of one's own group emerges early in infancy and is in large part based on familiarity. Such an orientation, which no doubt has survival value in that it serves to align the child with those who are like her and therefore more likely to offer safety, is a clear sign that even in these early months, babies do not occupy socially neutral space.

6. Lukianoff and Haidt, *Coddling*, 58.

> Distinguishing between "like us" and "not like us," they first express very simple forms of preference, such as accepting an object from one person rather than another.[7]

Additionally, Banaji and Greenwald discuss the human mind's remarkable ability to quickly and efficiently categorize not only ideas and things, but people.[8] One strength of this design feature is it allows us to make split-second decisions at the elephant level ("Is that person safe or dangerous, friend or foe, teammate or opponent?"). This low-road, automatic elephant sifting and sorting capability frees up the rider to handle the cognitive load of more challenging problems when they arise.

While this design feature is quite elegant, it has an underbelly. The elephant is wired for survival, not accuracy. Left unchecked, our tribal cognition can easily drive us to unfair stereotyping and discrimination. This tribal instinct can manifest in overt forms of favoritism and exclusion, but more often it lurks beneath our conscious awareness in the form of hidden biases.

Consider the story of Carla Kaplan, a young Yale University professor with a penchant for quilting. One evening while she was washing the dishes, a broken bowl sliced Carla's hand from palm to wrist. Carla was rushed to the emergency room, where her boyfriend explained to the attending physician her love of quilting. Given the severity of the wound, he was rightfully concerned about damage to the fine motor skills in her hand. The doctor understood and assured the couple that all should be well if they got going on the stitches right away.

While the doctor prepped her hand, a student volunteer recognized Carla and exclaimed, "Professor Kaplan! What are you doing here?" Immediately, the surprised doctor asked, "You're a professor at Yale?" Within moments, Carla was wheeled out of the emergency room to the surgery center. A few hours later the best hand surgeon in the state had restored Professor Kaplan's hand to full capacity.

Banaji and Greenwald tell this story to illustrate how our hidden biases can create unintended discrimination. The well-intentioned physician was providing adequate care to Carla, but when the patient shifted from "Carla the quilter" to "Carla the professor," a fellow Yale faculty member, the level of care significantly elevated. Would an average patient,

7. Banaji and Greenwald, *Blindspot*, 130.

8. Banaji and Greenwald, *Blindspot*, 71–93.

who lacked Yale tribal status, have received this extra special level of care? The answer is clear.[9]

In their book *The Coddling of the American Mind*, Jonathan Haidt and Greg Lukianoff offer another relevant story. In a tribalism study, participants are placed inside an fMRI then exposed to videos of other people's hands receiving either a sharp pinprick or the light brush of a cotton swab. When the pinpricked hand is identified as belonging to a person of the same religion, "the area of the participant's brain that handles pain showed a larger spike of activity than when the hand was labeled with a different religion."[10] In another part of the study, participants were separated into arbitrary groups by flipping a coin. Despite belonging to their newly minted "heads" or "tails" tribe for only a few moments, participant brains still showed a larger spike of activity when the hand of a fellow tribe member was pricked. The takeaway: "We just don't feel as much empathy for those we see as 'other.'"[11]

In a TED Talk entitled "This Is Your Brain on God," Michael Ferguson describes another fMRI tribal study. Citing Haidt's Moral Foundations Theory, he and his team wondered if an in-group authority bias might be observed when their Mormon participants were exposed to comments made by a range of spiritual teachers. Quotations would be accompanied by the name and picture of the attributed teacher. One set of comments were attributed to three Mormon leaders; the other set to three non-Mormon Christian leaders—Pope Francis, Desmond Tutu, and Billy Graham. After reading each comment, participants were asked "to rate how meaningful the teaching was and how strongly they felt the spirit." But there was a surprising twist. Unbeknownst to the participants, none of the teachings were correctly attributed. In fact, all of the quotations came from one source—C. S. Lewis! Ferguson describes the results of the study accordingly: "What we saw was so beautiful from the point of view of cognitive science. Believing Mormons consistently ranked the teachings of their own leaders as more meaningful and as more spiritually evocative than the teachings of out-group authority figures, even though in reality they were all from the same source."[12]

9. Banaji and Greenwald, *Blindspot*, 140–41.

10. Lukianoff and Haidt, *Coddling*, 58.

11. Lukianoff and Haidt, *Coddling*, 58.

12. Ferguson, "Your Brain on God."

All of these stories underscore the degree to which tribalism is woven into our DNA. But what happens when we bring God more directly into the conversation? Is there a correlation between our conception of God and our treatment of others? Earlier in this chapter, I made the case for an inclusive understanding of divine love, but there are other passages of Scripture that seem to point in a different direction—toward a tribal deity who plays favorites. After all, both the Old and New Testament contain passages about God's elect and chosen people. If this is so, then how do we square these apparently exclusive passages with the *teleiotic* teaching of Matthew 5?

I think the correct biblical balance is struck by missiologist Lesslie Newbigin, who believed the most stubborn heresy in the history of Monotheism is the claim that some are chosen for privilege rather than service.[13] The problem isn't with the biblical doctrine of election. No, the problem is with twisting election into some kind of exclusive club. Treating election like a platinum card ("Membership has its privileges") constricts the *teleiotic* scope of God's love and drives a social wedge between chosen and unchosen, elect and non-elect, favored and unfavored. According to Newbigin, Israel was never selected by God for exclusive privilege, but rather to be a missionary tribe—a light to all the world. God promised Abraham that every nation would be blessed through Isaac. In the same way Christians are chosen for service, blessed to be a blessing.

An inclusive view of God is expansive and life-giving, while an exclusive view of God is constrictive and potentially hazardous to your health. Timothy Jennings, the author of *The God-Shaped Brain*, writes, "Does it even matter whether our view of God is good, bad, or ugly? It does matter, more than we ever realized—to the point of changing our brain structure! Although we have power over what we believe, what we believe holds real power over us."[14] In a review of *How God Changes Your Brain*, *Washington Post* columnist Michael Gerson develops Jennings's point: "Contemplating a loving God strengthens portions of our brain—particularly the frontal lobes and the anterior cingulate—where empathy and reason reside. Contemplating a wrathful God empowers the limbic system, which is 'filled with aggression and fear.' It is a sobering thought: The God we choose to love changes us into his image, whether he exists or not."[15]

13. Newbigin, *Open Secret*, 32.

14. Jennings, *God-Shaped Brain*, 9.

15. Gerson, "Newberg on the Brain and Faith."

So if our brain is shaped by the kind of God we worship (whether that God actually exists or not), then we better get busy worshipping the *teleiotic* Father of Jesus rather than a God of preferential treatment. Given our deeply tribal DNA, what other hope do we have of loving our enemies?

Heineken and Homeboys

Now that the case has been made for loving our enemies, the next question is how do we go about responding to the most difficult command ever uttered? While we are hopelessly tribal, the good news is our brains are plastic and capable of being rewired well into adulthood. With the twin assumptions of divine *teleiosity* and mental mobilism, let's consider some strategies for expanding the tribe.[16]

Think back to Treble Tactic Three, "Swap Stories." In that chapter, we considered the following quote from Alan Alda: "People's minds will sync up in the presence of story, but the process relies heavily on there being some similarity between the storyteller and the listener. . . . The more the commonality between the storyteller and the listener, the more an MRI will show brains in sync."[17] Banaji and Greenwald pick up on this theme in a section of their book entitled "Do Neurons care about 'us' versus 'them'?" The co-authors describe a Harvard study in which students were shown faces and brief biographies of two young men: John and Mark. John was described as a typical East Coast liberal Democrat, while Mark was characterized as a Midwestern fundamentalist Christian conservative. After reading the bios, participants were then asked a series of questions while their brains were scanned. Most Harvard students resonated more with John, the liberal. That wasn't surprising. Banaji and Greenwald describe what was:

> To most of us, it would seem sensible to assume that the neurons recruited to answer the questions about John would be the same ones figuring out the answers about Mark. Yet as the brain activation observed in this study showed, that was not the case. The brain, it turns out, engages two different clusters of neurons in thinking about other people, and which cluster gets activated depends on the degree to which one identifies with those others.

16. As a reminder, we covered the difference between *fixism* and *mobilism* in chapter 4. The kind of self-directed neuroplasticity we will be discussing in Part III requires a commitment to *mobilism*.

17. Alda, *If I Understood You*, 178.

> . . . From previous research at Dartmouth University, we know that the ventral mPFC is more engaged when we think about our own selves than when we think about others. The Mitchell study at Harvard suggests that, by extension, we engage the same region of the brain when we try to anticipate what somebody who is similar to ourselves would do. Psychologists call this recruitment of the brain regions associated with ourselves a *simulation* of the mind of the other person. But apparently we recruit that particular area of the brain in thinking about someone else only if we identify with that person.[18]

This tells us that the majority of Harvard students *simulated* the mind of John, but not the mind of Mark. Understanding this kind of "selective neural activation" is key if we are going to empathize across a divide.

Let's return to Ferguson's "This is Your Brain on God" TED Talk for a moment. We learned that his elegantly designed study clearly demonstrated preference for in-group over out-group spiritual statements even though all of the comments were actually derived from C. S. Lewis. That was only the first half of his experiment, however. Without revealing the Lewisian twist to the subjects, the second half of the experiment included exposing participants to a similar batch of in-group and out-group statements, only this time it was after they had engaged in thirty minutes of prayer and spiritual study. The result? The vast majority demonstrated a higher degree of appreciation and warmth toward the out-group statements. This shows that spiritual disciplines that humanize the other can turn up the treble and increase our capacity for compassion. Timothy Jennings makes a similar point: "Brain research shows that fifteen minutes a day in meditation or thoughtful communion with the God of love results in measurable development of the prefrontal cortex, especially in the anterior cingulate cortex (ACC). This is the area where we experience love, compassion, and empathy. The healthier the ACC, the calmer the amygdala (alarm center), and the less fear and anxiety we experience."[19]

Another common-ground strategy is working with your "other." Andrew Newberg and Mark Robert Waldman, co-authors of *How God Changes Your Brain*, point to encouraging studies that show "when [children] are placed in a mixed cultural group and given a project that requires everyone's assistance, prejudices fall away, hostility fades, and group cooperation

18. Banaji and Greenwald, *Blindspot*, 138–39.

19. Jennings, *God-Shaped Brain*, 132–33.

flourishes."[20] Author Jonathan Rauch, a senior fellow at the Brookings Institution, makes a similar observation: "Psychological research shows that tribalism can be countered and overcome by teamwork: by projects that join individuals in a common task on an equal footing. One such task, it turns out, can be to reduce tribalism. In other words, with conscious effort, humans can break the tribal spiral."[21]

In 2017, the Heineken beer company engaged in a social experiment that was captured in a short film entitled *Worlds Apart*. The documentary-style film showed three vignettes, all set in the same gritty urban warehouse. In each story, two strangers were assigned a shared task. While the audience quickly learned that each pairing included polar political opposites, the subjects of the social experiment knew nothing about their partner. As each pairing worked together to accomplish the assignment, they learned each other's story. You could literally see elephants leaning toward each other as the project advanced and conversation flowed. By the end of the experiment, a pub-style bar had emerged.

Over the loudspeaker, the participants were let in on the social experiment. Videos of each participant were projected on the wall, complete with their opinions on issues such as feminism, global warming, immigration, and transgender rights. After learning of their work partner's polar opposite political views, they were then given a choice. They could either leave or stay and discuss their differences over a beverage. All participants bellied up to the bar and engaged in civil, friendly dialogue. The spot ends with one gent quipping to his transgender work partner: "I'll give you my phone number and you give me yours, [but] I'll have to tell my girlfriend that I'll be texting another girl."[22]

Working together humanizes the other person. No one knows this better than Father Gregory Boyle, a Jesuit priest and founder of Los Angeles's Homeboy Industries, "the largest gang intervention, rehabilitation and re-entry program in the country."[23] Nearly thirty years ago, Boyle was pastoring the poorest Catholic parish in LA, the home of eight rival gangs. He began working with gang members and discovered that superficial approaches were not solving the drug and violence problem in his parish. You had to go deeper. In conversation with gang members, he discovered that

20. Newberg and Waldman, *How God Changes Your Brain*, 139.

21. As quoted in Lukianoff and Haidt, *Coddling*, 267.

22. Aaron Whittier Channel, "Worlds Apart."

23. See Homeboy Industries website.

many were willing to work but could not get hired. With the motto "nothing stops a bullet like a job," Boyle founded Homeboy Industries, which provides mental and physical health support services and employs former gang members and felons in a range of Homeboy businesses, from food service to clothing apparel.[24]

At Homeboy Industries, enemies work side by side. Father Boyle tells the story of Youngster and Puppet, former gang rivals, who worked next to each other in the silkscreen factory. At first, they refuse to shake hands. The enmity is deep. But they want these coveted jobs, so they suck it up and work a few feet from each other. Six months go by. One evening, ten gang members attack Puppet on his way back from the corner grocery store. He is beaten mercilessly, beyond recognition, and put on life support. Within forty-eight hours, he will be dead. Shortly after the beating, however, Father Boyle is sitting alone in his office. The phone rings. It's Youngster. He says, "Hey, that's messed up about what happened to Puppet." Father Boyle agrees. Youngster eagerly volunteers, "Is there anything I can do? Can I give him my blood?" The line goes silent "under the weight of it all." Finally, a tearful Youngster continues, "He was not my enemy . . . he was my friend. We worked together." Boyle concludes this story by asking the question, "Can I say that always happens at Homeboy Industries? Yeah. Are there any exceptions? No." How can Homeboy claim a perfect success rate of turning enemies into friends? According to Boyle, it's simple: "Human beings can't demonize people they know."[25]

The command to love our enemies is really a command to expand the circle of our tribe. As Father Boyle puts it, "How do we create and imagine a circle of compassion, and then imagine no one standing outside that circle?"[26]

Atheists for Jesus

Let's return to where this chapter began: Blackwell's Bookshop. Imagine you are there for a Richard Dawkins book-signing event. As you are standing in line to get *The God Delusion* inscribed, you flip through the pages. The name C. S. Lewis pops out at you on page 117. In a few short paragraphs, Dawkins

24. For a more comprehensive history of the Homeboy Industries story, see Boyle, *Tattoos*.

25. Boyle, "Compassion and Kinship."

26. Boyle, "Compassion and Kinship."

dismisses Lewis's famous Lord, Liar, Lunatic argument with these words: "A fourth possibility, almost too obvious to need mentioning, is that Jesus was honestly mistaken [about his identity]. Plenty of people are."[27]

As Dawkins signs your copy of the book you ask him about his dismissal of the divinity of Jesus. Politely he throws you a bone: "I don't think Jesus was any more divine than you or I, but this might surprise you—I actually like Jesus. In fact, if he were here today I think he'd be an atheist. He might even turn water into a pint for me at the The White Horse pub next door! But seriously, you should read an article I wrote called, 'Atheists for Jesus.'" You shake his hand and thank him for the inscription.

When you return to the hotel, you notice that Dawkins has included the website for his "Atheists for Jesus" article under his signature. Intrigued, you read it as you settle in on your first night in Oxford. You are stunned by some of the lines in the article. Dawkins describes the love-your-enemy Jesus ethic as "super niceness." He believes such super niceness is "just plain dumb" from a Darwinian survival-of-the-fittest perspective, but it is the kind of stupidity we should nurture and spread like an epidemic.[28] You wonder if Dawkins is onto something. By spreading the super niceness or *teleiosity* of Jesus might we build up herd immunity against the plague of restrictive tribalism? Such a task seems far beyond what humans can do in their own strength, but if an ornery atheist wants to make the world a little less Darwinian and a bit more Christlike, who are we to say no.

27. Dawkins, *God Delusion*, 117. For an interesting discussion of what qualifies as an "honest mistake," see Morris, *Making Sense*, 173–74. It is also worth noting that Lewis was open to the idea that atheists like John Stuart Mill could possibly become believers once their "honest ignorance" or "honest error" has been corrected beyond the grave. See Lewis, "Man or Rabbit?," 110.

28. Dawkins, "Atheists for Jesus."

Chapter 8

Treble Tactic Eight: Exorcise Demonization

Bass-Pounding Fallacy: The Whole World Is Divided into Clean and Unclean

> "We've broken the world into us and them, only emerging from our bunkers long enough to toss rhetorical grenades at the other camp. We write off half the country as out-of-touch liberal elites or racist misogynist bullies. No nuance. No complexity. No humanity. . . . This path has brought cruel sniping, deepening polarization and even outbreaks of violence. I remember this path. It will not take us where we want to go."[1]
>
> —MEGAN PHELPS-ROPER

Fifteen years before Leonardo DiCaprio starred in *Once Upon a Time in Hollywood*, he played Howard Hughes in *The Aviator*. This Martin Scorsese-directed film received eleven Academy Award nominations, including DiCaprio for best leading actor and Alan Alda for best supporting actor.

The Aviator opens in 1913 Houston with Hughes's mother giving eight-year-old Howard a bath. As she teaches him the word "Q-U-A-R-A-N-T-I-N-E," they discuss recent outbreaks of cholera and typhoid. The scene concludes with her earnest words to young Howard: "You are not safe."[2]

1. Phelps-Roper, "Why I Left."
2. Scorsese, dir., *Aviator*.

The movie chronicles Hughes's life as both a Hollywood producer and aeronautical trailblazer. During his career, he made seventeen films and set several airspeed world records enroute to becoming one of the wealthiest men alive. Despite his many professional accomplishments, however, he is arguably best known for his legendary germaphobia. Near the end of his life, the reclusive Hughes would lie naked in a dimly lit hotel room, believing he had created a pathogen-free environment. When moving around he would wear tissue boxes to keep the bottom of his feet from touching the floor. If he did venture out and encounter anyone who was sick, he would quickly burn the clothes he had been wearing.

Those who worked for Hughes were required to follow strict protocols when preparing his food. He compiled "a staff manual on how to open a can of peaches—including directions for removing the label, scrubbing the can down until it was bare metal, washing it again and pouring the contents into a bowl without touching the can to the bowl."[3] His servers would deliver his food to him with layers of paper towels covering their hands.

If you had read the preceding paragraphs a few years ago, Hughes would likely have struck you as the pathological poster child for Obsessive Compulsive Disorder (and he is). In our current COVID conditions, however, he seems almost normal. Funny how a pandemic can flip the script. As I write this chapter, more than a hundred years removed from Hughes's cautious childhood upbringing, his hometown has become an epicenter of the outbreak. Yesterday, Texas reported its highest daily increase in confirmed cases and Houston-area hospitals were nearly overrun. Cleanliness has never been more critical.

But, as we have been discussing in this book, our country is in the midst of another epidemic, as well: a deepening culture war in which the whole nation is divided into clean and unclean tribes. While our side is viewed as good, pure, and safe, the other team is evil, dirty, and infected. The 2020 outbreak not only heightened our awareness of actual malicious microbes, it increased our sensitivity to ideological and political pathogens. Far too many of us believe the cure is to either to quarantine ourselves from the other side's infectious ideas or to spray them with copious amounts of verbal pesticide. Dehumanizing our opponents, however, will not expand the tribe.

3. Dittman, "Hughes's germ phobia."

The Dehumanization of Disgust

An episode of *Black Mirror* illustrates well the danger of dehumanization. In "Men Against Fire," implants are surgically inserted into the brains of soldiers to help them kill the enemy—a group of people labeled *Roaches*. When the implant is functioning properly, soldiers don't see the enemy as they really are; instead, they see monstrous sub-human mutants. The implant also mutes the senses of the soldiers so they don't hear the cries of their victims or smell their blood following a kill.

In one scene soldiers invade a farmhouse, where they suspect a villager of harboring *Roaches*. While the soldiers sweep the house, the commander tries to convince the devout owner to hand over the fugitives.

> That cross on the wall there—you got principles. [You] think all life is sacred. And I get it. I agree. All life is sacred, so you even got to protect the *Roaches*, right? It's not their fault they're like that. They didn't ask for this. I get it. We get it. There's s**t in their blood that made them that way. The sickness they're carrying, that doesn't care about the sanctity of life or the pain about who else is gonna suffer. If we don't stop the *Roaches*, in five, ten, twenty years from now, you're still gonna get kids born that way, and then they're gonna breed. And so it goes on. That cycle of pain, that sickness, and it could have been avoided. Every *Roach* you save today, you condemn God knows how many people to despair and misery tomorrow. You can't still see them as human. Understandable sentiment, granted, but it's misguided. We gotta take them out if humankind is gonna carry on in this world. That's just the hard truth. Gotta make sacrifices.[4]

Later in the episode, a soldier experiences a glitch with his implant. As it malfunctions he is able to see the enemy for who they really are, not as vile insects, but actual human beings with dignity and value. Instead of shooting, he saves a boy and his mother. The renegade soldier, however, is captured and taken back to the base. In a meeting with a military psychologist the soldier pushes back: "The whole thing is a lie. *Roaches*, they look just like us." The psychologist replies, "Of course they do. That's why they're so dangerous. Humans, you know, we give ourselves a bad rap, but we're genuinely empathetic as a species. I mean, we don't actually really want to kill each other . . . until your future depends on wiping out the enemy. . . . [And] it's a lot easier pulling the trigger when you're aiming at

4. *Black Mirror*, "Men Against Fire."

the bogeyman."[5] Dehumanization and disgust are powerful tools when they are psychologically weaponized.

John Gottman, an emeritus professor of psychology at the University of Washington, is one of the nation's leading marriage-stability researchers. According to the data, he can predict with a 91 percent accuracy whether or not a couple is going to stay together or get divorced. And he can do it in as little as five minutes. Here's his method: Married couples spend the night in a fabricated on-campus apartment, affectionately labeled the "Love Lab." During their stay, they consent to have their conversations videotaped. Gottman later evaluates the footage. In his book *The Seven Principles for Making Marriage Work*, Gottman discusses how he predicts divorce. One of the key signs is whether or not contempt is present.

> Sarcasm and cynicism are types of contempt. So are name-calling, eye-rolling, sneering, mockery, and hostile humor. In whatever form, contempt . . . is poisonous to a relationship because it conveys disgust. It's virtually impossible to resolve a problem when your partner is getting the message you're disgusted with him or her. Inevitably, contempt leads to more conflict rather than to reconciliation.[6]

If you want to cause the other person's elephant to either recoil or stampede, conveying disgust is a surefire method. What Gottman describes is not reserved for married couples; any relationship will suffer when contempt rears its ugly head. Just think how often sarcasm, cynicism, name-calling, eye-rolling, sneering, mockery, and hostile humor are present in our cultural disagreements. The ubiquity of these seven deadly expressions of disgust is patently obvious.

In 2016, a few weeks before the presidential election was decided, TED curator Chris Anderson sat down with Jonathan Haidt for a conversation entitled "Can a Divided America Heal?" The twenty-minute discussion covered a lot of ground, including the three principles of moral psychology, but eventually settled into this dangerous emotion of disgust. While admitting that politics has always been a nasty business, they both agreed that there is something different about our current polarized climate. Let's listen in on part of the exchange:

5. *Black Mirror*, "Men Against Fire."
6. Gottman and Silver, *Making Marriage Work*, 29.

ANDERSON: The tone of what's happening on the Internet now is quite troubling. I just did a quick search on Twitter about the election and saw two tweets next to each other. One, against a picture of racist graffiti: "This is disgusting! Ugliness in this country, brought to us by #Trump." And then the next one is: "Crooked Hillary dedication page. Disgusting!" So this idea of "disgust" is troubling to me. Because you can have an argument or a disagreement about something, you can get angry at someone. Disgust, I've heard you say, takes things to a much deeper level.

HAIDT: That's right. Disgust is different. Anger—you know, I have kids. They fight ten times a day, and they love each other thirty times a day. You just go back and forth: you get angry, you're not angry; you're angry, you're not angry. But disgust is different. Disgust paints the person as subhuman, monstrous, deformed, morally deformed. Disgust is like indelible ink. . . . So this election is different. Donald Trump personally uses the word "disgust" a lot. He's very germ-sensitive, so disgust does matter a lot more for him, that's something unique to him—but as we demonize each other more, and again, through the Manichaean worldview, the idea that the world is a battle between good and evil as this has been ramping up, we're more likely not just to say they're wrong or I don't like them, but we say they're evil, they're satanic, they're disgusting, they're revolting. And then we want nothing to do with them.[7]

Common Humanity vs. Common Enemy Engagement

Haidt is an expert in disgust. A major part of his research has focused on how intuition and reason interact when confronted with stories of purity and revulsion. Early in his career, he would write various fictious disgust vignettes, then interview study participants to gauge how the low-road elephant interacts with the high-road rider. The incest vignette, considered in the introduction to this book, is one example of the rider offering post-hoc rationalizations in an attempt to justify the elephant's immediate and unyielding revulsion to siblings engaging in sex. Even when the experimenter would successfully shoot down each line of reasoning, the subject refused to deny his active intuitions.[8] Why? Because intuitions come first, strategic reasoning second.

7. Haidt, "Divided America."

8. Haidt, *Righteous Mind*, 38–40.

The first principle of moral psychology is also confirmed by what Haidt calls the "roach juice" experiment. In this activity a can of apple juice was poured into a cup. The participant was asked to take a sip. No problem. Then a white plastic box appeared. The lid was lifted to reveal a batch of sterilized cockroaches. The participant was assured the roaches had been raised in a sterile environment followed by intense heating at temperatures too high for any germs to survive. Using a tea strainer, one of the roaches was dipped into the apple juice. Study participants were then asked to take a sip. While all participants took the initial roach-free sip, approximately two-thirds refused to put the "roach juice" to their lips. Despite all of the sterilization guarantees, for most people the initial gut-level repulsion was too much to overcome. The *sanctity/degradation* intuition would not be swayed by any amount of rider-focused logical assurance.[9]

Now, the same *sanctity/degradation* intuition that is activated by the incest vignette and "roach juice" experiment is triggered when opponents are tainted with disgust. As Haidt points out, passionate disagreement is not the problem in our disputes. The problem is when our intensity escalates into disgust. When this happens, our gag reflex kicks in and we find the other person revolting and nauseating. If people with competing political/religious/moral convictions can be equated in our mind with incestuous behavior or bug nectar, the chance for bridge-building, peacemaking, and persuasion is about as likely as me eating cockroach casserole for dinner.

So how do we fix our current obsession with demonization and disgust? Haidt and Lukianoff believe one answer is to shift from a *common enemy* to *common humanity* approach. We are all members of identity tribes with a range of concerns, but the methodology we choose to advance our causes matters immensely.

> *How* identity is mobilized makes an enormous difference—for the group's odds of success, for the welfare of the people who join the movement, and for the country. Identity can be mobilized in ways that emphasize an overarching common humanity while making the case that some *fellow human beings* are denied dignity and rights because they belong to a particular group, or it can be mobilized in ways that amplify our ancient tribalism and bind people together in shared hatred of a *group* that serves as a unifying common enemy.[10]

9. Haidt, *Righteous Mind*, 37.
10. Lukianoff and Haidt, *Coddling*, 60.

Haidt and Lukianoff identify Martin Luther King, Jr. as an exemplar for the *common-humanity* approach. King "appealed to the shared morals and identities of Americans by using the unifying language of family, referring to people of all races and religions as 'brothers' and 'sisters.' He spoke often of the need for love and forgiveness, hearkening back to the words of Jesus."[11] King's inclusive nonviolent methodology made it clear that his purpose was to "repair and reunite," not to "destroy America."[12]

Think back to the story of Drew Brees from chapter 6. The comments that landed him in hot water were made during a Zoom interview with Yahoo! Finance. We've already discussed his redemption story, so I want to focus on something else here. What many people don't realize is that Brees's comments about "never agreeing with anyone disrespecting the flag" came *after* an initial attempt to answer the standing/kneeling dispute. The Yahoo! Finance conversation began with this question: "You are a leader. You took the knee several years ago, along with all of your teammates, but you've also talked about that sometimes protests or demonstrations for instance in the middle of the national anthem might be divisive. So what is the action we should take now?" Brees offered this response:

> Well that's not an easy question to answer. But at the end of the day, my response via social media today was to reinforce my belief that God created us all equal and we all have a responsibility to love each other and respect each other. I try to live my life by two basic Christian fundamentals: that is love the Lord with all your heart, mind, and soul and love your neighbor as yourself. And I think we accomplish greater things as a community, as a society, and as a country when we do it together. And I think we are all equipped with great talents, abilities, and strengths and we can use that with each other and for each other. I think we can accomplish some amazing things. And obviously these are trying times during our country certainly coming out of this COVID crisis and then entering into another crisis or really these two compounding with each other. I think we all recognize the changes that need to take place. . . . Everybody is going to social media and kind of saying their piece. Obviously there are riots and there are protests, people are certainly out there showing their frustration, as well, but I think at the end of the day, we need to find ways to work together

11. Lukianoff and Haidt, *Coddling*, 60.

12. Lukianoff and Haidt, *Coddling*, 61.

> to provide opportunities for one another to continue to move our country forward to a bigger and better place.[13]

Notice that this first attempt to answer the standing/kneeling question did not include a single reference to the flag. Instead, Brees laced his response with *common-humanity* language. He said, "God created *us all equal*," "we *all* have a responsibility to *love* each other and *respect* each other," "we accomplish greater things as a community, as a society, and as a country when we do it *together*," and "we need to find ways to *work together*." Like MLK, Brees used unifying language to focus on commonality and he did so without mentioning the controversy of standing or kneeling. The problem arose when the next Yahoo! Finance questioner pressed Brees for a more specific response. Perhaps it's a good thing that the follow-up question was asked, because the controversy that erupted led to Brees realizing that the flag is not seen by all people as a unifying symbol due to widespread racial inequality. For our present purposes, however, I simply point out that Brees's initial attempt to answer the standing/kneeling question was loaded with *common-humanity* references, something to which we should all aspire if we want to move past demonization and disgust.

One of the reasons Brees received so much blowback, however, was because his initial response was not included in the video that went viral. Instead, all that circulated was an apparently divisive statement without the contextual benefit of the broader overarching theme of unity that Brees emphasized before and after his lightning-rod remark. This is why social-media sound bites can be so perilous. I suspect most people who piled onto Brees didn't take the time to go back and watch the full Yahoo! Finance conversation.

The resulting demonization and disgust thrown at Brees, however, illustrate well the *common-enemy* approach so prevalent today. Many who responded to Brees chose to assume the worst rather than extend the benefit of the doubt. Even after the apology, many chose to view his words with skepticism rather than charity. This is an excellent example of our current call-out culture, which rewards people for publicly shaming and demonizing those we perceive to be on the wrong side of an issue. Our *common-enemy* call-out culture is problematic on many levels, but one issue is tribal leaders are the ones who decide who deserves empathy and who doesn't.

Let's return to Haidt's TED conversation with Chris Anderson. When the discussion turned to empathy, Haidt said: "Empathy is a very, very hot

13. Brees, "Kneeling protests."

topic in psychology, and it's a very popular word on the left in particular. Empathy is a good thing, and empathy for the preferred classes of victims. So it's important to empathize with the groups that we on the left think are so important. That's easy to do, because you get points for that. But empathy really should get you points if you do it when it's hard to do."[14] Haidt sounds an awful lot like Jesus here. Compare his comments with Matthew 5:46–47, "If you love those who love you, what reward will you get? Are not even the tax collectors doing that? And if you greet only your own people, what are you doing more than others? Do not even pagans do that?" In other words, Jesus is saying you get points or credit (reward) when it is hard to extend grace and empathy, not when it is easy.[15] While a *common-enemy* approach has the veneer of virtue, beneath the surface it actually drives us deeper into disgust and fans the flames of tribal warfare.

Hope After Westboro

Ultimately, this chapter is about bringing exorcisms back. Not exorcising demons, but exorcising demonization. Megan Phelps-Roper knows a thing or two about demonization. She joined her family and other Westboro Baptist Church members on the picket line for the first time when she was five years old. Moments before, she was playing with her dolls in the air-conditioned van. Now, in the scorching Kansas sun, her little arms were waving a sign she did not understand: "Gays are worthy of death."[16]

For the next twenty years, Megan's childhood and adolescence were filled with fervent coast-to-coast protests, in venues ranging from baseball games to military funerals. She believed there are two kinds of people in this world: the clean, comprised of the few hundred members of the Westboro church, and the unclean, everyone else—"Only Jacob or Esau! Elect or reprobate!"[17] From the earliest days, Megan was a sold-out disciple: "Like the

14. Haidt, "Divided America." Lukianoff and Haidt also point out that trying to extend empathy to the other side can put your tribal status in question: "One gets no points, no credit, for speaking privately and gently with an offender—in fact, that could be interpreted as colluding with the enemy." Lukianoff and Haidt, *Coddling*, 71.

15. Readers should not confuse the language of reward, credit, and points in this context with support for works-righteousness salvation.

16. Phelps-Roper, "Why I Left."

17. Phelps-Roper, *Unfollow*, 118.

rest of my ten siblings, I believed what I was taught with all of my heart and pursued Westboro's agenda with a special sort of zeal."[18]

Megan's wit, intelligence, and faithfulness made her the perfect right-hand complement to her mother, Shirley, the daughter of Fred Phelps, Westboro's founding pastor. When reporters would travel from around the world to interview the Phelps clan, they were often surprised to find a family full of educated, articulate lawyers rather than backwoods hillbillies. They were also bewildered to learn that the same Fred Phelps whom Megan describes as a man overflowing with "a toxic sense of certainty in his own righteousness" also once used his legal training to defend African American clients during the civil rights movement.[19] While Fred garnered most of the attention, Shirley was the logistical whirlwind that kept the family's personal and professional schedules from spiraling out of control. Megan was right by her side, providing a range of support services including social media management.

As the official curator of the Westboro online presence, Megan took her crusade to Twitter. At first, the digital sparring mirrored the many hostile encounters she had experienced on physical picket lines. Before long, however, harsh judgmental tweets gave way to civil, curious dialogue. "How had 'the other' come to such outrageous conclusions about the world?"[20] Megan began to realize that she had been "inoculated against outside ideas" and maybe dividing the world into clean and unclean, Jacob and Esau was a mistake.[21] Feelings of empathy even began to emerge for those she had previously been taught to deny compassion.

> The truth was that I had started to feel sad in response to tragedies . . . On Twitter, I came across a photo-essay about a famine in Somalia, bursting into tears at the sight of the first image: a tiny emaciated child. My mother heard and immediately walked over to my desk, asking what was wrong. I pointed to the photo on my screen and shook my head. "Would you send me that link, hon?" she said eagerly, "I'm going to write a GodSmack about it!" The disparity between my response and my mother's gave me pause, but she didn't seem to notice. She was already caught up in composing a celebratory blog post. In the past, this discrepancy would have made me wonder what was wrong with me, but now

18. Phelps-Roper, "Why I Left."
19. Phelps-Roper, "Amends."
20. Phelps-Roper, "Why I Left."
21. Phelps-Roper, "Oxford Union."

> I thought of the prophet Elisha, weeping at his prophecy of the destruction of Israel. As I watched my mother's fingers fly over the keys, a small part of me began to wonder if there was something wrong with Westboro.[22]

Megan had been raised to believe that the definition of love was "truth." That meant "any expression of truth was, by definition, loving. Truth was love regardless of context, target, or tone—even when it involved holding a sign that read THANK GOD FOR DEAD SOLDIERS on the sidewalk near a military funeral, while singing praises to the homemade bombs that killed them."[23] One Twitter follower whispered to Megan's elephant with sincere compliments about her wit and intelligence. Once the elephants were friendly, however, he challenged Westboro's tactics. As Megan pounded on "commandments and truth," he would counter with "humility, gentleness, and compassion. To him, our message and methods clearly lacked these qualities—no matter how truthful we believed our words to be."[24] It was becoming clear to Megan that all bass, no treble might not be so loving after all.

Sometimes the electronic and physical worlds blurred. A blogger named David, who runs the site "Jewlicious," encountered Megan in New Orleans. He brought her a "Middle Eastern dessert from Jerusalem where he lives, and I brought him kosher chocolate and held a 'God hates Jews' sign. There was no confusion about our positions, but the line between friend and foe was becoming blurred. We started to see each other as human beings and it changed the way we spoke to one another."[25]

The dominos were set in motion. Megan opened up to her dialogue partners and began to see internal contradictions in Westboro's theology. "The truth is the care shown to me by these strangers on the internet was itself a contradiction. It was growing evidence that people on the other side were not the demons I had been led to believe."[26] All the dominos eventually toppled and Megan left Westboro in 2012 to carve out a new life for herself.

The decision to leave was difficult, because she realized it would mean a lifetime of estrangement from her family. Megan had seen previous family

22. Phelps-Roper, *Unfollow*, 119.
23. Phelps-Roper, *Unfollow*, 117.
24. Phelps-Roper, *Unfollow*, 117.
25. Phelps-Roper, "Why I Left."
26. Phelps-Roper, "Why I Left."

members leave the church. She had felt the heartache of siblings turning into demons, deserters, and traitors overnight. She knew she would also be viewed as Judas Iscariot, an evil reprobate Esau whose true colors finally surfaced in God's perfect, divinely ordained timing. She would be demonized by the family that loved and nurtured her for twenty-six years. They would treat her with contempt and disgust. But the scales had fallen from her eyes; she had no other choice.

Today, Megan speaks widely trying to make amends for the pain she has caused. Her transformation is inspiring. It demonstrates that no one is beyond hope—even her antagonistic grandfather, Fred, who in his final days of hospice care declared to a group of LGBT folks: "You're good people."[27] The most amazing thing about Megan's story, however, is that she refuses to give up on the rest of her family, despite the painful demonization that has come her way. "I see my parents as good people who have been trapped by bad ideas. . . . How dare I not have hope for them, considering my own journey. If I could be persuaded by kind, compassionate strangers, who listened to where I was coming from, considered my perspective, and made their case [then there is hope for them, as well]."[28] Perhaps the most touching expression of her enduring hope can be found on her book's dedication page: "To my beloved parents, Shirley and Brent, whose tenderness fills my memories. I left the church, but never you—and never will. I am humbled to be your daughter."[29]

Overcoming Tribal OCD

In Scorsese's telling of the story, Howard Hughes calls upon a UCLA professor to serve as a meteorological consultant while shooting his first film, *Hell's Angels*. When Leonardo DiCaprio was chosen to play Hughes in *The Aviator*, he likewise sought consultation from a UCLA faculty member—Dr. Jeffrey Schwartz, a research psychiatrist in the university's school of medicine. As an internationally recognized expert in Obsessive Compulsive Disorder, Schwartz received "a phone call at 3 p.m., a script before 5 p.m., and the next afternoon he was there, sitting with Leonardo

27. Phelps-Roper, *Unfollow*, 282.

28. Phelps-Roper, "Amends."

29. Phelps-Roper, *Unfollow*, front matter.

DiCaprio, exploring the intricacies of one of the most debilitating mental illnesses in medicine."[30]

Schwartz would not teach DiCaprio how to imitate someone with severe OCD; "instead, he would show him 'how to become a person with OCD,' so his brain was 'like the brain of a person who has the disease.'"[31] DiCaprio was up for this immersive challenge; so much so that he developed a mild case of OCD during the filming of the movie. According to science reporter Steve Volk, "It reportedly took him about a year to get back to normal. And today, his willful descent into the illness and subsequent recovery represents one of the most dramatic public examples in our popular culture of neuroplasticity—the ability of the brain to change in shape, function, configuration or size."[32]

Schwartz has developed a focused strategy for helping people who struggle with OCD. His therapeutic approach is grounded in a *mobilist* view of human cognition and a robust belief in free will—that our choices play an important role in wiring and rewiring our brain. So for Schwartz, his approach to OCD isn't just neuroplasticity, but *self-directed* neuroplasticity.

We will return to Schwartz's method in a moment, but first we must revisit the rider and the elephant. This book has discussed the power of the elephant to drive much of our thinking and behavior, but the rider can influence the elephant, as well. In Romans 12:2, the Apostle Paul writes: "Do not conform to the patterns of this world, but be transformed by the renewing of your mind." Now, the full counsel of Scripture makes it clear that we are fallen and incapable of transforming ourselves. We must lean into the Holy Spirit, to be sure but we also have a role to play in the sanctification process. Our role is to cooperate with divine grace, which requires that we "take captive every thought to make it obedient to Christ."[33]

Let's explore self-directed neuroplasticity in light of the elephant-rider metaphor. There are actually two different kinds of neural pachyderms in this metaphor: first-nature and second-nature elephants.[34] First-nature elephants represent the universal intuitions and skills that naturally occur at the appropriate stage of human development. For instance, most people

30. Volk, "Rewiring the Brain."

31. Volk, "Rewiring the Brain."

32. Volk, "Rewiring the Brain."

33. 2 Corinthians 10:5.

34. For a more technical discussion of these two low-road forms of natural cognition, see McCauley, *Religion Is Natural*, 26–30.

begin to walk and chew at about the same developmental time—between eight and eighteen months for walking and between two and three years for chewing. These activities take place at the automatic, sub-conscious level. When we walk and chew, we aren't consciously thinking about leg and jaw movement. It just happens naturally and automatically at the first-nature elephant level.

Second-nature elephants, on the other hand, represent particular intuitions, dispositions, and skills that develop through intentional rider-focused choice, practice, and muscle-memory maturation. Consider, for instance, learning how to play a musical instrument or shoot a basketball. While some people are born with natural gifting for music or sports, these undeveloped proclivities still require cultivation through intentional practice. This is where the rider gets involved with training the second-nature elephant. Our high-road strategic reasoning plays an important role in whether or not we will invest the necessary time and effort to cultivate the desired musical or athletic proficiency. If all goes well, after hours, weeks, and sometimes years of practice, the automatic elephant will be wired to perform according to the rider's wishes. When the bright lights turn on, muscle memory kicks in and it is now second nature to hit all the right notes or that baseline jump shot without direct rider involvement. In fact, if you overthink it at the key moment, you will probably mess up.

If you aren't a musician or an athlete, consider another example that most of us can relate to—driving a car. Think about a time when you were driving, then all of a sudden you realized you hadn't been thinking about driving at all. Yet, for the last ten minutes, you somehow made all the correct turns. How did this happen? Because through countless hours of practice, driving has become so second nature that you were driving at the elephant subconscious level without any assistance from the rider. This is more likely to happen when you are driving in familiar surroundings. But what happens when you take the wheel in unfamiliar territory? This happened to me a few years ago when my wife and I went to Scotland, where they drive on the left side of the road. I drove over 700 miles—from Edinburgh to Oban to Inverness to St. Andrews—but it was my rider not my elephant that was engaged most of the time. Why? While driving is second nature for me, doing so on the left side of the road is not. Negotiating the Scottish highways and byways required constant conscious vigilance to overcome my right-side-of-the-road, second-nature habits. It was hard work, but I am proud to report no accidents!

Here is the point: Most of life happens at the automatic elephant level. There is good reason for this: it frees up energy for our rider to focus on the more complex problems that can only be handled by strategic reasoning. But what happens when the second-nature elephant gets wired in unhealthy ways? What happens when someone engages in irrational obsessive compulsive behavior due to faulty wiring?

Schwartz has developed a four-step strategy to rewire the elephant. The four steps are: 1. Relabel, 2. Reframe, 3. Refocus, and 4. Revalue. These four steps help his patients overcome unhealthy OCD patterns of behavior, such as an obsession with cleanliness. These four steps, however, can also help us overcome our tribal OCD. As we've been discussing in this chapter, most of us struggle with viewing people outside our tribal community as toxic, impure, and contagious. Consequently, non-tribal members are a threat to the safety and well-being of our in-group. Tribal OCD is reinforced by the *in-group loyalty* and *sanctity* intuitions. While *in-group loyalty* and *sanctity* have their place, an overemphasis increases the us-them divide and undermines the quest to love our enemies as Jesus commanded. We are naturally wired to be tribal and communal, so in-group loyalty isn't the problem. The problem is the restrictive way in which our in-group loyalty intuition gets engaged. So, how can Schwartz's OCD strategy help us expand the tribe and love our enemies more faithfully? Let's look more closely at the four steps.

Relabel. The first step is to recognize your negative compulsive *otherizing* feelings and sensations are not a true reflection of who you are or aspire to be, but rather the result of faulty brain wiring. As a Christ-follower, you are a new creation in Christ and called to renew your mind. This includes loving your enemies. Over time, however, your elephant has been wired to automatically respond to the other with anger, resentment, fear, and disgust, but this is not a permanent condition. When these feelings and sensations surface, instead of treating them as an accurate representation of reality, we must relabel them as faulty, broken thinking—part of your old sinful nature. This process requires the practice of mindfulness, which is better understood as an activity rather than a passive state of mind. Schwartz explains:

> Mindfulness, like any activity, requires effort, vigilance, and a willingness, because in each moment of your life you are choosing whether to be mindful or not. And, like most activities where focus and skill are involved, the more you practice, the better your abilities become. In this way, mindfulness literally is a training ground for

> your mind—a mental gym where you strengthen your powers of observation and awareness so that you become more proficient at seeing what is happening in each moment of your life.[35]

By practicing mindful awareness, we are better able to identify and relabel the feelings and sensations that are keeping us from expanding the tribe.

Reframe. In the second step we become aware of cognitive distortions or fallacies. One common fallacy is black and white thinking.[36] At this stage, we might catch ourselves reducing the other person to either evil or stupid. As we get our rider involved under the guidance of the Holy Spirit, we can begin to reframe our view of the other person in a more generous and charitable manner.

Refocus. Once our cognitive field is clear, we are now able to focus on our goal of expanding the tribe. This is the stage in which our brain can be rewired through intentional choice by concentrating on our common ground and shared humanity with the other person. When you think about it, we all have more than one tribe. In fact, we are members of multiple tribes. For instance, here are some of my tribal groups: Christians, men, husbands, fathers, dog lovers, professors, authors, Americans, Indiana residents, sports fans, Ohio State sports fans, Big Ten Conference sports fans, political centrists, Avett Brothers music fans, and Coen Brother movie fans. Of course, this list is just a sampling of the tribes that I am either formally or informally a part of. As we seek to find common ground with our "other," a good starting point is determining where you have shared allegiance or a tribal connection point. Once you begin to view each other as teammates, fruitful conversations about your differences are more likely. The takeaway here is to find a tribal intersection point with your other. Build on the warmth of this shared allegiance first. Remember, elephants must lean toward each other before fruitful dialogue can take place.

Revalue. When you consistently practice the first three steps, this final step begins to kick in automatically—revaluing the other. When the cognitive distortion of viewing your other as disgusting and sub-human surfaces, you will be able to call these deceptive thoughts and feelings for what they really are—as Schwartz puts it: "trash . . . not worth the gray

35. Schwartz and Gladding, *You Are Not Your Brain*, 147–48. See 144–78 for more specific mindfulness exercises.

36. For a helpful quick reference list of common cognitive distortions, see Lukianoff and Haidt, *Coddling*, 38.

matter they rode in on."[37] By practicing these steps, we will begin to naturally see the other person as one of "us" instead of one of "them." After all, if Leonardo DiCaprio could come all the way back from recreating the obsessive-compulsive mind of Howard Hughes, then overcoming tribal OCD should be a no-brainer.

37. Volk, "Rewiring the Brain."

Chapter 9

Treble Tactic Nine: Focus on Reconciliation

Bass-Pounding Fallacy: Winning Isn't Everything; Looking Good Matters Too

> "When it clicks, when you're in sync with someone, even for the briefest moment, it feels like reconciliation. We're no longer apart. We have an actual two-way conversation. We go from 'No, you're wrong' to 'Oh. Maybe you're right.' And *boom*. Dopamine."[1]
>
> —ALAN ALDA

I use a lot of video clips in my classes, but the most popular ones come from the hit TV show *The Office*, which garnered forty-two Emmy nominations during its nine-year run on NBC. Clips, however, aren't enough to satisfy my *Office*-obsessed students—props are essential, as well. On the day we watch Jim successfully condition Dwight with breath mints (illustrating Pavlov's dog), an Altoid tin accompanies me to class.[2] When I introduce the Apostles' Creed to my theology students, I wear my beloved Creed Bratton t-shirt. During the final exam, a Michael Scott bobblehead keeps a watchful eye over the test-takers. No one can leave without giving Michael a love tap.

So you can imagine my concern when the show finally came to an end in 2013. Would future students get my *Office* references and appreciate my

1. Alda, *If I Understood You*, 195.
2. *The Office*, "Dwight's Speech."

antics? Then miracle of miracles, NBC signed a deal with Netflix and *The Office* became the platform's most popular show.[3] A whole new generation has since fallen in love with Michael, Dwight, Jim, Stanley, Phyllis, Toby, Creed, Ryan, Kelly, Oscar, Kevin, Angela, and Andy, whose college a capella group was called "Here Comes Treble." Oh, and, of course, everyone's favorite receptionist—Pam.[4]

Catering to this second wave of interest, best friends Jenna Fischer and Angela Kinsey, who played Pam and Angela, launched an enormously popular podcast called *Office Ladies*. Each week, the hosts rewatch an episode and offer fans priceless behind-the-scenes nuggets of *Office* gold. At the time of this writing, they are thirty-five episodes in. Only 166 to go.

One of my favorites is episode five of season two, "Halloween." All employees show up for work in costume. Michael has a paper-mâché head of himself on his shoulder (two-headed Michael); Dwight is a Sith Lord; Pam, Angela, and Phyllis are cats; Toby is Hugh Hefner; and Jim has three vertically stacked circles on the right side of his shirt (three-hole-punch Jim). Despite the festive attire, Michael is required to fire someone by the end of the day. After considering the strengths and weaknesses of everyone in the office, he settles on Creed. In full vampire garb, Creed talks Michael out of it, suggesting Devon instead. Dressed like a hobo—foreshadowing his impending unemployment—Devon tries to convince Michael to trust his initial instinct.

> **DEVON:** Creed's an idiot, you know that. No, no, no, no, no . . . You had it right the first time.
>
> **MICHAEL:** Well, maybe I did.
>
> **DEVON:** Exactly, you gotta go with your gut, man.
>
> **MICHAEL:** No, I can't—no. I can't go back. I'd look like an idiot.
>
> **DEVON:** That's why I'm being fired? So you won't *look* like an idiot?[5]

To soften the blow, Michael hands Devon a gift certificate to Chili's. Devon rips it up and storms out of the office, but not before inviting a select group

3. Rao, "Netflix made it a phenomenon."

4. Not to mention Jan, Meredith, Roy, Darryl, Hank, Karen, Gabe, Erin, and many others.

5. *The Office*, "Halloween."

of co-workers to join him for a drink. This episode painfully illustrates the lengths to which Michael will go to avoid looking bad.[6]

Michael, however, is not alone. Blaise Pascal once wrote, "We would cheerfully be cowards if that would acquire us a reputation for bravery."[7] This Pascalian quotation captures well our obsession with public perception, even if it means, as in Michael's case, firing the wrong person. The ubiquity of this human characteristic is due, in part, to the rider's natural tendency to serve as a public-relations practitioner for the elephant. Additionally, as tribal creatures, we work tirelessly to prove our worth as good, faithful, and loyal teammates. So when it comes to the kinds of culture clashes under consideration in this book, is it any wonder that many of us focus on our own vanity and image rather than the well-being of those across the aisle?

The Pleasure of Reconciliation

As Christ-followers, however, we have a higher calling. Instead of obsessing over our own image, the Apostle Paul instructs us to focus on restoring relationships: "All this is from God, who reconciled us to himself through Christ and gave us the ministry of reconciliation: that God was reconciling the world to himself in Christ, not counting people's sins against them. And he has committed to us the message of reconciliation" (2 Corinthians 5:18–19).

If our goal is to expand the tribe and not just make ourselves look good, then during our interactions with others we must think less about our own image and more about the well-being of our dialogue partner. We should be asking, "What can I do in this conversation that will facilitate reconciliation with God and others?" Alan Alda encourages us to approach challenging interactions as "a dance with a partner. Not a wrestling match with an opponent."[8] Alda continues:

> Practicing contact with other people feels good. It's not like lifting weights. It feels good while you're doing it, not just after you stop.

6. *Office* fans know how important not looking like an idiot is to Michael, who once asked Dwight: "What is the most inspiring thing I ever said to you?" Dwight responds, "Don't be an idiot. Changed my life." *The Office*, "Business School."

7. Pascal, *Pensées*, 45 (147).

8. Alda, *If I Understood You*, 195.

> When it clicks, when you're in sync with someone, even for the briefest moment, it feels like the pleasure of reconciliation. We're no longer apart. We have an actual two-way conversation. We go from "No, you're wrong" to "Oh. Maybe you're right." And *boom*. Dopamine.
>
> It's a good feeling. I think we crave it.[9]

In the previous chapter, we discussed Jonathan Haidt's research into the emotion of disgust. In this chapter, we will consider another area of his research—moral elevation. According to Haidt, the moral emotions of disgust and elevation are actually the polar opposites on a vertical axis. As we saw in chapter 6, Haidt believes the human mind "automatically perceives a kind of vertical dimension of social space," with the divine at the top and the demonic down below.[10] The emotion of disgust is organically linked to demonization in this vertical space, whereas the emotion of elevation is associated with the divine.[11] While expressions of contempt and disgust can make us "feel dirty" and "bring us down," stories of service, sacrifice, and reconciliation can "lift us up" and inspire us to make the world a better place. Haidt's research shows that "people really do respond emotionally to acts of moral beauty, and these emotional reactions involve warm or pleasant feelings in the chest and conscious desires to help others or become a better person oneself."[12] This elevating response is often accompanied by a release of oxytocin, a hormone associated with "calmness, love, and desire for contact that encourages bonding and attachment."[13] This is why inspiring stories can often leave us with a natural high.

In the remainder of this chapter, we will consider several elevating reconciliation stories, starting with one of my students, who, if memory serves correctly, is also a fan of *The Office*.

Reconciling Teammates

On the first day of class Tony introduced himself and I learned he was a student athlete. We exchanged pleasantries and he found a spot in the back row, where he remained for the entire semester. Tony was quiet in

9. Alda, *If I Understood You*, 195.
10. Haidt, *Righteous Mind*, 103.
11. Haidt, *Righteous Mind*, 106.
12. Haidt, *Happiness Hypothesis*, 196.
13. Haidt, *Happiness Hypothesis*, 196.

class, but when I read his "Who Is My Other?" paper, the first part of the Matthew 5 assignment, I could tell he was a passionate young man with strong convictions.

In his paper, Tony identified fellow Christians who support LGBT marriage equality as his other. "Some people try and argue that God made them that way, and that He wants them to live exactly like He made them," wrote Tony. "However, when I look at Scripture I see no place in which there is any talk or even hint of it being okay. One of my biggest pet peeves is when people try and bend the Holy Word of God and make it match their own arguments. . . . It is very hard for me to show love to these people because I genuinely question their faith and understanding of the Gospel."

As the semester progressed, Tony learned the same treble tactics we have been covering in this book. When we got to the final part of the Matthew 5 assignment, I was very interested to see if Tony would employ any of these strategies in his quest to better understand his other. I was moved by what I read.

While Tony's first paper was heavy on bass, his second one was saturated with treble. He described how a good friendship with a teammate had disintegrated after the two vehemently disagreed over the subject of marriage equality. Tony admits, "The very first time I heard his opinion on this topic, I immediately thought less of him." Tony viewed his teammate as "ignorant," while his teammate saw him as "judgmental and hateful." Heated arguments were interspersed with icy silence. The estranged teammates eventually agreed to avoid the topic altogether, but this did not make the tension go away. That is, until Tony took the first step toward reconciliation. I'll let Tony tell the rest of the story:

> When I began working on the "Understanding My Other" assignment, I thought of no better person to interview than my teammate. The only difference is that this time I approached the conversation with the ten treble tactics, and the outcome was so much different. I asked this friend of mine if he would be willing to Facetime and talk about this issue, and when the conversation started, I opened by apologizing for the way I originally handled our previous discussions. He in turn apologized, and the conversation already had a different tone to it. We both wanted to learn, grow, and understand one another. As the conversation continued, I asked him what experiences led him to his current beliefs. I found out that his brother, who happens to be one of his best friends, recently came out as homosexual. I can now very much

> see and understand why he would want so badly to believe that this is not a sin. It took a lot of intentionality and effort, but I was able to empathize with him after I approached the conversation humbly and actually listened to what he had to say.
>
> This was such a moving experience for me, as me and my teammate finally felt like brothers again. We still disagreed, but we wanted to reconcile our relationship and we were both very loving in the words we said. One thing I did pick up on, however, was the difference in our moral intuitions. He seemed to be far more focused on care, liberty, and fairness, whereas my convictions were more rooted in loyalty, authority, and sanctity. These differences can help explain why two people can read the same situation so differently, and it helps us to empathize more.
>
> When I actually gave my teammate the chance to share his story and explain his reasoning, I was able to see him as a legitimate person with legitimate opinions. Prior to knowing his background, I saw him as an uneducated Christian who obviously knew nothing about the Bible, whereas now I see him as someone who loves his brother and would go to almost any extent to support him. While I still openly disagree with his stance on the issue, I disagree from a place of love and understanding. I am incredibly grateful for the experience me and my teammate had, because it remarkably healed our friendship, and also taught me how to love those I don't agree with in the future. From here on, I will always seek to listen and understand before I seek an argument. I hope and pray that my relationship with this teammate will reflect my future relationships with people I disagree with, because I love him to death and even though we don't agree, we love, and we do it because Christ loved first.

Tony did so many things well in this encounter. First, he started by apologizing, which elicited a similar response from his friend. This is quite common. We all tend to reflect back the attitudes and behaviors of those around us due, in part, to something called *mirror neurons*.[14] If we start a conversation with defensiveness and anger, we will likely experience the same negativity coming back at us. If we start with warmth and kindness, however, elephants are more likely to lean toward each other and sync up. Haidt believes setting the correct tone is the key to conversational synchrony: "If you start with some appreciation, it's like magic. This is one of the main things I've learned . . . I still make a lot of stupid mistakes, but I'm incredibly good at apologizing now and at acknowledging what somebody

14. For more on mirror neurons, see Goleman, *Social Intelligence*, 40–44.

was right about. And if you do that, then the conversation goes really well and it's actually really fun."[15]

Tony also did a great job of approaching his estranged friend with humility and a desire to understand. Before, he had assumed the posture of teacher and judge. Now, he wanted to listen and learn from his friend's story. Consequently, the issue moved from theoretical to concrete and his friend became a "legitimate person with legitimate opinions"—a fellow human being instead of a disgusting, demonic "other."

Finally, by paying attention to moral intuition, Tony identified not only his friend's sacred values, but his own, as well. As a result, mutual empathy emerged. This work at the elephant level restored their friendship. As Tony puts it, they "felt like brothers again." These reconciled teammates are now in a much better position to have a compassionate, respectful, and nuanced rider-to-rider discussion about their differences should they choose to do so.

When a Common Enemy Is Common Ground

In an episode entitled "The Merger," Michael Scott is charged with the task of integrating several workers from another branch into his office. At first, it's not going well. In an effort to unite the old and new employees, Michael decides to let the air out of everyone's tires and blames another business for the prank. When the employees go outside to check, one of the new workers asks Michael why the tires to his Sebring are still inflated. Michael replies, "Why? I will tell you why. Because they saved the worst for me. They put a hate note under my windshield wiper. Check this out. It's so hateful. 'You guys suck! You can never pull together as one and revenge us. That is why you suck.'" Upon hearing this, the disgruntled employees march back up the stairs. When Michael returns to his office he observes everybody huddled together and talking about him. Peering through the shades of his office window, he quips to the camera: "Mission accomplished. They are like a bunch of fourth graders. Sometimes what brings the kids together is hating the lunch lady. Although that'll change because by the end of fourth grade, the lunch lady was actually the person I hung out with the most."[16]

In the previous chapter, we discussed the importance of adopting a *common-humanity* instead of a *common-enemy* approach if we are going

15. Haidt, "Divided America."

16. *The Office*, "The Merger."

to expand the tribe. That said, a common-enemy approach can be fruitful when the common enemy is not a person, but a sacred cause. Consider the story of Jim Daly and Ted Trimpa. In 2005, Daly became president of Focus on the Family, which had earned a reputation for leading the charge for conservative Christians on many culture war issues, including the definition of marriage. Daly did not want to change the convictions of the organization, but he did want to find a way to turn up the treble.

In a conversation facilitated by Gabe Lyons, Daly and Trimpa, one of the nation's leading gay rights activists, tell how they became unlikely allies and close friends.[17] Daly begins by describing a Focus on the Family radio broadcast that centered on sex trafficking. During the broadcast, he learned that 100,000 youth are annually trafficked in the United States. He also found out that the state of Colorado, where Focus on the Family is based, had recently received a "D" rating for its response to this human rights calamity. This avalanche of information upset Daly and he thought about who might be interested in collaborating on a solution. A Denver-based LGBT advocacy group came to mind.

Daly called the Gill Foundation and was put in touch with Trimpa, who represents the legal interests of the group. When he heard that the president of Focus on the Family was on the line, his first thought was, "Is it April 1?" The two set up a meeting. After both men made their unflinching marriage equality convictions known, they turned to the primary purpose of the conversation. Daly described how Colorado was failing to address the sex trafficking of minors. Trimpa recalls, "My first reaction was one of shock. How can this be in a state that I consider to be somewhat progressive?" As the two men discussed the issue, it became clear that while they disagreed on the definition of marriage, they had a shared sacred value—the stability of families and the protection of children. With Daly's ties to conservative Christians and Trimpa's connections to progressive politicians, they forged a broad-based, bipartisan coalition that led to significant legislative change in the prosecution of sex trafficking cases. Both men hope to continue their collaboration on other shared concerns.

Daly and Trimpa have learned much from their surprising friendship. Daly no longer stereotypes people from the LGBT community. "We think of each other's tribe in a very monolithic way. [For instance] the gay community is this way. This is what they think about religious freedom,

17. Lyons, "Unlikely Allies." All of the quotations included in this section of the chapter come from this interview.

this is how they want to take it away. . . . So one of the first things I learned getting to know Ted is he has a deep respect for religious liberty. He's concerned about it." Daly also discovered that a surprisingly large percentage of LGBT folks share many of his core doctrinal beliefs. "At least a third of the LGBT community is at least somewhat religious if not very religious," says Trimpa. "Belief in God and even being evangelical, it's there and there are a lot of them."[18] This friendship has also provided Trimpa a "more authentic base" from which to speak when he hears negative evangelical stereotypes among his colleagues.

Perhaps the most important takeaway is the power of reframing. "I hate using the term compromise, because it is a negative frame," says Trimpa. "Everyone feels like they are giving up something. I love the term *common ground* because [it] is a positive frame." While some Christians have celebrated Daly's innovative common ground approach, others view it as dealing with devil. Daly has received phone calls from donors who said, "If you are going to work with people like him, then I'm not going to support you anymore." His response? "Keep your cash." Daly believes this kind of bass-pounding arrogance is poisoning the church.

> Ted is not my enemy. He is somebody that Christ died for, just like me. . . . The one thing that really offended me was Christian leaders who knew I was reaching out not just in Ted's direction but with those in other areas of conflict with the traditional Christian viewpoint (abortion, things like that). They would send me a note and say, "How could you betray us like this?" And I'm sitting here thinking it's a taste perhaps of what the Lord felt when the Pharisees, I'm afraid to say it, would ridicule the Lord for engaging people who didn't think the way the Pharisees thought. Right? We think that behavior is gone and we've gotten beyond being pharisaical, [but] it is alive and well and we've got to recognize it in the church. And we've got to run from it, because there's two things I see in the New Testament: salvation through Christ and don't become a Pharisee. My thing is to always be true to that. . . . It's a dangerous place to be when you are judging other people in a way in which it's not your position to do that. What I want Ted to see in our relationship is the love of Christ, certainly the truth of what I believe—and I think our friendship is strong enough that Ted can bear that and vice versa. At the end of the day that's what the Lord will either smile about or frown upon. And I trust in that process.

18. For corroboration of this claim, see Marin, *Us Versus Us*.

Trimpa calls their friendship "infectious," while Daly describes it as "irresistible." Daly continues, "I think there's something really special about the Lord saying, 'Love your neighbor.' By doing that, that sincerity of care, when you feel that, you are drawn together. You have a greater openness to that human being. . . . [There is] a knittedness that occurs when you actually sincerely care about somebody. It's in us because we're made in the image of God."

As the conversation comes to a close, Daly describes his motivation to expand the tribe: quite simply, it is to spread the love of God. Turning to his friend, Trimpa says, "And I mean this very sincerely. I feel [the love of God] every time I am with you. I went through open heart surgery last August. It was a complete surprise. One day I was fine and three weeks later I was in New York going under the knife. And someone I knew was always praying for me, always checking on me, and I could feel the presence, was Jim. And that's something I will never forget."

Befriending the KKK

During his music career, Daryl Davis has played with several legends including B. B. King and the father of rock and roll, Chuck Berry. While Davis has accompanied many famous musicians through the years, he is best known for his ability to harmonize with a very different group of people—the Ku Klux Klan. Davis chronicles his provocative story in the book, *Klan-Destine Relationships: A Black Man's Odyssey in the Ku Klux Klan,* and in the film documentary *Accidental Courtesy.*

As the young son of a state department foreign service officer, Davis lived in several different countries before his family settled in a small Massachusetts town when he was ten. While living abroad, he experienced his own personal melting pot and United Nations education. Davis learned how to get along with everyone, so his first encounter with racism came as a shock. It came when he, the only person of color in his Boy Scout troop, was carrying the American flag in a parade. All went well until people started hurling projectiles at him. His first thought was, "These people must not like the Boy Scouts." [19] Later that day his parents informed him that he was the target of a hate crime, due solely to his skin color. This experience set Davis on a life-long quest to discover why anyone would hate someone they do not know simply because of their pigmentation.

19. Ornstein, dir., *Accidental Courtesy.*

This question prompted Davis to reach out to members of the KKK. He has engaged in countless civil conversations in restaurants and bars. At other times, he has hosted Klansmen in his home. On one occasion, he funded a family's cross-country trip to visit their Klansman husband and father in prison. Davis came along for the ride. Another time, he loaned his private tour bus to a group who needed transportation to a Klan rally. Some of these encounters have led to real, live, authentic friendships. While not agreeing with the majority of what his KKK conversation partners promote, Davis has worked hard to understand their perspective. Out of a sense of fairness, he even corrected a misrepresentation of the Klan during a discussion on CNN. For this deed, the president and imperial wizard of the Traditionalist American Knights, the largest KKK group in the country, presented Davis a certificate of friendship.[20]

Davis's desire for understanding and reconciliation has earned the respect of many KKK members and has led directly to dozens of resignations from the Klan, some of whom were high-ranking officials. Many of these former Klansmen have given Davis their memorabilia, including robes and hoods. He hopes one day to open a Klan history museum in which these paraphernalia can be put on display.

Not everyone in the African American community has supported Davis's work, however. Near the end of the *Accidental Courtesy* documentary, he has a tense encounter with Black Lives Matter leaders in Baltimore. During the exchange, one young protester by the name of Kwame Rose asks Davis how many robes he has collected.

> **DAVIS:** Roughly, I'd say twenty-five or twenty-six.
>
> **ROSE:** How long you been doing that for?
>
> **DAVIS:** Since about 1990.
>
> **ROSE:** And you only got twenty-six robes? So since 1990, which is longer than I've been alive, you've been trying to infiltrate the Klan but what does that do for people?
>
> **DAVIS:** I will tell you what it does. The state of Maryland had a large Klan organization. When the imperial wizard, which means national leader, turned in his robe to me, the Maryland Ku Klux Klan fell apart. Today, there is no more Ku Klux Klan in the state of Maryland.

20. Ornstein, dir., *Accidental Courtesy*.

ROSE: Infiltrating the Klan ain't freeing your people. . . . Stop wasting your time going into people's houses who don't love you. A house where they want to throw you under the basement.

DAVIS: So you believe nobody can change?

ROSE: I believe you believe the *wrong* people can change. . . . White supremacists can't change. But I can change your mind because you look like me. You ain't doing nothing but collecting something that is going to build your own credibility. You're nothing but a pimp in a pulpit.[21]

After the exchange, Davis says he has met young men like Rose before. While he doesn't agree, he understands the reaction. "A Klansman hates a white person who sells out, so to speak, more than they hate a black person. Just like [Rose] hated me more than he hated some white guy because he felt I sold out my own race. He was very definite that white people can't change. How is he going to advance any agenda in this country, as diverse as it is?"[22]

That tense encounter, however, was not the final word on the Davis-Rose relationship. When the film debuted in New York City, the producers asked both men to attend the premiere and participate in a talkback session. They agreed and spent the day getting to know each other better. After the film, Rose said, "The time I spent with Daryl today, I wish I could have spent with him before sitting down." Davis concurs: "He may not agree with me, but he understands me a lot better today and I understand him a lot better today. And it took us sitting down and just hanging out and talking."[23]

Davis and Rose were able to reconcile and it didn't require either man compromising his convictions. Davis supports the social justice work that Rose is doing in Baltimore, but will continue to expand the tribe one person at a time: "In the movie, Kwame stated that I am not freeing my people. Well, I consider everybody in this room—the Klan, Neo-Nazis, whatever—they're all my people. And granted . . . some of them will never change, but we have an obligation to make this a better society."[24]

21. Ornstein, dir., *Accidental Courtesy*.

22. Ornstein, dir., *Accidental Courtesy*.

23. Sound & Vision, "Accidental Courtesy Follow-Up."

24. Sound & Vision, "Accidental Courtesy Follow-Up."

A Doorjamb Away

Minneapolis resident Mary Johnson knows the healing power of reconciliation. During a dispute at a party, sixteen-year-old Oshea Israel shot and killed Mary's only son, twenty-year-old Laramiun Byrd. Israel was sentenced to twenty-five years, but released after serving seventeen. Israel packed up his meager belongings and moved back into Mary's neighborhood—not one block away, not one house away, but literally "one doorjamb away" from Mary.[25]

Cold. Cruel. Unthinkable. Or was it? Instead of a hard-hearted bureaucratic edict, this re-entry placement was an act of grace—something Mary requested.

After her son was murdered, Mary reacted like any mother would: "I wanted justice. He was an animal. He deserved to be caged."[26] After a dozen years of agonizing, hateful resentment, however, Mary decided to visit Oshea at Minnesota's Stillwater State Prison. As a committed Christian, she was motivated by her faith to seek reconciliation and forgiveness. With great fear and trepidation, Mary entered the prison and sat down with Oshea. She told him, "I don't know you. You don't know me. My son didn't know you. You didn't know my son. We need to lay a foundation. We need to get to know one another."[27]

Mary started by asking to hear Oshea's story. "That's the thing that made it comfortable and easy, because instead of attacking me she wanted to know about me," said Oshea. In turn, Mary began sharing details of Laramiun's life and her son became real to his killer.[28] When it was time for Mary to leave she broke down in tears and Oshea hugged her like he would his own mother. Mary recalls thinking, "I just hugged the man who murdered my son. And I instantly knew that all that anger and animosity, all the stuff I had in my heart for twelve years . . . I knew it was over, that I had totally forgiven [him]."[29]

Oshea forgiving himself was a different story. "I haven't totally forgiven myself yet," he admits. "I'm learning how to forgive myself and I'm still

25. CBS, "Power of Forgiveness."
26. CBS, "Power of Forgiveness."
27. ForgivenessVideo, "Forgiveness Project."
28. Atlanticphil, "Beyond Belief."
29. Atlanticphil, "Beyond Belief."

growing towards [that]."[30] Part of the healing process includes speaking about the power of reconciliation at churches, prisons, and schools.

Today, Mary and Oshea feel and act like family. "She's my mother now. She's my second mother." Mary agrees, "I treat him like my son. I talk to him like a son."[31] While she is grateful to have Oshea in her life, Mary admits that her original motivation was to free herself from the bondage of anger. "Unforgiveness is like cancer," says Mary. "It will eat you from the inside out. It's not about the other person. Me forgiving him does not diminish what he's done. Yes, he murdered my son. But the forgiveness is for me."[32] The forgiveness might have been for Mary, but this story is a powerful reminder to us all of what can happen when we focus on the goal of reconciliation.

Yes, And

In *The Office* episode entitled "Email Surveillance," Jim hosts a barbecue. Everyone receives an electronic invitation, except Michael. While Michael eventually crashes the party, he begins the night at his weekly improv class. Michael's improv character in each scene is an alter ego he calls Michael Scarn. As soon as someone sets up a scene, Michael pulls out fake guns (actually his hands) and starts shooting people. Eventually he shoots everyone in the scene, as well as all onlookers. Michael explains why he is fixated on guns: "Think about this. What is the most exciting thing that can happen on TV or in movies or in real life? Somebody has a gun. That's why I always start with a gun because you can't top it. You just can't."[33] The improv teacher finally has to take away all of Michael's faux weaponry.

Michael is an excellent example of bad improv, because he hijacks and derails each scene instead of respecting what his acting partners have introduced. Tina Fey, who was trained at Chicago's Second City, explains the four principles of improv in her book *Bossypants*. The first principle is *agree and say yes*. When improv partners are on stage, they need to function as teammates. When one person sets up the scene, the partner must affirm what has been created. The second principle is *yes, and*. We should not only agree with our partner, but add something of our own in a way that

30. CBS, "Power of Forgiveness."

31. Emergence Pictures, "Smooch."

32. CBS, "Power of Forgiveness."

33. *The Office*, "Email Surveillance."

advances the scene. The third principle is *make statements*. While questions can be helpful, sometimes asking questions puts too much pressure on the other person. So make sure you mix in statements. The fourth principle is *there are no mistakes*. Each conversation should be viewed through a positive lens without passing judgment on yourself or the other person. No mistakes, only opportunities.[34]

In a Google interview, Fey mentions that improv has not only advanced her professional life; these four principles have also changed her worldview and helped her improve her communication skills.[35] These improv principles can help us in our difficult conversations, as well. By beginning with affirming what the other person has introduced, we are practicing *agree and say yes*. When we build on common ground by adding something to it, we are applying *yes, and*. When we *make statements*, we participate in a real give-and-take conversation. Finally, when we resist judgment and embrace the *no mistakes*, only opportunities mind-set, we allow the conversation to organically emerge—sometimes in surprising directions.

Alan Alda discusses the power of improv when teaching the art and science of communicating well. He even explains how these principles can diffuse difficult situations. One example is the story of Larry Gelbart, a writer on the TV show *M*A*S*H*. Larry was unlocking his front door one night when a young man put a *real* gun to his head. The man wanted valuables inside the house. They went inside, but instead of protesting or putting up a fight, Larry went with it and said, "You don't need to do this. You're too smart. What if I help you get a job?" Alda says the conversation likely went much longer, "but I remember it this way because it startled me so much when Larry told me. The kid put away the gun and the next day Larry got him a job. Yes And."[36]

Some Good News

Stephen Merchant, co-creator of the original BBC version of *The Office*, reveals that one of the key inspirations for the Jim character ("Tim" in the British version) was Hawkeye Pierce, the star of *M*A*S*H*, played by none other than Alan Alda.[37] Hawkeye was charming, smart, and quick-

34. Fey, *Bossypants*, 84–85.
35. Talks at Google, "Tina Fey."
36. Alda, *If I Understood You*, 88.
37. Baumgartner, "The Pitch."

witted—just like Jim. One of the reasons *The Office* has experienced so much enduring success is because it feels real, almost like the lines are improvised. While many of the actors have been trained in improv, most of the dialogue is scripted by talented writers. Another reason for the show's enormous success is its heart. It isn't just about Michael's many cringeworthy faux pas, it is also full of well-timed and perfectly placed tender moments that elevate the spirit.

One of my favorites comes in an episode entitled "Niagara"—Jim and Pam's wedding.[38] Just as Pam is ready to walk down the aisle, Chris Brown's song "Forever" breaks out over the sound system and each member of the wedding party boogies down the aisle with memorable dance moves. This was actually an example of art imitating reality, because they re-enacted a real wedding video that had recently gone viral.[39]

One of the most elevating experiences for me during the pandemic was watching John Krasinski, the actor who played Jim, broadcast a homemade Internet show called *Some Good News*—complete with a charming banner constructed by his kids. During those dark days, Krasinski would report nothing but heartwarming stories, some humorous, others inspirational. Guest appearances included heavy hitters like Oprah and the cast of *Hamilton*. On one segment, Krasinski showed a clip of a couple who had recreated Jim's proposal to Pam outside a gas station. Due to the pandemic, however, their wedding ceremony was postponed. Through the power of Zoom, Krasinski, who had acquired an online minister's license for the occasion, performed the ceremony with Jenna Fischer as the maid of honor. After the ceremony, the rest of *The Office* cast performed an encore of their memorable down-the-aisle dance moves.[40] While there were many moments of disgust and sadness during the pandemic, this was a moment of pure, heartwarming, uplifting, inspirational joy.

The elevating reconciliation stories shared in this chapter remind us that we need to seek synchrony with those on the other side of the aisle if we are going to expand the tribe. And if we do that, our conversations will have a chance to look more like a dance down the aisle rather than a fight across one.

38. *The Office*, "Niagara, Part 2."

39. TheKeinz, "JK Wedding Dance." This video has been viewed on YouTube more than 100 million times.

40. *Some Good News*, "Cast Reunites."

Chapter 10

Treble Tactic Ten: T.H.I.N.K. Before You Post

Bass-Pounding Fallacy: All Is Fair in Love, War, and Social Media

> "We can begin to see the way that social media amplifies the cruelty and 'virtue signaling' that are recurrent features of call-out culture. . . . Mobs can rob good people of their conscience, particularly when participants wear masks (in a real mob) or are hiding behind an alias or avatar (in an online mob). Anonymity fosters deindividuation—the loss of an individual sense of self—which lessens self-restraint and increases one's willingness to go along with the mob."[1]
>
> —GREG LUKIANOFF AND JONATHAN HAIDT

The *Black Mirror* episode "Nosedive" was written by two cast members from *The Office*—Michael Schur, who played Dwight's cousin Mose, and Rashida Jones, who portrayed Karen.[2] "Nosedive" was nominated for several awards, including a Screen Actors Guild nod for Bryce Dallas Howard, who played lead protagonist Lacie Pound.

The episode is set in a world in which every daily interaction elicits a one to five rating from fellow citizens. Ratings are entered on cell phones, while eye implants allow people to see each other's current cumulative score

1. Lukianoff and Haidt, *Coddling*, 73.
2. That said, Schur's primary role on *The Office* was as a producer and writer.

and running social feed. Fluctuating scores not only affect self-esteem, they determine each person's socio-economic status.

Lacie is a 4.2—good, not great. While she does everything possible to refine her social skills and overall likeability, she has seemingly hit her ceiling. When Lacie learns that an upscale apartment is beyond her financial reach, she is told that a discount is awarded to residents with a 4.5 rating. In an effort to nudge her score higher, Lacie seeks advice from an image coach who tells her favorable ratings from "up-scale folks" will produce the desired boost.

Armed with this newfound knowledge, she posts a photo of a raggedy doll that she and childhood friend Naomi made together when they were five years old. The nostalgia of the photo seemingly causes the aloof and highly rated Naomi to invite Lacie to deliver the maid-of-honor toast at her upcoming nuptials. Lacie is thrilled because she believes Naomi's high-powered social circle will provide her the much-needed bump in her ratings.

Unfortunately for Lacie, several mishaps on the way to the wedding lower her rating. An hour before the ceremony, Naomi calls and tells her not to come. She admits to Lacie that the only reason she invited her in the first place is because "the authenticity of a 'vintage-bond low-4' at a gathering of this caliber played fantastically in all the simulations we ran. . . . But now you're a 'sub-3.' Sorry."[3]

By the end of the episode, Lacie has fallen to a socially unacceptable level. She is taken out of circulation and locked up in a cell, but only after her phone is confiscated and the implants removed from her eyes. This cautionary tale illustrates many of the pitfalls associated with a cyber-centric society, including its addictive quality, our need for perpetual validation, and the tendency to slip into a mob mentality. All of these dangers work against the goal of expanding the tribe.

Shoot an Iraqi

Three years after a drone strike brutally killed his brother, Iraqi artist Wafaa Bilal set up a controversial interactive exhibition in a Chicago art gallery. The gallery named it *Domestic Tension*; Bilal wanted to call it *Shoot an Iraqi*.[4] The idea came after Bilal watched an interview with an American soldier who orchestrates long-distance missile attacks from

3. *Black Mirror*, "Nosedive."

4. Zaki, *War for Kindness*, 144.

the safety of her Colorado base. When asked if she feels any regret over killing Iraqi citizens, she said, "No, these people are terrorists and I trust my government."[5] Bilal was struck by her carefree words, as if she were playing an innocuous video game.

Concerned with the hardening effects of technology, Bilal moved items from his apartment into the gallery, set up a website with a video chatroom, and attached a paintball gun that could be remotely fired by anyone who visited the site. For the next thirty days, he chatted with people from all over the world while attempting to dodge around-the-clock paintball strikes. His only respite came at night when he tried to grab a few winks behind protective Plexiglass. By the end of the experiment, 60,000 paintballs were fired and representatives from 138 different countries had pulled the trigger, "often while mocking him through chat messages."[6] Jamil Zaki observes:

> People who shot paintballs at Waffa Bilal and those who wish each other violent deaths in comments sections work under cover of virtual darkness. Trolls spend vast amounts of time and energy sowing pain. Anonymity tempts people to try on cruelty like a mask, knowing it won't cost them. It does, of course, cost their targets. Online harassment can follow people into their homes, their rooms, and their beds. This might help explain why teenagers who are cyberbullied contemplate and attempt suicide even more than victims of traditional bullying.[7]

Why do so many of us transform into Mr. Hyde when technology is at our fingertips? While not everyone would inflict physical pain upon Bilal, meting out emotional and mental misery is a different story. I've had countless students tell me that they post things on social media that they would never dare say directly to a person's face. Nearly all of the students I've spoken to regret something they have posted online. As a random meme points out: "Social media has made too many of you comfortable with disrespecting people and not getting punched in the mouth for it."[8] While this statement is painfully true, I've found many of my students are becoming increasingly *uncomfortable* with their online behavior. They'd like to change, but can't

5. CityLightsBooks, "Waffa Bilal discusses Shoot an Iraqi."

6. Zaki, *War for Kindness*, 145.

7. Zaki, *War for Kindness*, 148–49.

8. See https://ifunny.co/picture/social-media-has-made-too-many-of-you-comfortable-with-Bd6Gu1cO7.

seem to stop. They don't understand how reading a random tweet or post can suddenly turn them into a different person.

Of course this challenge is not unique to college students. Controlling one's online behavior is a widespread problem for older adults, as well. Tristan Harris, who has been called "the conscience of Silicon Valley," says this isn't an accident; it's by design.[9] Formerly a design ethicist for Google, Harris now runs the Center for Humane Technology, where he encourages leaders to engineer tech with a moral rudder.

Harris explains that all online platforms are vying for one thing: user attention. And "the best way to get someone's attention is to know how their mind works."[10] Harris knows what he is talking about. He was trained at Stanford's Persuasive Technology Lab, where he learned a range of psychological techniques to keep users engaged and coming back for more. These seemingly innocuous techniques include tactics like YouTube's auto-play feature that takes you from one video to the next in order to keep you on their site longer. Nearly every streaming service now uses this feature. Another is Snapchat's Snapstreaks, which tracks how many days two users have communicated with each other. This feature is designed to give "two people something they don't want to lose."[11] Many users have become so obsessed with this feature that when they go on vacation, friends are recruited to keep *all* of their streaks alive. Some wonder if this is no big deal, just the latest iteration of "talking on the phone." Harris demurs: "In the 1970s, when you were just gossiping on the telephone, there wasn't [sic] a hundred engineers on the other side of the screen who knew exactly how your psychology worked and orchestrated you into a double bind with each other."[12]

Outrage is an especially powerful and addictive technique to get not only individuals but groups hooked in. Harris says social media platforms benefit from intense emotional engagement and would rather flood newsfeeds with heated instead of calming content. "Outrage is a really good way also of getting your attention because we don't choose outrage, it happens *to* us. And if you're the Facebook newsfeed, whether you'd want to or not, you actually benefit when there's outrage because

9. Harris, "Can Truth Survive Big Tech?"

10. Harris, "Tech companies control billions of minds."

11. Harris, "Tech companies control billions of minds."

12. Harris, "Tech companies control billions of minds."

outrage doesn't just schedule time [and] space for you—we want to share that outrage with other people."[13]

A few years ago *The Wall Street Journal* created an online project called "Blue Feed, Red Feed."[14] The website allows visitors to pick a controversial topic, such as abortion or immigration, and then displays liberal and conservative Facebook newsfeeds side by side. The focus, tone, facts, and imagery of these competing stories are wildly different, reinforcing concern over social media echo chambers in which tribal communities are never exposed to different perspectives. According to Zaki, however, one thing is the same: both sides "are sickened, saddened, and outraged—all based on their empathy for victims—but each side's victims are the other's perpetrators."[15]

In a talk given at Stanford a few years ago, Chamath Palihapitiya, one of the early Facebook thought leaders, shared his remorse for the online world he helped design: "I think we have created tools that are ripping apart the social fabric. . . . The short-term, dopamine-driven feedback loops we've created are destroying how society works."[16]

The Pitchfork Posse

Back to *Black Mirror*. Ches once had a solid social score, but has now nosedived to a 3.1. On his way to work, he picks up smoothies for everyone in the office in an effort to redeem his score. After accepting the drink, Lacie rewards Ches with a high interaction rating. He breathes a sigh of relief as his score receives a slight bump. A puzzled Lacie notices nobody else is taking the smoothies. As Ches walks away, a co-worker explains that the office doesn't like him anymore and they are going to freeze him out by reducing his rating. Later in the episode, Ches begs Lacie for a few stars so he can enter the building. She refuses. Ches is officially *persona non grata*. The mob has won.

An online journalist shares how he once unwittingly whipped the Twitter world into a frenzy after exposing a fellow writer for plagiarism: "You turn around and you suddenly realize you're the head of a pitchfork mob . . . Why are they acting like heathens? I don't want to be associated with

13. Harris, "Tech companies control billions of minds."

14. *Wall Street Journal*, "Blue Feed, Red Feed."

15. Zaki, *War for Kindness*, 148.

16. Zaki, *War for Kindness*, 150.

this at all. I want to get out of here."[17] In *So You've Been Publicly Shamed*, Jon Ronson writes about the rise of online mobbing. Ronson fondly recalls the early days of Twitter as a time of hopeful idealism. The platform empowered voiceless people to speak out against legitimate abuse. "When powerful people misused their privilege, we were going to get them," remembers Ronson. "This was like the democratization of justice. Hierarchies were being leveled out; we were going to do things better."[18] But today, it isn't just the powerful; anyone is fair game.

Consider the story of Justine Sacco. A young New York City public relations executive with a modest Twitter following, Justine would periodically tweet snarky observations to her 170 Tweeps. On the first leg of a December flight from New York to South Africa, she quipped: "Weird German Dude: You're in first class. It's 2014. Get some deodorant.—Inner monolog as I inhale BO. Thank god for pharmaceuticals."[19] During a layover at London Heathrow, she decided to up the ante. About an hour before boarding a flight to Johannesburg, she tweeted: "Going to Africa. Hope I don't get AIDS. Just kidding. I'm white!" No response. Ronson imagines Justine likely experienced "that sad feeling when nobody congratulates you for being funny, that black silence when the Internet doesn't talk back."[20]

Justine boarded the plane, powered down her phone, and settled in for the eleven-hour flight. When the plane touched down and her phone powered up, she was stunned to discover that she had become the number-one worldwide trending topic on Twitter.[21] How did this happen? Cyber contact tracing revealed that someone from her tiny circle had forwarded the tweet to an online journalist who reposted it to his 15,000 followers. From there, "it was like a bolt of lightning. . . . While she slept, Twitter took control of her life and dismantled it piece by piece."[22]

Thousands of tweets like these flooded the Twittersphere that night: "'In light of @JustineSacco['s] disgusting racist tweet, I'm donating to @CARE today,' and 'How did @JustineSacco get a PR job?! Her level of racist ignorance belongs on Fox News. #AIDS can affect anyone!' and 'No words for that horribly disgusting, racist as f*** tweet from Justine Sacco. I am beyond

17. Ronson, *Publicly Shamed*, 50–51.
18. Ronson, "Online Shaming."
19. Ronson, *Publicly Shamed*, 68.
20. Ronson, *Publicly Shamed*, 68.
21. Ronson, *Publicly Shamed*, 68.
22. Ronson, "Online Shaming."

horrified.'"[23] While Justine slumbered, people in crowded pubs around the world were eagerly anticipating her imminent demise: "Seriously. I just want to go home to go to bed, but everyone in the bar is so into #HasJustineLandedYet. Can't look away. Can't leave."[24] Another person revised his holiday wish list: "All I want for Christmas is to see @JustineSacco's face when her plane lands and she checks her inbox/voicemail."[25]

Ronson recalls checking his own Twitter feed that night and noticing the growing throng. His gut reaction was to grab a pitchfork himself, but then he paused. "I'm not entirely sure that joke was intended to be racist," he thought to himself. "Instead of gleefully flaunting her privilege she was mocking the gleeful flaunting of privilege. There is a comedy tradition of this like *South Park* or Colbert or Randy Newman. Maybe Justine's crime was not being as good at it as Randy Newman."[26] When Ronson met with Justine a few weeks later, she confirmed his suspicion. "Unfortunately, I am not a character on *South Park* or a comedian, so I had no business commenting on the epidemic in such a politically incorrect manner on a public platform," admitted Justine. "To put it simply, I wasn't trying to raise awareness of AIDS, or piss off the world, or ruin my life. Living in America puts us in a bit of a bubble when it comes to what is going on in the third world. I was making fun of that bubble."[27]

Justine's name was typically Googled around thirty to forty times a month. In the two weeks following Justine's fall from grace, her name was searched 1,220,000 times.[28] Ronson interviewed an Internet economist who estimated that Google profited "between $120,000 and $468,000 on Justine's annihilation, while those of us doing the actual shaming, we got nothing. We were like unpaid shaming interns for Google."[29]

By the end of the ordeal, Justine had lost her job, her reputation, and nearly her sanity. She had culpability, to be sure. Twitter is a challenging platform for subtlety, nuance, and oblique humor. That said, Ronson had known within a matter of moments that her "tweet, whilst not a great joke, wasn't racist, but a reflexive comment on white privilege—on our tendency to

23. Ronson, *Publicly Shamed*, 69.
24. Ronson, "Online Shaming."
25. Ronson, *Publicly Shamed*, 69.
26. Ronson, "Online Shaming."
27. Ronson, *Publicly Shamed*, 73.
28. Ronson, *Publicly Shamed*, 71.
29. Ronson, "Online Shaming."

naïvely imagine ourselves immune from life's horrors."[30] How had the Twitter world missed Justine's intent—calling her out for white privilege while white privilege was the very thing *she* was attempting to call out?

And why did so many people gang up on Justine? Her story illustrates well a widespread phenomenon known as "cancel culture," which encourages us to call out those whom we perceive to be misusing their privilege.[31] "Social media amplifies the cruelty and 'virtue signaling' that are recurrent features of call-out culture," explain Greg Lukianoff and Jonathan Haidt. "Mobs can rob good people of their conscience, particularly when participants wear masks (in a real mob) or are hiding behind an alias or avatar (in an online mob). Anonymity fosters deindividuation—the loss of an individual sense of self—which lessens self-restraint and increases one's willingness to go along with the mob."[32]

Additionally, as we have learned, outrage offers a dopamine hit. Raising your pitchfork in solidarity with others intensifies the pleasure. Ronson says, "With social media, we've created a stage for instant artificial high drama. Every day a new person emerges as a magnificent hero or a sickening villain."[33] Ronson underscores the addictive quality of this phenomenon by describing his own withdrawal symptoms: "I began to feel weird and empty when there wasn't a powerful person that we could get. A day without a shaming began to feel like a day picking fingernails and treading water."[34]

Online mobbing creates widespread damage—not only to the individual under attack, but to society as a whole. While Twitter might have begun as a way to "democratize justice" and level the playing field, Justine's story illustrates how quickly and easily a person's dignity can be stripped. Distance diminishes our ability to view others as fellow human beings, entitled to due process and the benefit of the doubt. "When shamings are delivered like remotely administered drone strikes nobody needs to think

30. Ronson, *Publicly Shamed*, 73.

31. For more on "cancel culture," see Kristian, "Cancel Culture is a class issue." In this article, Kristian points out that Sacco was eventually hired back by the company that fired her.

32. Lukianoff and Haidt, *Coddling*, 73.

33. Ronson, *Publicly Shamed*, 78–79.

34. Ronson, *Publicly Shamed*, 89.

about how ferocious our collective power might be," warns Ronson. "The snowflake never needs to feel responsible for the avalanche."[35]

For Whom the Bell Trolls

One of the key takeaways from the saga of Justine Sacco is that she wasn't ripped apart by trolls emerging from their deep, dark cyber caves; she was destroyed by "nice people like us."[36] Online anonymity and pitchfork detachment can turn normal human beings into desensitized monsters. But the reverse can happen, as well. Monsters can turn back into human beings. Don't believe me? Consider the story of Lindy West.[37]

As an Internet personality and author of *Shrill: Notes from a Loud Woman*, Lindy takes controversial stands on various issues, including body size.[38] One might even call her the poster child for Meghan Trainor's *All About That Bass* body-positive message. Lindy's outspoken nature, not surprisingly, has attracted an army of trolls. She has learned how to live with most of them, but one went too far.

One day Lindy started receiving mean tweets from her father. She noticed that he had created a new Twitter account. She immediately knew something was fishy. Her dad had never been mean to her a day in his life. But the real giveaway? Her father was dead.

Lindy was devastated by this cruel act. Why would someone go so far to hurt her? She was used to personal attacks, but someone posing as her recently deceased father? Unconscionable. She didn't know how to react. "Conventional wisdom says never feed the trolls," says Lindy. "Don't respond. It's what they want." This time, however, she couldn't help herself. She chose to talk about the pain of this experience online. Then something surprising happened—the troll reached out to her. He sent an email with an apology and receipt from a donation made to the Seattle Cancer Care Alliance, where her dad had received treatment. The email led to a phone call between the two. Here's part of the exchange:

LINDY: How did you even find out that my dad died?

35. Ronson, *Publicly Shamed*, 56.

36. Ronson, "Online Shaming."

37. West, "For Whom the Bell Trolls." The direct quotes in this section all come from this podcast.

38. West, *Shrill*. The Hulu series *Shrill* is based on Lindy's life story.

TROLL: I went to my computer. I Googled you, found out you had a father who had passed. I found out that he had—you had siblings. I forget if it was three total.

LINDY: I have two siblings. Did you read his obituary?

TROLL: I believe I did. I knew he was a musician.

LINDY: Yeah, I wrote that. I wrote his obituary.

TROLL: What I did was this. I created a fake Gmail account using your father's name. Created a fake Twitter account using his name. The biography was something to the effect of, my name is—um, sorry, I forget the name—the first name.

LINDY: His name was Paul West.

TROLL: I wrote, my name is Paul West. I've got three kids. Two of them are great and one of them is an idiot.

LINDY: Yeah, you said, "Embarrassed father of an idiot."

TROLL: OK.

LINDY: "Other two kids are fine, though."

TROLL: That's much more worse.

LINDY: And you got a picture of him.

TROLL: I did get a picture of him.

LINDY: Do you remember anything about him? Did you get a sense of him as a human being?

TROLL: I read the obit and I knew he was a dad that loved his kids.

LINDY: How did that make you feel?

TROLL: Not good. I mean, I felt horrible almost immediately afterwards. You tweeted something along the lines of, "Good job today, society." Or something along those lines.

LINDY: Yeah.

TROLL: It just wouldn't—for the first time, it wouldn't leave my mind. Usually, I would put out all this Internet hate and oftentimes I would just forget about it. This one would not leave me. It would not leave me. I started thinking about you because I know you had read it. And I'm thinking, how would she feel? And the next day, I wrote you.

LINDY (in tears): Yeah. Well, I—

TROLL: And I truly am sorry about that.

LINDY (in tears): Yeah, I mean, have you lost anyone? Can you imagine? Can you imagine?

TROLL: I can. I can. I don't know what else to say except that I'm sorry.

LINDY (in tears): Well, you know, I get abuse all day, every day. It's part of my job. And this was the meanest thing anyone's ever done to me.

TROLL: Oh.

LINDY (in tears): I mean, it was really fresh. He had just died. But you're also—you're the only troll who has ever apologized. Not just to me. I've never heard of this happening before. I mean, I don't know anyone who's ever—who's ever gotten an apology. And I just—I mean, you know, thank you.

TROLL: I'm glad that you have some solace.

Lindy admits that the conversation did provide solace. She was able to offer forgiveness and feel empathy, as well. Elsewhere in the exchange, her troll explained that he struggled with his own body image and rudderless life. Trolling helped fill that void, albeit in a terribly destructive way. He told Lindy that his trolling days had come to an end. She believes him. "It's so difficult to believe that anyone ever really changes," says Lindy. "And he did it. I found immense comfort in that."

This inspiring exchange brings together many of the treble tactics we've considered in this book: speaking to the elephant, exhibiting humility, listening to the other person's story, cultivating empathy, tapping into the imagination, resisting demonization, finding the humanity in the other, extending forgiveness, forging reconciliation, expanding the tribe. They are all here in one powerful conversation.

It's also a tale of two polar opposite emotions: disgust and elevation. At the beginning of the story, who doesn't despise Lindy's troll? He's a despicable low-life, as bad as it gets, beyond redemption. By the end, however, you feel something for him. At least I did. And Lindy did, too. "Trolls still waste my time and tax my mental health on a daily basis," admits Lindy. "But honestly,

I don't wish them any pain. Their pain is what got us here in the first place. That's what I learned from my troll. . . . I can't give purpose and fulfillment to millions of anonymous strangers, but I can remember not to lose sight of their humanity the way they lost sight of mine."

Redeeming Technology

It's easy to think the Internet is nothing but a bottomless pit of bile, but Lindy's story reminds us that there are tales of inspiration and empathy to be found online as well. Sixty-thousand paintballs were fired at Wafaa Bilal, yet at the end of thirty days he was also moved by the compassion of strangers. Reflecting upon 33,000 pages of chatroom exchanges, which included an encouraging number of uplifting messages, Wafaa says, "This project changed my life forever and it gave me hope in humanity."[39] Megan Phelps-Roper originally took to Twitter to spread the Westboro gospel of hate, but the kindness she encountered online transformed her life. "Twitter is a cesspool because we make it a cesspool," says Megan. "We get to decide how we are going to engage people. We can give in to the very human impulses to respond in outrage when we see things that are outrageous or we can decide there's a human being on the other side of this. . . . The way out was not to shame me but to help me see outside of it."[40]

Tristan Harris is working to create a more ethical and compassionate cyber experience. Imagine a world in which software is designed to not only check for spelling and grammar, but for compassion as well. What if every post ran through a kindness filter and gave the user a moment of pause and reflection before pressing send? Harris also suggests instituting a Hippocratic oath for the technology industry. As doctors are required to do no harm, software and platform developers would make a similar principled pledge to creating a more life-affirming online world.[41]

The final scene of "Nosedive" shows Lacie Pound sitting in her cell. She and a fellow inmate begin to belittle each other. Their exchange escalates without restraint until the mutual verbal assault reaches a deafening crescendo. The lesson? While incarcerated, they are finally free. Free from their devices, free to say whatever they want, free from mob mentality, free from the fear of social judgment. While this might give the illusion

39. CityLightsBooks, "Shoot an Iraqi."

40. Phelps-Roper, "Amends."

41. Harris, "Tech could protect us."

of liberty, we can do better. Abusing people face to face is no better than doing it through technology.

Sometimes, perhaps, we just overthink it. One day a random meme popped up on my feed. It offered some commonsense advice in the form of the acronym T.H.I.N.K.: Before we post, we should ask ourselves the following five questions: Is it True? Is it Helpful? Is it Inspiring? Is it Necessary? Is it Kind?[42] If we would just stop and T.H.I.N.K. before posting, there'd be a little more treble in our bass-pounding world.

42. Pilakowski, "T.H.I.N.K. Before You Post."

Conclusion

"In any given moment, we can turn empathy up or down like the volume knob on a stereo: learning to listen to a difficult colleague, or staying strong for a suffering relative. Over time, we can fine-tune our emotional capacities, building compassion for distant strangers, outsiders, and even other species."[1]

—JAMIL ZAKI

A decade after appearing in three episodes of *The Office*, Amy Adams starred in *Arrival*, a film that received eight Academy Award nominations. Adams plays the role of internationally respected linguist Louise Banks. When a dozen alien space craft simultaneously land at strategic locations throughout the world, Banks is recruited by the United States military to decipher their intent.

Banks begins to communicate with two of the seven-limbed aliens through a transparent barrier. When Banks has assembled a rudimentary shared lexicon, she asks the visitors why they have come to earth. They tell her to "offer weapon." This news travels quickly around the world. China, Russia, Sudan, and Pakistan all declare war. The aliens are given twenty-four hours to leave our planet.

Banks, however, is not convinced of hostile intent. The term translated as "weapon" is ambiguous and open to other possible interpretations. She learns from a US colonel that China has been communicating with the aliens by using a zero-sum game. Banks explains the challenge with this approach:

1. Zaki, *War for Kindness*, 15.

"Well, let's say that I taught them chess instead of English. Every conversation would be a game. Every idea expressed through opposition, victory, defeat. You see the problem? If all I ever gave you was a hammer . . ." The colonel finishes the sentence: "everything looks like a nail."

As the world prepares for battle, Banks feverishly rushes to crack the code. Just before the war of the worlds is launched, she discovers the aliens aren't offering a "weapon," but rather a "gift." Their *language* turns out to be the offering, rewiring the brain and allowing humans to perceive the future.[2]

One of my former students (who also happens to be my son, Ryan) saw *Arrival* when it came out in November 2016. He posted the following on Facebook:

> The past few days have been for me, like many others, pretty hard. I was in shock about the results of Tuesday's election. I've never been a supporter of Hillary Clinton (and please don't take this post as support for her now) but Trump scared me.
>
> The next day I was blindsided by the grief I felt knowing he would be our next president. I worried about my health issues and what would happen with my health insurance. I worried about my friends of different races and sexual orientations and the persecution they could face. I worried about the entire direction I thought this country was headed.
>
> Then last night, after a slightly less depressing day, I went to see the movie *Arrival* and it could not have come at a better time. This movie inspired me. It showed me that we shouldn't assume things about others when we don't understand them. It showed me that one of the biggest dangers to our country and our world is how divided we have become. It also taught me not to be afraid of the future. To have hope, that if we can come to each other with open hearts and open minds we can heal as a nation. . . . I don't know how to fix our country but I believe that if we can start taking steps toward understanding, with love and compassion, then we will be on our way.
>
> "So now I am giving you a new commandment: Love each other. Just as I have loved you, you should love each other."—John 13:34[3]

2. Villeneuve, dir., *Arrival*.

3. R. Burson, "Arrival." Ryan is not only a lover of movies, he is a filmmaker himself. To see his portfolio, go to: https://vimeo.com/281039744.

As Ryan points out, this film contains several lessons for our current militant moment. People on the other side of our cultural divide seem like hostile aliens. We don't understand *them*. Rather than doing the hard work of figuring *them* out, we'd rather vilify and demonize—assuming the worst. This movie, however, inspires us to pursue the more noble path of engaging the elephant, honoring the sacred, and expanding the tribe.

As we've learned in the preceding pages, stories, in whatever form, have the power to elicit hope and elevate the spirit. At a time when our country has been fighting a pandemic on the one hand and a culture war on the other, hope and elevation are two sentiments in short supply. It is my prayer that the stories shared in this book have offered encouragement. I, personally, am moved by the warmth of Tony and Bart Campolo; the imagination of empathy leaders Sue Rahr and the two Bobs; the convicted civility of Richard Mouw; the contrition of Drew Brees; the chútzpah of Gregory Boyle; the surprising friendship of Jim Daly and Ted Trimpa; the courage of Daryl Davis; the grace of Mary Johnson; the good news of John Krasinski; the strength of Lindy West; and the tenacity of Megan Phelps-Roper, who continues to hold out hope for her Westboro family. All have turned up the treble in pleasing ways.

On that note, let's conclude with one final elevating story. Whitney Tilson was walking his dog one Sunday outside his Fifth Avenue apartment when he noticed a group of people descending upon Central Park like foreign invaders. There was a flurry of activity with trucks unloading boxes, tarps, and supplies. Hours later tents were rising up out of the ground. Tilson learned that the group was called Samaritan's Purse, a medical mission ministry founded by Franklin Graham. They were there to build a field hospital to treat overflow COVID patients. Tilson hadn't heard of the organization, but decided to volunteer. His assistance was gladly accepted.

A former hedge-fund manager who publishes a financial newsletter out of his high-rise apartment, Tilson had been looking for a way to lend a hand. New York City was on the leading edge of the pandemic and he'd felt powerless to do anything about it. He threw himself into the work, volunteering from dawn to dusk for several consecutive days. He helped construct tents. He donated sleds and shovels to transport and spread mulch. He and his daughters made several runs to Costco, packing the car with drinks and snacks for the overworked and famished medical staff. He recruited friends to donate their time and resources.

Not everyone was so enthusiastic about Samaritan's Purse coming to town. Rumors began to circulate that Graham's organization was demanding volunteers to sign anti-gay pledges. Others said they were forcing people to convert before treatment would be administered. Neither rumor was true. Tilson, who is not religious, chose to record a video to address the rumors and explain his involvement.[4] Filming in his home office, an emotional Tilson made it clear that while he doesn't agree with Samaritan's Purse on issues such as LGBT equality and women's reproductive rights, he is willing to set his ideological differences aside for a common cause.

> I'm not going to have arguments with them over those beliefs. We can do that later. I probably will do that later with some of these people who I now consider my brothers and sisters. It is very emotional to me. Look, I'm not a religious person but they're here doing God's work. And what motivates them is not proselytizing and this other nonsense I'm hearing. It's because they believe God is telling them to go heal people and help people in distress and save lives. That's what they're doing here. It's not some sham. . . . These people have been doing this for a long time. They are a well-oiled machine. It's amazing in four days they've put up a world-class critical-care facility with sixty-eight critical-care beds with ventilators [and] a whole team of nurses and doctors.[5]

For his volunteer work and kind words, Tilson received a personal thank you from Franklin Graham and an invitation to visit the organization's North Carolina headquarters. "He's a great human being," Graham said of Tilson. "He might disagree with me, and I might disagree with him, but that's not going to stop us from working together to help people."[6] As we learned from previous stories, something beautiful and powerful happens when we use our talents as gifts rather than weapons. People on the other side of an issue move from aliens from another planet to fellow tribe members.

So what are we waiting for? Let's roll up our sleeves and get to work.

4. Tilson, "Thank you to Samaritan's Purse."
5. Tilson, "Thank you to Samaritan's Purse."
6. Shimron, "Samaritan's Purse Finds an Unlikely Champion."

Bibliography

Aaron Whittier Channel. "Heineken Worlds Apart OpenYourWorld 1." April 26, 2017. Video, 4:25. https://www.youtube.com/watch?v=dKggA9k8DKw.

ABC. "Marshall Curry Accepts the Oscar for Live Action Short." February 9, 2020. Video, 1:46. https://www.youtube.com/watch?v=DJR3Tz-oaS8.

Adichie, Chimamanda Ngozi. "The Danger of a Single Story." Filmed October 2009 at TEDGlobal 2009. Video, 18:34. https://www.ted.com/talks/chimamanda_ngozi_adichie_the_danger_of_a_single_story.

Akins, Robert. "Segment 1." The Digital Collections of the National WWII Museum. 2015. Video, 1:21:34. https://www.nationalww2museum.org/about-us/notes-museum/robert-ray-akins.

Alda, Alan. *If I Understood You, Would I Have This Look on My Face? My Adventures in the Art and Science of Relating and Communicating*. New York: Random House, 2017.

AnnArborIsAW**** Channel. "Ohio State-Michigan ESPN commercials." December 5, 2006. Video, :57. https://www.youtube.com/watch?v=Zvo_EpF5SyY.

Atlanticphil Channel. "Beyond Belief." February 4, 2014. Video, 4:26. https://www.youtube.com/watch?v=p6bLw4-2i8A.

Baker, Mike, Jennifer Valentino-DeVries, Manny Fernandez, and Michael LaForgia. "Three Words. 70 Cases. The Tragic History of 'I Can't Breathe.'" *New York Times*, June 29, 2020. https://www.nytimes.com/interactive/2020/06/28/us/i-cant-breathe-police-arrest.html?auth=login-facebook&campaign_id=9&emc=edit_nn_20200629&instance_id=19843&nl=themorning®i_id=57721415&segment_id=32114&te=1&user_id=86d0e9a281880326d1a253598a1df880.

Banaji, Mahzarin R., and Anthony G. Greenwald. *Blindspot: Hidden Biases of Good People*. New York: Bantam, 2016.

Barrett, Justin L. *Born Believers: The Science of Children's Religious Belief*. New York: Free, 2012.

Basinger, David. *The Case for Freewill Theism: A Philosophical Assessment*. Downers Grove, IL: InterVarsity, 1996.

Baumgartner, Brian. "OK, Here's the Pitch." *An Oral History of the Office* (podcast). July 14, 2020. https://open.spotify.com/episode/1xMkBMHjRlVyoCUuWlImhP.

Black Mirror. "Men Against Fire." Series 3, episode 5. Directed by Jakob Verbruggen. Written by Charlie Brooker. Netflix, originally aired October 21, 2016.

———. "Nosedive." Series 3, episode 1. Directed by Joe Wright. Story by Charlie Brooker. Written by Michael Schur and Rashida Jones. Netflix, originally aired October 21, 2016.

Bloom, Paul. *Against Empathy: The Case for Rational Compassion*. New York: HarperCollins, 2016.

———. *Descartes' Baby: How the Science of Child Development Explains What Makes Us Human*. New York: Basic, 2004.

Boyle, Gregory. "Compassion and Kinship: Fr Gregory Boyle at TEDxConejo 2012." TEDx Talks. June 20, 2012. Video, 20:39. https://www.youtube.com/watch?v=ipRokWt1Fkc.

———. *Tattoos on the Heart: The Power of Boundless Compassion*. New York: Free, 2010.

Brees, Drew. "Drew Brees beams with pride as he discusses his late grandfather." New Orleans Saints on NOLA.com Channel. December 27, 2017. Video, 5:10. https://www.youtube.com/watch?v=wGYZ1i7VfdM.

———. "Drew Brees talks return of NFL season and potential return of kneeling protests." Yahoo! Finance website. June 3, 2020. Video, 12:23. https://finance.yahoo.com/video/drew-brees-nfl-season-well-154642768.html.

Brewer, Jerry. "Drew Brees was the saddest kind of wrong." *Washington Post*, June 4, 2020. https://www.washingtonpost.com/sports/2020/06/04/drew-brees-is-wrong-he-can-be-reached/.

Burson, Ashley. "Saw Joker this afternoon and all I want is to be his friend." Facebook, October 2019.

Burson, Ryan. "Arrival." Facebook, November 11, 2016.

Burson, Scott R. *Brian McLaren in Focus: A New Kind of Apologetics*. Abilene, TX: Abilene Christian University Press, 2016.

Burson, Scott R., and Jerry L. Walls. *C. S. Lewis and Francis Schaeffer: Lessons for a New Century from the Most Influential Apologists of Our Time*. Downers Grove, IL: InterVarsity, 1998.

Campolo, Tony, and Bart Campolo. *Why I Left, Why I Stayed: Conversations Between an Evangelical Father and His Humanist Son*. New York: HarperCollins, 2017.

CBS. "The Power of Forgiveness." June 7, 2011. Video, 3:28. https://www.youtube.com/watch?v=02BITY-3Mp4&t=58s.

Cikara, Mina. "Us Versus Them." The Brainwaves Video Anthology Channel. October 3, 2018. Video, 5:31. https://www.youtube.com/watch?v=YJgQQ_SXBm8.

CityLightsBooks Channel. "Waffa Bilal discusses Shoot an Iraqi." July 23, 2008. Video, 2:21. https://www.youtube.com/watch?v=DcyquvDEeoo.

Clemins, Patrick. "African Elephants." Dr. Dolittle Project website. https://speechlab.eece.mu.edu/dolittle/proj_afelephant.html.

CNN. "Drew Brees faces backlash for remark about taking a knee during national anthem." June 4, 2020. Video, 9:57. https://www.youtube.com/watch?v=nBFryxQ3SLI.

———. "Obama discusses Kaepernick's anthem protest." September 28, 2016. Video, 3:41. https://www.youtube.com/watch?v=VPqOotT_ta8.

Covey, Stephen R. *The 7 Habits of Highly Effective People: Powerful Lessons in Personal Change*. New York: Fireside, 1989.

Curry, Marshall. "The Neighbors' Window—Oscar Winning Short Film." December 21, 2019. Video, 20:37. https://www.youtube.com/watch?v=k1vCrsZ80M4.

Davis, Daryl. *Klan-destine Relationships: A Black Man's Odyssey in the Ku Klux Klan*. Far Hills, NJ: New Horizon, 2005.

Dawkins, Richard. "Atheists for Jesus." The Rational Response Squad website. December 11, 2006. https://www.rationalresponders.com/atheists_for_jesus_a_richard_dawkins_essay.

———. *The God Delusion*. New York: Mariner, 2008.

———. "Richard Dawkins in Conversation with Julia Sweeney—June 9, 2015 in Rochester, MN." Richard Dawkins Foundation for Reason & Science Channel. October 29, 2015. Video, 1:38:04. https://www.youtube.com/watch?v=cYpk20XwPgQ.

Demby, Gene. "A Decade of Watching Black People Die." *Code Switch* (podcast). May 31, 2020. https://www.npr.org/2020/05/29/865261916/a-decade-of-watching-black-people-die.

Des Hammond Channel. "The Very Best of Sergeant Schultz." March 20, 2017. Video, 5:43. https://www.youtube.com/watch?v=OsXrpx04uCo.

Dittman, M. "Hughes's germ phobia revealed in psychological autopsy." *Monitor on Psychology* vol. 36, no. 7 (July/August 2005). https://www.apa.org/monitor/julaug05/hughes.

Duriez, Colin. *The C. S. Lewis Handbook*. Grand Rapids: Baker, 1994.

Emergence Pictures. "Smooch–Early Trailer." November 18, 2010. Video, 4:21. https://www.youtube.com/watch?v=OqkcLQrtwPg.

ESPN. "Maria Taylor shares a passionate message on Drew Brees' comments and apologies, First Take." June 5, 2020. Video, 6:49. https://www.youtube.com/watch?v=BKR1kKO-TV4.

Etter, Nicole Sweeney. "Listening to the Animal Kingdom." *Discover: Marquette University Research and Scholarship* (2008)14–15.

Feinberg, John S. "God, Freedom and Evil in Calvinist Thinking." In *The Grace of God, the Bondage of the Will*, vol. 2, edited by Thomas R. Schreiner and Bruce A. Ware, 459–83. Grand Rapids: Baker, 1995.

Ferguson, Michael. "This Is Your Brain on God." TED Talks Channel. October 7, 2016. Video, 14:03. https://www.youtube.com/watch?v=ocuqguH1OIw.

Fey, Tina. *Bossypants*. New York: Reagan Arthur, 2011.

Fischer, Austin. *Young, Restless, No Longer Reformed: Black Holes, Love, and a Journey In and Out of Calvinism*. Eugene, OR: Cascade, 2014.

ForgivenessVideo Channel. "The Forgiveness Project: Mary Johnson and Oshea Israel." October 17, 2014. Video, 6:47. https://www.youtube.com/watch?v=JJDqceiwR2U.

Gerson, Michael. "Neuroscientist Andrew Newberg on the Brain and Faith." *Washington Post*, April 15, 2009. http://www.washingtonpost.com/wp-dyn/content/article/2009/04/14/AR2009041401879.html.

G4ViralVideos Channel. "Trump Tells NFL Owners 'Get That Son Of A Bitch Off The Field' in Alabama Speech." YouTube, September 23, 2017. Video, 2:17. https://www.youtube.com/watch?v=zcHTifjFIxU.

Gladwell, Malcolm. "Chutzpah vs. Chutzpah." *Revisionist History* (podcast). Season 4, episode 9. http://revisionisthistory.com/episodes/39-chutzpah-vs-chutzpah.

Glass, Ira. "If You Don't Have Anything Nice to Say, SAY IT IN ALL CAPS." *This American Life* (podcast). January 23, 2015. https://www.thisamericanlife.org/545/if-you-dont-have-anything-nice-to-say-say-it-in-all-caps.

Goldman, Kim. "What's Your Son Worth?" *Confronting: O. J. Simpson* (podcast). Episode 8. July 24, 2019. https://wondery.com/shows/confronting-oj-simpson/#.

Goleman, Daniel. *Social Intelligence: The New Science of Human Relationships*. New York: Bantam, 2006.

Good Morning America. "This man left hand sanitizer and toilet paper on his doorstep for delivery workers." April 1, 2020. Video, :30. https://www.youtube.com/watch?v =EUXq58mMxro.

Gottman, John, and Nan Silver. *The Seven Principles for Making Marriage Work: A Practical Guide from the Nation's Foremost Relationship Expert*. New York: Three Rivers, 1999.

Gros, Frédéric. *A Philosophy of Walking*. New York: Verso, 2014.

Haidt, Jonathan. "Can a Divided America Heal?" Filmed November 2016 at TEDNYC. Video, 20:09. https://www.ted.com/talks/jonathan_haidt_can_a_divided_america_heal#t-1178581.

———. *The Happiness Hypothesis: Finding Modern Truth in Ancient Wisdom*. New York: Basic, 2006.

———. "The moral roots of liberals and conservatives." Filmed March 2008 at TED2008. Video, 18:08. https://www.ted.com/talks/jonathan_haidt_the_moral_roots_of_liberals_and_conservatives?language=en.

———. *The Righteous Mind: Why Good People Are Divided by Politics and Religion*. New York: Pantheon, 2012.

Haidt, Jonathan, and Sam Abrams. "The Top 10 Reasons American Politics Are So Broken." *Washington Post*, January 7, 2015. https://www.washingtonpost.com/news/wonk/wp/2015/01/07/the-top-10-reasons-american-politics-are-worse-than-ever-/?utm_term=.0a2ee0bb9df7.

Hallowell, Billy. "Lee Strobel Details Conversation He Had With Hugh Hefner About God, Gospel." *The Christian Post*, October 7, 2017. https://www.christianpost.com/news/lee-strobel-details-conversation-he-had-with-hugh-hefner-about-god-gospel.html.

Hansen, Collin. "Still Young, Restless, and Reformed? The New Calvinists at 10." 9Marks website, February 5, 2019. https://www.9marks.org/article/still-young-restless-and-reformed-the-new-calvinists-at-10/.

———. *Young, Restless, Reformed: A Journalist's Journey with the New Calvinists*. Wheaton, IL: Crossway, 2008.

Harris, Tristan. "Can Truth Survive Big Tech? Tristan Harris." July 21, 2020. Video, 4:08. https://www.youtube.com/watch?v=wHQQFOv7QgQ.

———. "How a handful of tech companies control billions of minds every day." Filmed April 2017 at TED2017. Video, 16:53. https://www.ted.com/talks/tristan_harris_how_a_handful_of_tech_companies_control_billions_of_minds_every_day.

———. "How better tech could protect us from distraction." Filmed December 2014 at TEDxBrussels. Video, 14:48. https://www.ted.com/talks/tristan_harris_how_better_tech_could_protect_us_from_distraction.

Henrich, Joseph, Steven J. Heine, and Ara Norenzayan. "The weirdest people in the world?" *Behavioral and Brain Sciences* 33, no. 2 (June 2010) 61–135.

Homeboy Industries. "Our Founder: Father Greg." Homeboy Industries Website. https://homeboyindustries.org/our-story/father-greg/.

James, Lebron. Twitter Post. June 3, 2020, 3:47 PM. https://twitter.com/kingjames/status/1268268213013327872.

Jenkins, Jerry. "Letter to the editor." *Christianity Today*, vol. 41, no. 5 (April 28, 1997) 8.

Jenkins, Malcolm. "Malcolm Jenkins Tells Drew Brees to STFU." Highlight Lab Channel. June 3, 2020. Video, 4:20. https://www.youtube.com/watch?v=ljO-TXjk3-Y.

Jennings, Greg. "Greg Jennings explains why Drew Brees' comments were a disappointment to many." First Things First Channel. June 4, 2020. Video, 13:03. https://www.youtube.com/watch?v=kq8P8lQUL50.

Jennings, Timothy R. *The God-Shaped Brain: How Changing Your View of God Transforms Your Life*. Downers Grove, IL: InterVarsity, 2013.

Kahneman, Daniel. *Thinking, Fast and Slow*. New York: Farrar, Straus and Giroux, 2012.

Kindy, Kimberly. "Creating Guardians, Calming Warriors." *Washington Post*, December 10, 2015. https://www.washingtonpost.com/sf/investigative/2015/12/10/new-style-of-police-training-aims-to-produce-guardians-not-warriors/.

Kristian, Bonnie. "Cancel Culture is a class issue." *The Week*, July 15, 2020. https://theweek.com/articles/925427/cancel-culture-class-issue.

KTVU. "Colin Kaepernick explains why he won't stand during national anthem." August 29, 2016. Video, 18:23. https://www.youtube.com/watch?v=ka0446tibig.

LeDoux, Joseph E. *The Emotional Brain: The Mysterious Underpinnings of Emotional Life*. New York: Simon & Schuster, 1996.

Lewis, C. S. "Christian Apologetics." In *God in the Dock*, 89–103. Grand Rapids: Eerdmans, 1970.

———. *Mere Christianity*. New York: Macmillan, 1960.

———. "Sometimes Fairy Stories May Say Best What's to Be Said." In *Of Other Worlds: Essays and Stories*, edited by Walter Hooper, 35–38. New York: Harcourt, Brace and World, 1966.

———. *Surprised by Joy*. New York: Harcourt Brace, 1956.

———. "Man or Rabbit?" In *God in the Dock*, 108–13. Grand Rapids: Eerdmans, 1970.

Lyons, Gabe. "Unlikely Allies: Ted Trimpa & Jim Daly." *Q* (podcast). May 18, 2016. Episode 8. https://qpodcast.libsyn.com/episode-008-unlikely-allies-ted-trimpa-jim-daly.

Lukianoff, Greg, and Jonathan Haidt. *The Coddling of the American Mind: How Good Intentions and Bad Ideas Are Setting Up a Generation for Failure*. New York: Penguin, 2018.

Marin, Andrew. *Us Versus Us: The Untold Story of Religion and the LGBT Community*. Colorado Springs, CO: NavPress, 2016.

Marty, Martin E. *By Way of Response*. Nashville: Abingdon, 1981.

McCauley, Robert N. *Why Religion Is Natural and Science Is Not*. New York: Oxford University Press, 2011.

McCoy, Terrence. "The inside story of the 'white dress, blue dress' drama that divided a planet." *Washington Post*, February 27, 2015. https://www.washingtonpost.com/news/morning-mix/wp/2015/02/27/the-inside-story-of-the-white-dress-blue-dress-drama-that-divided-a-nation/?utm_term=.abf67f9084ba.

McLaren, Brian D. "60 gifts I'm grateful for (Part 5)." brianmclaren.net website, May 8, 2016. https://brianmclaren.net/60-gifts-im-grateful-for-part-5/.

———. *A New Kind of Christianity*. New York: HarperOne, 2010.

Mohler, R. Albert, Jr., Bruce Ware, Gregory Wills, Jim Hamilton, and Stephen Wellum. "Panel Discussion—New Kind of Christianity?—Brian McLaren Recasts the Gospel." Filmed March 11, 2010 at Southern Baptist Theological Seminary, Louisville, KY. http://www.sbts.edu/resources/chapel/chapel-spring-2010/panel-discussion-a-new-kind-of-christianity-brian-mclaren-recasts-the-gospel/.

Morris, Thomas V. *Making Sense of It All: Pascal and the Meaning of Life*. Grand Rapids: Eerdmans, 1992.

Mouw, Richard J. *Adventures in Evangelical Civility: A Lifelong Quest for Common Ground.* Grand Rapids: Brazos, 2016.

———. *Calvinism in the Las Vegas Airport: Making Connections in Today's World.* Grand Rapids: Zondervan, 2004.

———. "Richard Mouw—A Journey Toward Convicted Civility." M. J. Murdock Charitable Trust. June 4, 2018. Video, 4:58. https://www.youtube.com/watch?v=IFoe3_-A3tE&list=PLgTCfn6PJIRi24XHTmiE_MmncdRwoonMm&index=2.

———. "Richard Mouw—Common Grace for the Common Good." M. J. Murdock Charitable Trust. June 4, 2018. Video, 9:42. https://www.youtube.com/watch?v=c55 7tDT1Blo&list=PLgTCfn6PJIRi24XHTmiE_MmncdRwoonMm&index=3.

Netflix Film Club Channel. "American Factory: A Short Conversation with the Obamas." August 21, 2019. Video, 3:09. https://www.youtube.com/watch?v=NRSoYDUf-Yc.

Newbigin, Lesslie. *The Open Secret.* Rev. ed. Grand Rapids: Eerdmans, 1995.

Newberg, Andrew, and Mark Robert Waldman. *How God Changes Your Brain.* New York: Ballantine, 2009.

New York Times. "Magazine—Can Babies Tell Right from Wrong?" May 13, 2020. Video, 5:12. https://www.youtube.com/watch?v=HBW5vdhr_PA&t=7s.

The Office. "Business School." Season 3, episode 17. Directed by Joss Whedon. Written by Brent Forrester. NBC, originally aired February 15, 2007.

———. "Dwight's Speech." Season 2, episode 17. Directed by Charles McDougall. Written by Paul Lieberstein. NBC, originally aired March 2, 2006.

———. "Email Surveillance." Season 2, episode 9. Directed by Paul Feig. Written by Jennifer Celotta. NBC, originally aired November 22, 2005.

———. "Halloween." Season 2, episode 5. Directed by Paul Feig. Written by Greg Daniels. NBC, originally aired October 18, 2005.

———. "Niagara, Part 2." Season 6, episode 5. Directed by Paul Feig. Written by Greg Daniels and Mindy Kaling. NBC, originally aired October 8, 2009.

———. "The Merger." Season 3, episode 8. Directed by Ken Whittingham. Written by Brent Forrester. NBC, originally aired November 16, 2006.

Ornstein, Matt, dir. *Accidental Courtesy: Daryl Davis, Race & America.* Los Angeles, CA: Sound and Vision Productions, 2015.

Pascal, Blaise. *Pascal's Pensées.* New York: E. P. Dutton, 1958.

Peterson, Robert A., and Michael D. Williams. *Why I am Not an Arminian.* Downers Grove, IL: InterVarsity, 2004.

Phelps-Roper, Megan. "I grew up in the Westboro Baptist Church. Here's why I left." Filmed in February 2017 at TEDNYC. Video, 15:10. https://www.youtube.com/watch?v=bVV2Zk88beY.

———. "Leaving the Westboro Baptist Church, Megan Phelps-Roper, Oxford Union." OxfordUnion Channel. December 10, 2019. Video, 45:41. https://www.youtube.com/watch?v=wGeQFLMrpBQ.

———. "Megan Phelps-Roper on Westboro Baptist Church and 'trying to make amends.'" *BBC HARDtalk* Channel. May 25, 2020, 24:40. https://www.youtube.com/watch?v=4jBcDao4ft4.

———. *Unfollow: A Memoir of Loving and Leaving the Westboro Baptist Church.* New York: Farrar, Straus and Giroux, 2019.

Phillips, Todd, dir. *Joker.* Burbank, CA: Warner Brothers, 2019.

Pilakowski, Melissa. "T.H.I.N.K. Before You Post." Technology Pursuit Website. October 18, 2015. https://technologypursuit.edublogs.org/2015/10/18/t-h-i-n-k-before-you-post/.

Piper, John. "An interview with John Piper." In *Suffering and the Sovereignty of God*, edited by John Piper and Justin Taylor, 220–21. Wheaton, IL: Crossway, 2006.

———. *Desiring God*. Sisters, OR: Multnomah, 1986.

Pippert, Rebecca Manley. *Out of the Saltshaker and into the World: Evangelism as a Way of Life*. Downers Grove, IL: InterVarsity, 1979.

Rao, Sonia. "'The Office' was always popular. But Netflix made it a phenomenon." *Washington Post*, June 26, 2019. https://www.washingtonpost.com/arts-entertainment/2019/06/26/office-was-always-popular-netflix-made-it-phenomenon/.

Rauch, Jonathan. "Have our tribes become more important than our country?" *Washington Post*, February 16, 2018. https://www.washingtonpost.com/outlook/have-our-tribes-become-more-important-than-our-country/2018/02/16/2f8ef9b2-083a-11e8-b48c-b07fea957bd5 story.html.

Richards, Sam. "A radical experiment in empathy." Filmed October 2010 at TEDxPSU. Video, 17:52. https://www.ted.com/talks/sam_richards_a_radical_experiment_in_empathy.

Rohr, Richard. *Eager to Love: The Alternative Way of Francis of Assisi*. Cincinnati: Franciscan Media, 2014.

Ronson, Jon. *So You've Been Publicly Shamed*. New York: Riverhead, 2015.

———. "When Online Shaming Goes Too Far." Filmed June 2015 at TEDGlobalLondon. Video, 17:03. https://www.ted.com/talks/jon_ronson_when_online_shaming_goes_too_far.

Schaeffer, Francis A. *The God Who Is There*, vol. 1, bk. 1 of *The Complete Works of Francis A. Schaeffer*. Westchester, IL: Crossway, 1982.

———. *The Mark of the Christian*, vol. 4, bk. 3 of *The Complete Works of Francis A. Schaeffer*. Westchester, IL: Crossway, 1982.

Schaeffer, Frank. *Portofino: A Novel*. New York: Berkley, 1996.

Schulz, Kathryn. *Being Wrong: Adventures in the Margin of Error*. London: Portobello, 2010.

———. "On Being Wrong." Filmed March 2011 at TED2011. Video, 17:12. https://www.ted.com/talks/kathryn_schulz_on_being_wrong.

Schwartz, Jeffrey M., and Rebecca Gladding. *You Are Not Your Brain: The 4-Step Solution for Changing Bad Habits, Ending Unhealthy Thinking, and Taking Control of Your Life*. New York: Avery, 2011.

Scorsese, Martin, dir. *The Aviator*. Burbank, CA: Warner Brothers Pictures, 2004.

Sharot, Tali. *The Influential Mind: What the Brain Reveals About Our Power to Change Others*. New York: Henry Holt, 2017.

Shimron, Yonat. "Under Fire From Many, Samaritan's Purse Finds an Unlikely Champion." *Word & Way*, April 22, 2020. https://wordandway.org/2020/04/22/under-fire-from-many-samaritans-purse-finds-an-unlikely-champion/.

Singer, Peter. *The Expanding Circle: Ethics, Evolution, and Moral Progress*. Princeton, NJ: Princeton University Press, 2011.

Skip and Shannon: Undisputed Channel. "Skip and Shannon react to Drew Brees' comments about protesting during national anthem." June 4, 2020. Video, 20:44. https://www.youtube.com/watch?v=Ou4Drn2hEhM.

———. “Shannon reveals his phone conversation with Drew Brees following anthem comments.” June 8, 2020. Video, 23:34. https://www.youtube.com/watch?v=_1cd3ewaWQE.

Some Good News. “The Office Cast Reunites for Zoom Wedding.” Episode 7. May 10, 2020. Video, 18:22. https://www.youtube.com/watch?v=NDjNX3nEfYo.

Sound & Vision. “Accidental Courtesy Follow-Up: Daryl Davis and Kwame Rose agree that black lives matter.” August 31, 2017. Video, 5:59. https://www.youtube.com/watch?v=1JMvRoVTyq8.

Stackhouse, John G. *Humble Apologetics: Defending the Faith Today*. New York: Oxford University Press, 2002.

Stonestreet, John. “A Meme of Mass Violence: ‘Joker’ and the Rise of ‘Demonic Anti-Heroes.’” *Breakpoint* (podcast). October 11, 2019. https://www.breakpoint.org/breakpoint-a-meme-of-mass-violence/.

Strobel, Lee. “Faith Under Fire—Hefner Interview.” *Faith Under Fire*, 2004. Video, 9:15. https://media.indwes.edu/media/1_7757fsff.

Stump, J. B., ed. *Four Views on Creation, Evolution, and Intelligent Design*. Grand Rapids: Zondervan, 2017.

Swaine, Jon, Oliver Laughland, Jamiles Lartey, and Ciara McCarthy. “Young black men killed by US Police at highest rate in year of 1,134 deaths.” *The Guardian*, December 31, 2015. https://www.theguardian.com/us-news/2015/dec/31/the-counted-police-killings-2015-young-black-men.

Talks at Google Channel. “Tina Fey: ‘Bossypants.’” April 21, 2011. Video, 56:36. https://www.youtube.com/watch?v=M8Mkufm3ncc.

Tarantino, Quentin, dir. *Once Upon a Time in Hollywood*. Culver City, CA: Columbia Pictures, 2019.

Taylor, Justin. “An Introduction to Postconservative Evangelicalism.” In *Reclaiming the Center: Confronting Evangelical Accommodation in Postmodern Times*, edited by Millard J. Erickson, 18–26. Wheaton, IL: Crossway, 2004.

TheKeinz Channel. “JK Wedding Dance Entrance.” July 19, 2009. Video, 5:09. https://www.youtube.com/watch?v=4-94JhLEiNo.

Tilson, Whitney. “My thank you to Samaritan’s Purse and thoughts on the coronavirus.” April 2, 2020. Video, 27:19. https://www.youtube.com/watch?v=a1cMV1myHWA.

Timpe, Kevin. *Free Will: Sourcehood and Its Alternatives*. 2d ed. New York: Bloomsbury, 2013.

Tippett, Krista. “On Being with Brian McLaren: The Equation of Change.” *On Being* (podcast). March 13, 2014. https://onbeing.org/programs/brian-mclaren-the-equation-of-change/.

———. “Reconnecting with Compassion.” Filmed November 2010 at TEDPrize@UN. Video, 15:07. https://www.ted.com/talks/krista_tippett_reconnecting_with_compassion.

Trainor, Meghan. “All About That Bass.” June 11, 2014. Video, 3:09. https://www.youtube.com/watch?v=7PCkvCPvDXk.

Van Biema, David. “The 25 Most Influential Evangelicals in America.” *Time*, vol. 165, no. 6 (February 7, 2005) 34–45.

Villeneuve, Denis, dir. *Arrival*. Hollywood, CA: Paramount Pictures, 2016.

Volk, Steve. “Rewiring the Brain to Treat OCD.” *Discover*, December 10, 2013. https://www.discovermagazine.com/mind/rewiring-the-brain-to-treat-ocd.

Wall Street Journal. "Blue Feed, Red Feed: See Liberal Facebook and Conservative Facebook Side by Side." https://graphics.wsj.com/blue-feed-red-feed/.

Walls, Jerry L., and Joseph R. Dongell. *Why I am Not a Calvinist*. Downers Grove, IL: InterVarsity, 2004.

WCPO 9. "Reds add to Wrigley Field history." April 23, 2014. Video, :50. https://www.youtube.com/watch?v=2Dn3yULs1NE.

———. "Where's Browning? Reds pitcher leaves World Series game after wife goes in labor." September 14, 2017. Video, 1:44. https://www.youtube.com/watch?v=WKtvcDEr3S8.

Webber, Robert E. *The Younger Evangelicals: Facing the Challenges of the New World*. Grand Rapids: Baker, 2002.

Wehner, Peter. *The Death of Politics: How to Heal Our Frayed Republic After Trump*. New York: HarperOne, 2019.

West, Lindy. "Act One: Ask Not for Whom the Bell Trolls; It Trolls for Thee." In "If You Don't Have Anything Nice to Say, SAY IT IN ALL CAPS." *This American Life* (podcast). January 23, 2015. https://www.thisamericanlife.org/545/transcript.

———. *Shrill: Notes from a Loud Woman*. New York: Hachette, 2016.

Wright, John, dir. *Leaving My Father's Faith*. Los Angeles: Matt Dean Films, 2018.

Zaki, Jamil. "Building Empathy: How to hack empathy and get others to care more." TEDx Talks Channel. October 18, 2017. Video, 13:18. https://www.youtube.com/watch?v=-DspKSYxYDM.

———. *The War for Kindness: Building Empathy in a Fractured World*. New York: Crown, 2019.

Index